Getting
along
with
yourself
&
others

Getting along with yourself & others

The art of solving people problems

Richard G. Hagstrom

Tyndale House Publishers, Inc.   Wheaton, Illinois

This book is dedicated to

PEOPLE who care about people—who quietly strive
  for genuineness and integrity
  in their people relationships.

YOU, to affirm and encourage you
  in your walk with Jesus.

Scripture quotations are from *The Amplified Bible* (AMP), © 1965 by
Zondervan Publishing House; *The New American Standard Bible*
(NASB), © The Lockman Foundation, 1960, 1962, 1963, 1968, 1971;
The New Testament in Modern English (Phil.), © J. B. Phillips, 1958,
1959, 1960, 1972; *Good News Bible, Today's English Version* (TEV),
© 1976 American Bible Society; *The Living Bible* (TLB), © 1971
Tyndale House Publishers, Inc.; *The New Testament in the Language
of the People* (Williams), © 1966 by Edith S. Williams.

Illustrations by Mrs. Jacqueline H. Prior

First printing, January 1982
Library of Congress Catalog Card Number 81-53033
ISBN 0-8424-0998-5 paper
Copyright © 1982 by Richard G. Hagstrom
All rights reserved
Printed in the United States of America

CONTENTS

Preface   7

One
People Problems Strike Everyone   11

Two
Stop, Look, and Listen   31

Three
Turn Clockwise, Not Counter-Clockwise   49

Four
Green Is Go   69

Five
Yellow and Red Are Slow Down and Stop   89

Six
Applying the Traffic Light Concept   107

Seven
Supervision—Where Is the *IF*?   135

Eight
Positive Supervision in Action   157

Nine
Taking the Negative Out of Evaluation—Realities
183

Ten
**Taking the Negative Out of Evaluation—
Doing It** 201

Eleven
Positive Relationships Are Genuine 223

Twelve
What to Do About Conflicts 247

Conclusion 269

Appendix A
Discovering Your Capabilities 273

Appendix B
Discovering Your Limabilities 275

Appendix C
Abilities 277

Appendix D
Questions for Discussion 279

PREFACE

"Why are you writing this book?" Margaret asked. "At first I saw four needs," I replied. "These four concerns turned into a deep sense of mission to communicate to others what I'm learning."

1. I saw huge reservoirs of people in every walk of life filled with feelings of inferiority, lacking a sense of self-worth. Typical comments were, "Compared to Ken, I'm no good," or "I'm only a homemaker," or "I'm just an amateur. I have so much to learn," or "I'm not a leader so let them do it," or "I feel like I'm drifting—I have no direction."

These comments add up to people downplaying who they are. As a result they are insecure and indecisive. Inferiority is their bondage. They are people problems, to themselves and others. They need help and encouragement.

2. I saw people leaving out God while making daily, practical decisions. Several years ago, I wouldn't have dreamed of asking, "Do you read your Bible and pray at least five out of seven days? Where are you in your walk with Jesus? Do you carry out prayer promises you make to others?" Today I ask those questions. I was wrongly assuming, for example, that the people I talked to were spending time alone with Jesus. I kept hearing, "I'm spiritually stagnant," or "I went into Christian work hoping to grow spiritually. Just the opposite is happening." They needed time alone with Jesus.

3. I saw many tired Christians—working hard trying to accomplish so much they were breathless and gasping for air. They were so intent on giving their all for Jesus that they were fast losing their effectiveness. I was stopped dead in my tracks by Oswald Chamber's statement in *Run Today's Race* (Fort Washington, PA: Christian Literature Crusade, 1968): "It is impossible to get exhausted in work for God. We get exhausted because we try to do God's work in our own way and refuse to do it in dependence on Him." People need to slow down and think things through occasionally.

4. I was appalled to see leaders so program-centered that little time is left over for listening and caring, with one person at a time, that is. Several years ago, I was doing research studies on how leaders get others to do things in the church. I stopped half-way through. I found little positive supervision going on: few knew how to pinpoint personal capabilities, and many relationships were filled with tension and conflict. I concluded that we need solutions to everyday, real-life people problems, not a research study. In other words, we need person-centered solutions.

"These four needs," I told Margaret, "moved me to formulate practical solutions to everyday people problems. Like many others, I feel people are the main testing ground. So we are never through solving people problems."

"Who is this book for?" Wanda asked.

"For homemakers, parents, supervisors," I replied, "and pastors, high school seniors, college students, presidents, vice presidents, carpenters, doctors, counselors, coaches, designers. . . ."

"Hold it," Wanda interrupted. "What you're telling me is that this book is for everyone."

"Not quite," I answered. "It's not for power-hungry, authority-oriented people whose main aim is success at the expense of other people."

"Instead," I continued, "it's for people who don't see themselves as leaders, who work unnoticed and unappreciated in today's fast-paced society; who are doing their best and accomplishing a lot with little thanks ever given them. Said differently, it's a book for people who care about people."

"What's the main message of the book?" Brian asked.

"Basically three truths," I answered.

The art of solving people problems

1. People problems are not solvable in the long run without God's help. ". . . for apart from Me, you can do nothing" (John 15:5, NASB).

2. In God's eyes, people are important and have equal value. God doesn't play favorites. "In this new life one's nationality or race or education or social position is unimportant; such things mean nothing. Whether a person has Christ is what matters, and he is equally available to all" (Colossians 3:11, TLB).

3. The three main causes of people problems in any setting (home, church, job, etc.) are (1) negative match-up between capabilities and responsibilities, (2) negative supervision, and (3) negative relationships. This book suggests positive workable solutions to all of these.

I am deeply grateful to a professional, quality research

organization—the Life Insurance Marketing and Research Association—where I worked thirteen years, studying, learning, teaching, supervising, and consulting. It was tough to leave them in 1976 to go out on my own.

Many people who have encouraged me to think and be practical are due my thanks: My brother Bob (I call him Rob) whose wise advice I trust and respect; Dr. Bruce B. Barton; Dr. Jim Galvin; Rev. Warren and Mrs. Connie Schuh; Rev. Norman E. Swenson; Mr. Robert and Mrs. Alison Wilson, and many others.

Other people have cared and prayed, especially my wife Marion, son Doug, and daughter Kristen. Thanks go to Barbara Eastman, Inez Lauterwasser, Jean Perkins, Beverly Pease, A. Barry White, as well as to countless others who pray for me—some of them I probably don't even know. I appreciate Mrs. Jackie Prior for making down-to-earth illustrations and Mr. Wightman Weese for being a caring and careful editor.

ONE
PEOPLE PROBLEMS
STRIKE EVERYONE

People problems appear in every area of real life. No one
escapes them or avoids them. When Floyd asked, "Aren't
there as many people problems as there are people?" I agreed
immediately. It's true. Most problems are people problems.
They strike everyone, everywhere.

Carol, in her mid-twenties, was talking about life since college
"Most of all, I want to be God's woman and lead a balanced
life. But these past four years have been anything but that.

"On my first job I was never encouraged. I didn't feel
appreciated since no one affirmed me. It seems I was tolerated
rather than built up. I was just expected to do what they said.
When no one listened to my ideas, I bottled up my feelings. I lost
respect for my supervisor. I couldn't believe a word he said.

"On top of this, I was counseling a teenager who had given up
on God, family, and friends. She later committed suicide. I felt
as if I had failed. Her suicide took the wind out of my sails. I felt
lifeless. It took several weeks to recover. Working was hard.

"I don't think I could have survived without my Sunday school
teacher. She and her husband really cared about me. They at
least tried to understand me by listening to me.

"Hoping things would get better, I moved to where I am
now. I'm disappointed. The climate in our office is negative.
There's constant conflict between people. My boss wears too

many hats, so he doesn't have time for people. He corrects me constantly. He's quick to point out my weaknesses and places I need to change. When he corrects and criticizes me, it's like pounding me further into the ground.

"Then I abandoned my quiet time and lost my appetite for God's Word. Just this week I've decided I can't go on without God, so I'm taking one morning each week to be alone with him.

"Am I expecting too much of my supervisor to care about me, to appreciate me? Staff meetings are OK, but they just don't seem interested in what I want to accomplish.

"I keep asking myself whether I should go into teaching, or another field of counseling. But then, why do I feel called to my present position?"

Sue, another example of people problems, committed her life to Christ several years ago. She cares for her two children alone, since she and her husband Carl separated three months ago. Sue related, "Six months ago, Carl asked Christ into his life but I've seen little change in him since. He hates his work at the hospital, seeing all the sick and injured people. And the pressure has gotten to him. Besides, no one cares about him. He feels locked in by his education to doing only the kind of work he's doing now.

"He tells me his heart is in farming. He loves the outdoors, using his hands, and doing physical work. He's a sensitive and creative person. But people tell him he's crazy to give up his present job. I think his job pushed our marriage downhill.

"We both distrust humanistic approaches to counseling. I can't speak for my husband, but I want to bring God into our problem. We can't really solve our problem without God's help and resources, can we?"

Jennifer, a college senior, confides, "I just can't wait to get out from under the rules and regulations of my college and parents and get married. I want to be free and make decisions on my own. I feel so stifled and put upon."

Lorraine, a homemaker, talks about six months of actual separation from her husband Dale. She says, "Actually we've been separated for several years. We've existed together arguing and bickering rather than living together like two grown-ups. I wonder what effect this will have on Tommy (age nine) and Rebecca (age three)?

"Must I live with a husband who's married to his job? Look at Tommy. He's angry. His father has no time for him.

"How can I get Dale to change? Is that too much to expect? When is he going to grow up and be a responsible husband and father? I've prayed myself into tears about this."

Lisa, for seventeen years a secretary for her organization, talks about her frustrations with her boss. "He just will not let me teach on seminars [one of her strengths] anymore. He says it's interfering too much with what I'm supposed to be doing—his secretarial work. He didn't even tell me that. I found out from his boss who happened to drop by one day. That made me angry.

"He says he knows my strengths. How can he? We've never talked about it. I feel suppressed. Now our relationship is sticky. Work isn't fun. Plus I don't trust him anymore.

"And do you know that studies reveal that secretaries quit not because they're overworked or underpaid, but because they're bored? Now I really believe that—I'm bored stiff. I'm just his slave now."

Two months later she resigned.

"All eighteen of my deacons and deaconesses agreed to visit one church member a month. I was so excited. I told my wife, 'They feel a sense of ownership too. It was their idea. I'm sure they'll do it.' "

This pastor continues, "Now three months later, am I disappointed! The first month four visits were made. The other fourteen said they would try harder next month.

"The next month, the same four visited but then began asking, 'Why should we? No one else is.' Meanwhile, the other fourteen were feeling guilty for not following through on their initial commitment.

"So now, three months later, we're back to ground zero. In fact, three deacons didn't come to our last meeting. I'm concerned."

Beth, a Sunday school superintendent, planned the fall teachers' meeting to a T. It was announced two months in advance, and two reminder notices were sent. After all, since the teachers said they wanted a teachers' meeting each quarter, she felt sixty of her seventy-five teachers would be there.

"Only eleven people came," she said. "I am feeling like a failure. Where did I go wrong?"

After a year and a half, Bill isn't cutting it as full-time youth worker. Youth meeting attendance is dropping and parents of youth increasingly hear comments like, "He doesn't seem to care about us. He doesn't listen. He seems more interested in getting the meetings over with and going home rather than being with us."

Frank, a committee person said, "He should be doing better. We all talked to him before we hired him. He has a written job description so he should know what to do."

Sally chipped in, "I agree. We all worked hard coming up with a detailed job description. I wonder what's the matter with him."

Lyle is, or has been up to now, a committed, loyal elder in his church. People say, "If you want to get something done around here, give it to Lyle."

"But I'm getting tired," Lyle said. "And I'm not forty yet! All I get around here is so-called affirmation, and it's leaving a bad taste in my mouth.

"If someone initiates an idea or project around here, he soon finds himself doing it all by himself. Leadership seems to be saying, 'Since it's your idea, why don't you do it?' That's killing our creativity and teamwork. All the so-called help a person gets is comments like 'Let me know if I can do anything.' A person gets the feeling they don't really want anyone to contact them.

"I get lots of pats on the back, so-called encouragement which I interpret as pretty shallow. But no one really cares about what I'm doing, or how, or the problems I'm encountering. Just because I'm president of my company doesn't mean I can do something alone or have all the answers. All I get is, 'Great job Lyle, keep it up,' pat, pat, pat. Frankly, right now I wish our church would stop growing."

Eleanor said, "He just doesn't understand. It's like hitting my head against the wall talking to him. The problem is communication. We aren't communicating. We end up arguing. Then each of us goes off and does his own thing. Teamwork? Tell me about it!"

"Will Doris ever straighten out her room?" parents ask.
"When will he learn to shut the back door?"
"If my son John volunteered to weed the garden I'd faint dead away."
"None of my children ever says, 'I'll do it.' "
"Who used the car last? The keys—where are they?"

Frances asks, "In a committee meeting people agree to do something. With two weeks to go, they tell me they can't. When people say they will, then don't, why don't they? Then I'm left holding the bag. It gets frustrating. What should I do?"

WHAT IS A PEOPLE PROBLEM?

My work of problem-solving and consulting in Christian settings boils down to these typical comments:
"How do we motivate them?"
"How do we get more people involved? Our people aren't committed enough. Just a certain few doing all the work."
"People are willing to help, but take on some leadership role? Now that's another story."

People problems break out when someone is not *doing* and *being* what is expected. To illustrate, people buy cars to do such things as take them to and from work. They also want their cars to be what they expect—to have certain qualities or attributes such as providing a smooth and comfortable ride. When either the engine quits or the shock absorbers go, we call it a car problem.

A person not *doing* what is expected of him may be, for example, missing deadlines, or not following through, or consistently arriving late for meetings. Someone not *being* what is expected may be uncooperative, or get angry too often, or show signs of a negative attitude. Such unmet expectations are what we call people problems.

Consider the unmet expectations in the examples of people problems mentioned earlier. Carol expected her supervisor to be more caring. Sue expected her husband, Carl, to change after committing his life to Christ. Jennifer chafed under rules and regulations. Tommy became angry when his father spent no time with him. Lisa, wanting to use her strengths more, felt underutilized as a secretary. In these and the other examples, notice that someone is not doing what is expected or being what is expected. As a result, people problems break out. Disappointment sets in, such as the pastor felt when visitation stopped.

People problems appear in every nook and cranny of real life experiences. One reason they appear is that everyone is a supervisor—each person has both a *do* and *be* expectation for someone else. This concept struck me like a bolt of lightning when a mother of three grown children said this about her neighbor's children. "What those kids need is good supervision. There's no discipline, their parents are always bickering. Those kids spend a lot of time with us because we give them attention. They need to be loved and cared for by their parents—they need good supervision."

The statement, "They need good supervision," got my attention fast. In fact, it revolutionized my thinking. I thought, *everyone is trying to get someone else to do something or be someone* with certain attributes. In that sense we're all supervisors. So is there any wonder most problems are people problems? Fred is asked to clear the kitchen table. Mary is told to straighten out her room. Priscilla says to her husband, "When are you going to clear the garage?" A deacon asks someone to be church greeter. The church nominating committee asks people to fill designated positions. A secretary is asked to take dictation. Parents urge their children to make the school honor roll. A corporation president asks his assistant to prepare the board report. Teachers ask students to complete assignments. A counselor asks the counselee to change his attitude toward his spouse; and on and on. We are all supervisors—husband, wife, father, mother, pastor, youth worker, teacher, committee member, mechanic, even teenagers arguing on the ballfield. We are all making "assignments" (the expectation) and overseeing their completion. It is done in committee rooms, ballfields, and

People problems break out when someone is not *doing* and *being* what is expected.

kitchens. John is expected to pick up a gallon of milk on his way home. If he doesn't, you know what happened the last time he forgot.

Some husbands expect their wives to have supper ready on time. The one time this month Jean is a few minutes late, Herman misses the first part of the trustees' meeting. And Herman "has a thing" about promptness. So fuses shorten quickly. Herman, like us, says things he later regrets. It is so difficult being Christ's person outside *and* inside our homes!

Our approach to people problems must put people and the situational needs first—yes, even before methods and techniques. Let's face it, putting people first means that our attempts to help people will often mean our being humiliated. We may be rebuffed with words such as "That's dumb" or "That's just what I was going to do."

Our attempts and approaches to solving people problems must include our doing often what isn't expected in many circles—such as going the second mile, or turning the other cheek, or being humiliated by someone in front of houseguests or office peers. To say that doing these things is not our role or job is often a cop-out. Christ's teachings about *doing* and *being* go beyond what is usually expected. A people-problem solver needs every ounce of God's grace and love because to be God's person goes against a person's natural grain, both outside and inside the home. We are often trying to impress. Yes, the problem is often us, not just them! Our fuse gets short too!

TODAY'S APPROACHES TO PEOPLE PROBLEMS

So what do supervisors, you and me, do when facing a people problem? Two possibilities appear: avoidance or immediate action. Either tendency is both risky and irresponsible.

Avoiding a people problem entirely is wishful thinking. Delaying action to think and pray, however, is not necessarily avoidance. Avoiding problems is also called "sweeping it under the rug." Rather than going away, the problem usually worsens. Parents, for example, can avoid the problem with their children by giving them money and presents instead of dealing with what is going wrong.

Francis, a supervisor in his mid-thirties, was asked to resign from his company after just eight months. Francis said, "Why didn't Dwight [his boss] tell me what I was doing wrong before yesterday? I had no inkling he was so dissatisfied."

Dwight confided, "I was hoping the problem would straighten itself out. But then people started complaining about Francis. Then I went on a two-week business trip. After that it was too late. People got so down on Francis I had no choice." Dwight's avoidance precipitated the problem; a people-first approach—carefully planned and thought through, could have prevented this problem.

Other reasons are given for avoiding people problems. Some are valid and honest feelings—others plain irresponsible.

We've all practiced avoidance.

"No one ever helped me, so why should I help them?" some might ask.

"It's not my job, so let someone else handle it."

"No time," others might say.

"He has a lot more education than I. I'm only a bricklayer."

"Me talk to him? He's a manager. Who am I to talk to him?"

"I don't want to hurt them."

"I tried before and things just got worse. In fact, I was the one who ended up with egg on my face. Never again."

"I really don't like the person. We've never really clicked. You might say there's a personality clash."

"Do you know how hard it was to get someone to do that? You tell me he's doing a lousy job, but remember he was the only one willing to teach that wild class. I respect his willingness. In the meantime, tell those other teachers they ought to put up with the noise."

"I don't know how—no one has ever told me what to do."

"Let's face it. I've only done half a job these past six months. So how can I expect someone else to do better."

"They ought to call in a professional—that's not my gift."

We've all practiced avoidance. Another response we might hear is, "Let the pastor handle it!"

Avoidance is an approach to take in problem solving, but doing nothing should be a conscious, deliberate decision. The decision might be made to do nothing and let someone fall flat on his face, for his own good. Sometimes that works, but don't count on it.

Avoidance should not mean forgetting and ignoring the person in trouble. So often the problem doesn't go away by itself, but the person does. Children "go away" to visit neighbors; a spouse may "go away" from home and have interests that exclude his mate. Or people, feeling uncared for, stop going to church.

To the other extreme of avoidance is the immediate action or confrontation approach, which too often is both risky and irresponsible. A mother said, "Our teenage son is getting more and more rebellious. All my husband really does with Roger is correct and criticize him, always harping on him for something he didn't do. There's no relationship."

Immediate action approaches are really hit-and-run efforts used mainly by people who don't have time for people, by those who are preoccupied with their own success and reputation. Direct confrontation seldom works. Raised voices around a table leave scars. People using such shortsighted problem-solving approaches forget that people take time. What those who use this approach are really trying to do is to get it over with. Hit-and-run approaches appear to be efficient because they don't take much time. But they aren't effective. They seldom work. Solving people problems takes time.

Neither avoidance nor direct confrontation works. Somewhere between these two extreme approaches are ways to solve people problems which recognize that our effort must be thought through carefully. We're dealing with people, not pawns on a chessboard.

People are God's creation.

TWO REMINDERS

Two facts should be remembered since they affect our
approach to people problems. First, we should determine
whether the other person's sense of worth is positive or
negative. Bernard bares his soul about his wife: "She feels
unloved—by me, by her family, and our kids. She resents me
because I'm not a dominant father. She feels I should be stricter
with employees in our business."

He added, "At rock bottom, I'd say she feels totally unwanted
and not worth anything—she says, 'What's the use? Why get
up in the morning?' "

I said, "People who lack a sense of worth often feel

insecure, inferior, indecisive—virtually immobilized.''

"Yes," Bernard said, "that's it, but what do I do?"

I said, "Be caring, and first accept her as she is, giving advice
sparingly. People like this may seem open to advice, but
someone feeling so negative about himself is usually incapable of
accepting advice. Instead of advising, be sincerely encouraging. Point out some little things to be supportive and affirming.
Make this concern a daily matter of prayer. Pray too about
your own attitude and ask for his Spirit to help you."

Things are improving gradually. He said, "I've quit advising
her. That was the main thing. It helped me be positive with her
rather than negative all the time."

Another example is Jim Chapman, who is scraping bottom.
Forty-four years old with a master's degree in education, he
hates teaching in high school. During our initial time together he
said, "I feel immobilized. I can't make a decision. I feel like a
ship at sea without a rudder—no direction." It took three months
for Jim to regain a positive sense of worth. But most of all, Jim
first needed someone to accept him and listen before advising
and arriving at solutions.

When solving people problems, I usually find myself on the
horns of a dilemma. Do I advise or not? Too often I've advised
before listening. I've found there are no rules or techniques that
tell me what to do. But I know that I must first accept the
person and be very sensitive to his or her needs and situation. I
have to consider his sense of worth and how he feels about
himself. I must pray for discernment so God's Spirit will enable
me with his wisdom. That is the best "technique" I know. If my
heart is hard, I can be sure it is not the best solution.

The second thing to remember is that people, unlike cars or
machines, care how they are treated. To solve a car's mechanical
problem is relatively simple. A person can usually follow a
checklist of possibilities to find out what's wrong. If the car still
doesn't run right, one can relieve his frustrations by slamming
his wrench against the engine, hitting the roof with his fist or
kicking the white sidewalls he just washed. And he can do it in
the privacy of his own garage.

People problems are a lot more complex. One can't just
follow a checklist of possibilities, then add up the facts, and apply

a technique and expect to solve the problem. Mechanistic, systematic approaches don't work except on robots. Yelling only sets off other short fuses.

So whatever approach we use, we must continually remind ourselves that we are dealing with people, God's creation. And God loves them. Like you, others are fallible and mistake prone. What if the Golden Rule were applied in just 50 percent of our attempts to solve people problems? What an improvement that would be!

LEADERS ARE INFLUENCERS

The concept of first accepting people before correcting them and first listening before advising suggests a special brand of leadership to solve people problems. Some may be thinking, "Leader? I'm not a leader." Wait a moment. Is such a view of leadership stopping people from stepping in and, for example, chairing a committee? I think so.

"I'm struggling over what leadership really is. Is it the concept of someone having power and authority?" Carl, a college professor asked, "Does leadership mean I've got to have people reporting to me? What I really want to do is teach and be a man of God as I teach. That is what I really desire. But everyone tells me I need to become a leader."

Beverly is a college graduate. She says, "I'm not a leader. I'm not a strong dynamic person. I don't enjoy the limelight."

Bob, a counselor, speaks up, "I'm really not a leader. I don't have charisma like Pauline and Fred. People seem to flock to them."

Carl, Beverly, and Bob had views of leadership that created guilt and inferiority. They were following views of leadership that ask, as the acid test, "Look around. Is anyone following you?"

A thirty-three-year-old Christian was asked: "Where do you want your Christian power base in five years?" The question angered me. Power is neither the means nor the end in a Christian setting. Secular business tactics demand power. The

Christian's power and resources are spiritual, not earthbound. To strive for power and authority in a Christian setting is destructive and divisive. In fact, it causes people problems. People sooner or later feel trapped. They will want to spring loose from its grip

And there is another reason people feel they aren't leaders. Typical answers to what a leader is include, "I'm not good in front of people, I can't express myself well in public." If that is the view of leadership, one will have difficulty being an effective people-problem solver.

Leadership isn't power and authority; it's not primarily the number of people following. So who are leaders and what is leadership? I'd like to suggest an all-inclusive definition. A leader influences either positively or negatively. Since we are all supervisors, in terms we described earlier, we are all leaders. Some influence positively, others negatively. A bank robber influences negatively, and so does a gossiper. Negative attitudes usually influence others negatively. Supervisors who either don't supervise or simply push people around, as if pushing some machine or piece of equipment into place, influence negatively. Many leaders influence, but the effects are negative.

Christ calls us to be positive influencers, who lead by serving and by helpful attitudes. A positive influencer takes hold of the teaching, "Blessed are the merciful" (Matthew 5:7) by demonstrating compassion for people in need, being loving and caring as he influences, particularly while solving people problems.

Today, Carl, the college professor, is positively influencing on campus and specializing in one area. Students love him, and he loves his work. He has no authority, no power, and no large following. No one reports to him, but he is a leader—a positive influence. He is a teacher, a resource, and a counselor to students.

Today, Beverly and Bob are leaders. They aren't speakers and both are in non-management jobs. Not to want power and authority is not to be second best. And people who lead like Beverly and Bob hardly know they are influencing, because their goal is God's glory, not self-glory. They are content to rest in Christ and silently *do* and *be* without fanfare. They usually go unnoticed except by those around them. In *My Utmost for His*

A leader is an influencer, influencing either positively or negatively.

Highest, Oswald Chambers writes: "The main thing about Christianity is not the work we do, but the relationship [with God] we maintain and the atmosphere produced by that relationship." Positive influencers create an atmosphere that causes people to be naturally drawn to them. The Vine we read about in John 15 is filling the branch. It can't be explained, planned, or forecasted.

Dr. Johnson said to me, "Dick, one of the biggest influences in my life was your brother's Sunday school class when I was in grade school. We loved Bob. I know he never felt qualified to teach but those days are memorable."

When I told my brother he said: "I never knew he felt this

way. Those were pretty rowdy boys." Serving influencers serve silently; they hardly know they are influencing.

Of all the people who have influenced us, most likely they don't know how much they impacted our lives. For example, my eighth-grade teacher encouraged me when I felt ostracized by my classmates. My first boss at a politically-oriented home office said, "Dick, around here it's best to listen for the first six months rather than talk or advise." He treated me like a son. His words stuck. He influenced silently and without fanfare.

One year I felt the high school Sunday school class I was teaching was a total failure. Discussion dragged and students never seemed to get into the lesson. Six years later a mother shared this comment from her daughter who was in that class: "Now I know what Mr. Hagstrom was talking about. It's beginning to make sense." In terms of immediate, measurable results, I had failed.

It is next to impossible for leaders to measure their influence. Results may occur immediately, but most likely they appear much later. It happens when a leader influences positively, in an atmosphere and environment that enables others to volunteer, to want to. There is no way of gauging, measuring, or predicting what God can do through an influencer who is rightly and vitally related to him. An effective people-problem solver must have this view of leadership.

Homemakers, carpenters, custodians, researchers, and designers are leaders. As God's love in a person increases, his influence is increasingly positive. Such a leader leads with a serving and helping attitude. He doesn't rely on this world's power and authority.

In his book, *No Little People* (Downers Grove, IL: Inter-Varsity, 1974), Francis Schaeffer writes, "To the extent that we want power, we are in the flesh and the Holy Spirit has no part in us. Christ put a towel around himself and washed his disciples' feet (John 13:4-14). We should ask ourselves from time to time, 'Whose feet am I washing?'"

What does this discussion of leadership have to do with solving people problems? A lot. As a pastor said, "In a volunteer organization, the rules seldom stick." Solving people problems in volunteer settings is 180 degrees different than in a business setting. As one lady said, "Getting people to do something around here [church] is like pushing a chain." The principles and methods are different. For example, standard business practice does not encourage turning the other cheek or looking out for the interests of the other person. Instead, it is results first, people last. Can you conceive of a business having as its standard operating procedures the "blessed" phrases from the Beatitudes? Not often!

A Christian president of a large secular firm says, "I want our business to be a spiritual hospital. Sometimes I'm the patient, at other times I'm on the attending staff. But Jesus is the physician and chief of staff." As I was talking to his people, they too were caught up in this philosophy.

Solving people problems is difficult because every situation is different. What worked last time may not work again. And it is hard to say whether a people problem is serious or not. We must not make hasty judgments. What seems inconsequential to one person is serious to another. Spats among teenagers may seem like nothing to a forty-year-old, but very serious to a sixteen-year-old.

I wish I could prove that each concept and method described in this book works and produce research data to prove it. I can't, because the results are hard to measure and their effect may not be known for years, if ever. And it seems presumptuous and audacious to separate from research data God's role and man's role. When and how his Spirit intercedes is his prerogative, not ours. We are his instruments, not his controller.

Solving people problems is a nebulous process. When a people problem is solved, it is often impossible to explain how it happened. Instead, it often appears as an experience of God's love and grace.

When facing a people problem, we should consider three questions once suggested by a homemaker and Sunday school superintendent: (1) What is God trying to accomplish *in that person?* (2) What is God trying to accomplish *through you* in that person? and (3) What is God trying to accomplish *in you* because of that person?

Leaders relying on power and authority do not solve people problems. Leaders relying on God's resources do. They influence positively and solve problems quietly and without fanfare. They let one person be their agenda, since people problems are usually solved one-on-one.

In the next chapters, we will see ourselves and others grappling with such real life issues as satisfaction and dissatisfaction, values, goals, climate, and expectations. Skipping these would be a mistake, since problems start and have solutions in a world where pressure, programs, and success bear down hard on all people.

Discussion Questions: Turn to Appendix D at the back of the book for discussion questions for this and other chapters of the book.

TWO
STOP, LOOK, AND LISTEN

Henry is a chemist and also very active in his church. He says, "I suffer from Monday-morning hangover [that was a new one to me!]. Sunday is not rest. It's just one thing after the other at church. I'm really dragging when I go back to work on Monday."

Comments like "I'm never through" or "There's always more to do" rattle about in our minds. We are functioning against the backdrop of rushing people, pressures, and programs that often turn out being the problem solver's worst enemy. Henry is still on his fast track, unwilling or unable to stop long enough to think. "I'm under constant stress," he admits.

Go-go-go, do-do-do is the norm. For many people, it is easier than stopping and thinking things through. Henry is an example. To ask questions such as "Why aren't more men active in our church?" is easy. Getting someone to think through, for example, what success really is is difficult. And when people do stop to think, others often feel they aren't doing anything. So guilt and discouragement set in.

Beetle Bailey is sitting against a tree, his arms folded and helmet down over his eyes. It looks as if he is dozing. Sarge comes by and asks, "What are you doing, Beetle?"

Beetle replies, "Just sitting here thinking, Sarge."

Then Beetle thinks to himself, "The trouble is, when I'm thinking, I look like I'm goofing off."

While at a church retreat, Silvia said, "I came here to get

some time alone. But people keep bothering me. They think something is wrong."

Against this backdrop, consider how Jesus spent the week before his crucifixion. Unlike today's fast pace, his life was unhurried, and he spent many hours alone in prayer with his Father.

The Apostle Paul writes about Timothy, "I have nobody else here who shares my genuine concern for you. They are all wrapped up in their own affairs and do not really care for the cause of Jesus Christ" (Philippians 2:20, 21, Phil.).

It is easy to get wrapped up in activity—even good activity—and forget that our relationship to God is most important and that as leaders we serve people to meet their needs. Stopping, looking at our life-style, and listening to God may point us to wait and avoid being hit by the onrushing locomotive of life.

Maureen and her husband have three children. Maureen feels trapped and unfulfilled by demands placed on her. "It's what I do, it's what I do," she repeated. "I just don't like housework, or even taking care of my family, for that matter. I feel boxed in and trapped by everyone else's demands.

"I don't feel good about myself. I can't accept myself and my situation. I must not be fun to live with. I'm not fruitful or loving. And I feel programmed by my church. Other people keep telling me what I ought to be doing. They're making my decisions, not me.

"Another thing—our marriage. Our roles seem reversed. My husband seldom talks or tells me what's on his mind. I'm making all the family decisions. When he gets home from work, he does absolutely nothing."

Bernard, in his mid-thirties, rose quickly in a national organization. Now a vice president, he says, "When my staff talk to me, I don't really hear them because of today's pressing problems. With sales down, my neck is out there. The pressure is intense."

A fifty-six-year-old bank president confides, "Is this what I've worked for all my life? Now that I'm here, what have I really got? Is this really success?"

People feeling pressured, programed, and unfulfilled are people problems.

Two years ago, Barbara, a Christian businesswoman, said, "If I'm dissatisfied most of the time, something must be wrong."
Today, she has her own business and says, "I just love it. I'm making less money but enjoying it more and more. I still have a lot of problems. It seems I'm always in process—I never seem to get *there,* wherever *there* is. But I'm satisfied and feel better about myself and life in general. I still have a lot of pressure, but it's bearable now."

People feeling pressured, programmed, and unfulfilled have people problems. Unhappy with themselves and others, they throw out vibrations of negative thinking to other people.

At this point someone may be saying, "I agree, life is a hassle, but I want to solve people problems. What's my real aim? Can you give me something to get my teeth into or to grab hold of as I solve people problems?"

The answer is yes, and in answering that question about aim, notice something that Barbara said: "But I'm satisfied and feel better about myself and life in general." Should helping a person become satisfied and fulfilled be one of the aims of a problem solver?

"Of course," someone may say. "Certainly God doesn't want dissatisfied people. Look at Maureen. She seemed very dissatisfied. She said she was not fruitful and loving, not fun to be with."

Bernard and the bank president were pressured and disillusioned; so they too are dissatisfied. Just imagine what kind of people they are at the family supper table.

Being dissatisfied most of the time is not right. Then, is the opposite true—that satisfaction is right and OK? I believe so, for Paul wrote: "Let everyone be sure that he is doing his very best, for then he will have the personal satisfaction of work well done, and won't need to compare himself with someone else" (Galatians 6:4, TLB). Another translation of this verse reads, ". . . the personal satisfaction and joy of doing something commendable [in itself alone] . . ." (Amp.).

To give aim and direction to problem-solving, I have pushed the concept one step further. People satisfied and fulfilled tend to be more fruitful (Galatians 5:22-23). Today Barbara, the Christian businesswoman, is satisfied with her work and situation. She is again having a daily quiet time studying God's Word and praying. Personal fulfillment and fruitfulness go hand in hand. Influencing people to that end is one aim of a problem solver.

It is also true that people who are dissatisfied and unfulfilled most of the time tend to be unfruitful (Galatians 5:19-21). Their fuse is short and they dislike themselves and others. Maureen disliked being a homemaker and feeling programmed, so relationships suffered.

Yet, like vice presidents and bank presidents, many people succumb unthinkingly to the rushing for success, money, and more things, which pushes aside the concept of fulfillment. It is either forgotten or overlooked. One aim of the problem solver is to help people regain the fulfillment perspective. It's not easy—you win some and lose some. I lost with Henry, the man with Monday-morning hangover.

Eloise needed to let Psalm 119:36 be her standard: "Help me to prefer obedience to making money" (TLB)

Eloise faced two job opportunities, one paying $14,000 and the other $11,000 a year. The $11,000 job matched her strengths and capabilities. The $14,000 job was outside her personal strengths. As we shall see, people are usually fulfilled when they are using their strengths and capabilities. But for Eloise, the overriding issue turned out to be money rather than fulfillment. Her husband was also locked into salary-only considerations. And he had every reason to be thinking this way, since they had two children in college. He said, "Well, couldn't she take the $14,000 job for just two years?"

I'm not suggesting that being financially responsible and having money concerns is wrong. What I am suggesting, however, is how easily we are overlooking the fulfillment issue when solving people problems. This couple, in full-time Christian work, did not think to ask, "Where will Eloise be most fulfilled and fruitful?" Eloise could have taken the $14,000 job for two years, but then I had to ask her husband, "Do you want an unfulfilled and unfruitful wife for two years?" As it turned out, she had to take the $11,000 job because the $14,000 job was filled by someone within that company. Today she is fulfilled.

One of our aims in solving people problems is to help them find fulfillment and fruitfulness. Talk about these goals is often repelled like water from a duck's back. Questions by a caring, positive influencer that will arouse the thinking of the person with the problem are often effective. "Success"—in terms of money and position—gets in the way constantly. As work is the bane of the drinking class, so today's success mentality is the bane of the problem-solving class.

WHAT IS SUCCESS?

The dictionary defines success as the gaining of wealth and position. This coincides with this world's values and standards, for it is saying, "What really counts is money, titles, and large offices." The bank president was disillusioned and unfulfilled.

Success eluded his grasp, even though he had gained wealth and a position. We need to heed the warning: "Then I observed that the basic motive for success is the driving force of envy and jealousy!" (Ecclesiastes 4:4, TLB). With careful planning, fulfillment and success (gaining wealth and position) can go hand-in-hand for some people. But often the only questions asked are: "How much money will I make?" and "What are the chances of advancement?" Money is important, but even more important is being personally satisfied and fulfilled. The world's success definitions crash in on Christians too. To not gain wealth and position doesn't mean failure. To be unfulfilled and fruitless does mean failure as a Christian. But the world's mind-set about success seems to prevail.

I was asked, "What was your most important success last year?" I replied, "Facilitating the process of helping someone who was unfulfilled in the number-one slot (therefore a people problem) to move into the number-two slot."

After a few moments, his head tilted a bit as he gave me that "You must be kidding me" look. Then he said, "Don't you help people advance and move up—to become more successful?"

I said, "While that may happen, my primary concern is personal fulfillment and the person's relationship to God." Fulfilled people who are walking with Jesus are less apt to be people problems—to themselves and to others.

Let us hold up the caution sign for a moment. Maybe someone has struggled with the concept of fulfillment because it sounds self-serving. The thought has troubled me for years. This struggle cleared up when I saw fulfillment as a means, not the end. The end is serving and glorifying God, not to serve ourselves and be self-fulfilled. "As each one has received a special gift, employ it in serving one another, as good stewards of the manifold grace of God" (1 Peter 4:10, NASB). Another translation of the last part of this verse reads "so that God may be glorified in everything" (Phil.).

Self-fulfillment is an end for many people, but not the end for a Christian who is serving God and people. Selfishness, insisting on my rights, is a constant problem. Self is not to be glorified. "And he [Jesus] said to them all, 'If anyone wants to come with me, he must forget himself, take up his cross every day and follow me" (Luke 9:23, TEV). Notice the words "every day."

In his book, *Psychology as Religion* (Grand Rapids: Eerdman, 1977), Paul Vitz writes:

It should be obvious—though it has apparently not been so to many—that the relentless and single-minded search for and glorification of the self is at direct cross-purposes with the injunction to love the self. Certainly Jesus Christ neither lived nor advocated a life that would qualify by today's standards as 'self-actualized.' For the Christian the self is the problem, not the potential paradise. Understanding this problem involves an awareness of sin, especially of the sin of pride; correcting this condition requires the practice of such unself-actualized states as contrition and penitence, humility, obedience, and trust in God.

Our end is not self-actualization, self-fulfillment, or self-satisfaction, Instead, the end is to serve God and man and to forget ourselves. Personal fulfillment, kept in its rightful place, is one means to this end. Someone unfulfilled is a people problem.

"Is a person always fulfilled?" you ask. No, because life demands we be doing unpleasant and unfulfilling things alongside of fulfilling things. We shall be looking at this more closely in chapter 5. A person needs to feel fulfilled enough to have a positive sense of worth and value. Because Christians are accepted by Christ, their own fulfillment, when coupled with a serving attitude, should be at least ten times more than someone whose end is self-fulfillment.

When I feel discouraged or find myself dealing with people who test my patience, I read Colossians 3:23, "Whatever you do, put your whole heart and soul into it, as into work done for the Lord, and not merely for men" (Phil.). It's like raising the caution sign. It tells me I serve God and man, not myself and man.

THE FULFILLMENT CYCLE

The Fulfillment Cycle (see Fig. 2.1) pulls together various components that most affect fulfillment. These components are not mutually exclusive or independent of each other. Instead, they interlock and all go together. So when parts of the cycle are negative or missing, fulfillment drops, as when relationships are negative or positive and caring supervision is missing.

The Fulfillment Cycle's three components (1) *personal strengths, limitations,* and *weaknesses;* (2) *values/priorities;* and (3) *goals/plans* form the basis of a sense of worth. The other six influences (left side of Fig. 2.1) also affect fulfillment significantly. Look at the Cycle, starting at the top: Sense of worth.

Reduced to bare bones, people with a positive sense of worth feel two things about themselves: a sense of competence and a sense of belonging—a place they fit in and feel comfortable.

First, people want a sense of competence—to feel they are good at something whether it is driving a vehicle, singing, doing math, or counseling. Recently someone said, "I don't want to be labeled as a no-good." None of us does. People want to view themselves as competent and to be viewed by others as

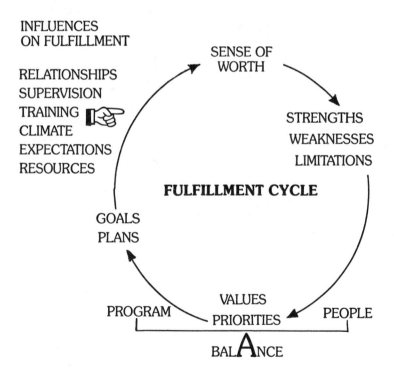

INFLUENCES
ON FULFILLMENT

RELATIONSHIPS
SUPERVISION
TRAINING
CLIMATE
EXPECTATIONS
RESOURCES

SENSE OF
WORTH

STRENGTHS
WEAKNESSES
LIMITATIONS

FULFILLMENT CYCLE

GOALS
PLANS

PROGRAM

VALUES
PRIORITIES

PEOPLE

BAL**A**NCE

FIGURE 2.1

competent. They like it when someone says, "Great job" after they have done something well. Nothing builds up people like a sincere "thank you."

Second, a sense of worth is also affected by whether or not people feel a sense of belonging—the "included, not excluded" feeling. A college senior says, "While I was growing up, there was constant fighting between my folks. I never felt at home." A pastor relates: "After two and a half years, my wife and I still don't fit into the church and community."

A thirty-four-year-old single girl says, "I don't fit in with married people, and I'm too old for college people. And looking for a job tells me more and more it's a man's world. Where do I fit?"

People new to a group feel uneasy at first. As relationships are established, they feel a sense of belonging. A stepson said, "He is my third dad. Mother divorced twice before. My present dad is just great. I've just decided to change my last name to his last name." For the first time in a long time he felt he belonged to a family.

People who feel competent and able to do something, who have a sense of belonging someplace, tend to have a positive sense of worth. They are more apt to be fulfilled, decisive, secure, and confident.

VALUES—PRIORITIES

Some people say values; others say priorities. Either way, values and priorities represent what is really important to a person. Values and priorities are one way of making choices about what to accept or reject. Ten years ago, I turned down an attractive position because it conflicted with my values. My friends thought I was crazy. My values helped make that choice. Values give added purpose and meaning to goal setting. Unrealized values and priorities contribute to lack of fulfillment and people problems.

Victor, a middle manager, loved his job but situational pressures and too much to do brought on stress. The quality of his work dropped, and he was working eighty hours weekly. It was his wife, Lorraine, who said in chapter 1, "Must I live with a husband who's married to his job?"

He asked, "Why can't I get things done around the house? I used to go home, put it in overdrive, do things with my wife, and take care of the usual projects around the house. But now I have no incentive. What's wrong?"

I told him that his fulfillment was dropping because two values were going unrealized: quality work and family. Added job pressure and stress caused his initiative to decline—no overdrive. Action plans were set in motion to gradually redo his work responsibilities and better plan his non-work time. Relationships are improving too.

There are many people like Victor today whose success drives and values are in conflict. Fulfillment is reduced and soon relationships go downhill fast.

Some people stop, look at their lives, and say, "I'm sick and tired of criticizing and griping and complaining. I want a more sensible life-style."

Some successful people (wealth and position) are fulfilled. For one thing, they have clarified their values. They aren't teetering on the brink of disaster, delaying their realization.

Values represent what and who is really important. Each person, on his own, must pinpoint his values and fit them into his overall life-style and goals.

Figure 2.2 illustrates values possibilities. It can be used as a worksheet to define your values using "your definition" if it doesn't correlate with the definition suggested. People find out the relative importance of their values by ranking them. Victor ranked his values (those numbers to the left) and commented, "It's the top six that are important." That is a common reaction. Five, six, or seven rise to the surface. The others tend to have little or no importance to a person.

Look at Victor's rankings. With family life and achievement ranked high, any wonder he felt unfulfilled? On top of this, he wanted to get another advanced degree—understandable, since personal growth is ranked second. In his situation this could be impossible to accomplish. So we worked out a less time-consuming self-development program.

All values can't be met in one fell swoop. Situations change, people change, and values may go unrealized for a time so another person can realize his. For example, Ruth is foregoing a community group involvement value while she helps finance her

VALUES

VALUE	A DEFINITION	YOUR DEFINITION
Achievement	Doing a quality job.	
Independence	Freedom to do pretty much as I wish; few controls on me as I do my job.	
Prestige	Respect others have for me, my situation, and my acomplishments.	
Leisure	The quality and quantity of time away from the job.	
Influence	The degree I can influence or direct the activities of others.	
Financial Compensation and Advancement	Income and the opportunity to achieve additional values or to enhance existing values.	
Helpfulness	The altruistic feeling of doing good or helping others.	
Family Life	The quality and quantity of time with my family.	
Security	Being relatively free from worries about the future or threatening situations.	
Personal Growth	The feeling of improving as an individual.	
Acceptance	Being accepted and liked by peers and enjoying social situations.	
Recognition	Being singled out for performing well.	
Location	The neighborhood and community where I live.	
Relatives	Proximity.	
Community and Civic Groups	Opportunity to be involved.	
Church	Opportunity to worship as I choose.	

FIGURE 2.2

husband's education. People need to be sensitive to each other's values to avoid conflict. Compromise enables one person to realize his values while another's go unrealized for a time. It requires constant give and take, which only caring people can do. But "takers," however, don't give.

Married couples who rank their priorities separately and then compare their values ranking often comment, "So that's why you're thinking this way and pushing for this." Understanding values throws new light on people's understanding of each other. While each has to compromise at points, people problems are nipped in the bud.

Several years ago, I read a study showing that the average family spends seven minutes *together* daily. That fact jolted me, so I tried spending time each day with each of our children. Often they were off doing their own thing, so one day I would spend little time with them and on another day they would want to do something together, so it took a lot more time. My point is that I had to decide consciously and set this time with family as a goal. Values give purpose and direction to goal-setting.

Christianity Today (May 25, '79) reported: "A study in a small US community shows that the average time per day fathers spend with their sons is about thirty-seven seconds."

Statistics and studies can be questioned. People sometimes falsify reports and rationalize their life away by saying, "Someday I'll straighten out my life." Like the caption under the Frank and Albert scene as they were reclining under a tree: "I'm going to reevaluate my priorities someday, but there are a lot of other things I've got to do first."

We mustn't wait; we must encourage others not to wait. Values need to be pinpointed and reviewed. Otherwise, the locomotive of life runs over us.

Marvin, in his early thirties, said, "My father and I didn't have much of a relationship. He was always busy."

Unlike Marvin, Bob, in his mid-forties, after his father died said, "I miss my dad. We were friends." People can't be forced to have this perspective, but we may be that person's positive influencer, for he may always remember a question we asked or a tidbit we shared. And we may never know we influenced him.

My father worked six days a week, but from my viewpoint it was not a people problem. I did not resent his long hours or feel neglected. I remember him to be warm, gentle, and caring. He encouraged me—never pushed me. He and my mother helped shape my present values. I felt I belonged to the family. We kids were their friends. While they were often busy, they always had some time for us. It is possible to realize values, even in today's busy world.

Most people find it easy and acceptable to rank family life high. Who can dispute it? But ranking family life high is no task to be undertaken by the fainthearted. Parents are often too busy for their children and spouses, so a people problem is in the making. To avoid this kind of people problem ask yourself, "Is my spouse my best friend? Are my children my friends?"

Determining our values has helped our family make choices. Early in our marriage, my wife and I decided we would not move for more money or a promotion (promotion in the sense of a more management-type job). We loved the place we lived in (and still do). Location is one of our values. We learned the hard way that things should not dictate our life-style. The first house we bought had house payments which were nearly one-third of my salary. Our house payments were dictating our decisions and life-style, so we decided to get out from under that burden. We lost money in the transaction. Then we bought our present house, which is much smaller than our first one. The other day my wife said, "Our home is home." Yes, where we live and our home is a value. Things, like a house, must not possess us and dictate our decisions. Solomon was right. "Sometimes it takes a painful experience to make us change our ways (Proverbs 20:30, TEV). Selling our house at a loss was painful, but it paid off in other ways.

Mildred, mother of four teenagers, has been widowed one year. She decided to go on a weekend retreat that allowed time for reflective thinking. On her return she said, "I needed time to be quiet and get those jumbled thoughts out of my mind. I relearned that God's first call is to be faithful to him. I was convicted about my prayer life. We talk to God, tell him what we want to do, saying 'I need this' and 'I want that.' When we pray, do we allow him to talk to us? Do we listen to him?" Mildred took time to stop, look, *and* listen—to think things through.

While preparing for a church seminar, I asked the assistant pastor about the needs of his people. He said, "I'm concerned about attitudes. I don't think people need to be challenged. What they need is a cot." A cot? That sounded funny, but it drove home the point that, like Mildred, people need to get away to think reflectively and get refreshed. Many people are tired, which affects attitudes—fuses shorten. Values need to be straightened out.

"Don't let the world around you squeeze you into its own mould" Romans 12:2 (Phil.). The world easily conforms us to what it perceives as success. One person asked: "Is our Christianity mainly an overlay on a non-Christian life-style?"

The harried manager of a travel agency said, "Customers keep changing their plans, the airlines put me on hold, phones ring. Every afternoon I take aspirins. My ear is sore, my throat is raspy, and I'm tired." The cruncher was when she said, "The whole system is wrong. The way we live is wrong. It's wrong, wrong, wrong." Aspirins aren't the cure.

When success, money, and things dominate, life ends up a hassle. Christians are victims when their life-style is but an overlay. We resent being squeezed. We feel trapped by lack of choices and become angry, resentful, and frustrated.

A housewife related, "I have three suppers to prepare each night, to meet my teenagers' and husband's schedule. Also, I never know when my husband will get home from work. I feel pressured by it all." Homemakers, travel agents, executives, all feel pressure.

To climb out of the pressure-cooker living, Edwin takes one day each year to evaluate and plan. He begins by evaluating his everyday living, challenged by Philippians 1:27: "But whatever happens, make sure that your everyday life is worthy of the gospel of Christ" (Phil.). Edwin reads and rereads the Sermon on the Mount as he thinks through his life-style and values. Then he makes plans for the year ahead. Edwin says, "What a difference this has made. I'm accomplishing more and feeling more at peace with God and myself."

We should encourage people to set time aside, to take a pencil and paper, and examine their values occasionally to see to what extent they are realizing their values. To what extent are they helping others realize their values? Have we selfishly pursued ours, without regard for other people? On the other hand, have we let our lives be controlled by others so that our own values have gone unrealized?

"But whatever happens, make sure that your everyday life is worthy of the gospel of Christ" (Philippians 1:27, Phil.).

If a person knew he had one year to live, would he want to live differently? If the answer is yes, he is teetering on the brink of disaster—you can be sure there is a people problem brewing somewhere in that life. While there are times everyone must go harder, these should be the exception rather than the rule.

People problems are impossible to solve when success, money, and things dominate. Yes, I mean impossible. Monday morning hangovers may be important signals to watch for. In such settings, people are ignored and left out. Personal fulfillment drifts downward.

Change is difficult. Discussing values and priorities clears the air and improves communication so some changes can gradually be made in life-style. A few hours stopping, looking, and listening pay fulfillment dividends that money can't buy.

For most people, success is not gaining wealth and position, for that only produces comparisons between people leading to jealousy and envy. People scrambling and clawing to the top walk over people, which also produces heaps of trouble. Instead, success is fulfillment and fruitfulness. And if wealth and position accompany that kind of success, fine. We also need people at the top who care first about people.

THREE
TURN CLOCKWISE, NOT COUNTER-CLOCKWISE

Jim Chapman, the forty-four-year-old high school teacher mentioned in chapter 1 told us about his lack of direction and of feeling like a ship at sea without a rudder. He said, "I'm fed up trying to apply all these so-called good approaches. They may work for others, but not for me. I've set goals until I'm blue in the face. Something is missing. I've felt this way for years."

I asked, "On a scale of ten-high, five-average, one-low, what is your level of fulfillment?"

He answered, "One to two."

Looking for solutions from the standpoint of the Fulfillment Cycle pointed out that Jim had never pinpointed his strengths and limitations. Doing that turned up strengths, such as working with his hands, building things out of wood, and refinishing woodwork. Although difficult, he accepted teaching as one of his limitations. To him, teaching is unfulfilling rather than fulfilling.

Missing in Jim's goal-setting process was the linking together of his goals with his strengths and values. The three—goals, personal strengths, and values go together. Today, Jim's level of fulfillment is about seven (it is hardly ever ten) and his sense of worth positive.

The way Jim was first trying to reach fulfillment is common today, which explains why people's fulfillment and sense of worth drop. And when that happens, serious problems settle in. Their life in Christ also drops. Carol, our first people problem example in chapter 1, experienced that. Luckily she is pulling out of her mucky situation and is back abiding in Christ.

But Eugene is another story and still teetering. He said, "No one cares enough about me to sit down long enough and pinpoint my strengths, or listen to me about what I would like to accomplish. It's all *their* goals and not ever mine." Then came the cruncher: "I've almost given up on my faith. I've stopped going to church, too. I was going through the motions of being a Christian. I haven't had a quiet time in five months." So Eugene is not trusting God, yet is trying to hang in there and continue to serve him. These are some of the sobering realities of solving people problems.

Eugene is still a victim of program-centered and goals-first approaches, where people are considered last. Goals-first approaches may build organizations, but they will not build up people. The first step in goal setting is finding out people's strengths, capabilities, and interests. Helping people pinpoint their personal strengths and capabilities will be discussed in a later chapter.

BALANCING PEOPLE AND PROGRAM

So often businesslike, program-centered approaches creep in and ensnare. While speaking at a seminar for full-time Christian workers, a Christian business executive said, "In my view, a leader is one who imposes his will on the group—other people don't call the shots for him. I always find myself in the position of having to manipulate people."

Several participants questioned that position (at that point, I quit taking notes). He retreated a little from his view of leadership, saying, "Of course, I'm speaking from the viewpoint of my business. In the church you'd strive for more consensus, and be a little more democratic." It is approaches like this—that impose and manipulate—that cause people problems. Two-hat Christians are not consistent. Being one way here (in church) and another way there (in business) is having double standards.

Leader-imposed goals are mainly program-centered. And in such a setting, assumptions about people's willingness cause problems, as when leadership, such as parental, church, or

Double standards cause people problems.

committee, assumes someone is automatically willing to do something. For example, leadership assumes a committee member is willing to carry out his responsibilities because he agreed to serve. This hoped-for willingness soon evaporates when follow-up stops or is done hurriedly.

So the chairman is left holding the bag. Why? Committee goals are being set first, rather than being linked up with people's strengths and ideas about what they would like to do. Then the leader tries to impose his will on people, which is counterproductive. It seldom works. Unfulfilled people drop out. Their parting salvo is, "Let them do it." Eugene is an example of a program-centered approach.

People everywhere fall victim to such approaches. Parents

who plan a family vacation and skip listening to their children's ideas are being program-centered. Curriculum planning that goes ahead without consulting teachers and students is program-centered.

Being person-centered is to listen before deciding. Listening that hears and considers other people's ideas enables genuine give-and-take between people. Balancing people and program builds people up. Such listening takes place in a setting where people are co-partners, co-laborers, with someone leading who utilizes the whole group in the decision-making process. Ideal? Yes. Does it work all the time? No. Someone has to make decisions that may be unpopular. But people's reactions to a decision hinge on whether people feel listened to and whether or not leadership cared about their opinions.

But simply asking people for their ideas and then sweeping them aside is worse than not asking in the first place.

Charlie, a deacon, said, "Our chairperson asked each deacon to tell what he wanted to do. Lots of practical ideas were suggested like doing something in evangelism, working with inner city people, and helping handicapped people. But the whole thing dropped. You see, leadership had already decided what they wanted. What we said didn't fit into their plans. Our list of ideas was never brought up again. We all felt let down and misled." A people-problem solver must watch out for counter-clockwise approaches and solutions that put program before people.

Starting with people first runs counter to what is usually done. Sally, a Sunday school superintendent, relates: "Before Shirley, our director of Christian education, arrived, I would appoint teachers who wanted to teach and who felt teaching was one of their strengths. And most important, I tried to find out about their walk with Jesus. I feel a class is only as good as its teacher and his or her love for Jesus. So I spent time first finding out about teachers."

"I'm learning Shirley does the opposite. She wants to get a teacher and then spend time promoting the class. I feel locked in by that approach. I'm losing interest in my job."

It's so easy to consider program before people. A housewife admitted that asking, "Who are we going to get?" is often the last question considered when planning. She said, "Come to

"As each one has received a special gift, employ it in serving one another, as good stewards of the manifold grace of God" (1 Peter 4:10, NASB).

think of it, we've already decided on our topic, location, and time for our Tuesday Bible study. We're now asking, 'Who are we going to get to lead it?' " In a volunteer setting, we should strive for balance. Ignoring people, or worse yet, ignoring what they say creates people problems.

REALISTIC GOAL-SETTING

We should help individuals set realistic goals. While long-term goals have their place, for most people it is more realistic to think about short-term goals.

Charlie Brown strikes out again. In disgust he says, "Rats!" Back on the players' bench, and with chin in hands, he says to Lucy, "I'll never be a big league ballplayer. All my life I've dreamed of playing in the big leagues, but I know I'll never make it."

Lucy says, "You're thinking too far ahead, Charlie Brown. What you need to do is set yourself more immediate goals."

"Immediate goals?" asks Charlie.

"Yes," says Lucy. "Start with this next inning when you go out to pitch. See if you can walk out to the mound without falling down."

Bradford and Marilyn have three children. Early Sunday morning, they have breakfast together to talk over plans for the week ahead and dovetail schedules. They occasionally examine their life-style, values, spiritual growth, and how they can help each other more. It has made a big difference in their marriage. Their "next inning and walk to the mound" is the next seven days. And they like to key in on doing one thing, using as their guide: ". . . the one thing I do . . ." (Philippians 3:13, TEV). Last year the one thing they worked on was to enable Marilyn to lead a neighbor Bible study. Leading discussion is one of her strengths. Bradford helped behind the scenes.

Esther is a seventy-three-year-old widow. As we were walking to a meeting she said, "Every New Year's Day I write one thing I want to accomplish that year. The first Sunday of each month, I read it again to see how I'm doing. I've quit trying to change the world. I'm trying to change me so I'll be doing his will." I didn't press Esther to tell me more about her goals when she was putting her goal-envelope back into her Bible. It seemed anticlimactic. She really didn't have to and they seemed too precious to her to talk about right there.

Jesus said, "My food is to do the will of Him who sent me, and to accomplish His work" (John 4:34, NASB). Realistic goals represent that which is to be accomplished (started, done right, and completed). Goal-setting isn't a mysterious, complicated process. If "short-term and one-thing," they should fit into an envelope like Esther's.

The areas the goals include will be different for each person; however, everyone should include these two areas: (1) spiritual-fitness goals and (2) goals to meet people needs.

SPIRITUAL-FITNESS GOALS

The Apostle Paul writes: "Now I long to know Christ and the power shown by his resurrection" (Philippians 3:10, Phil.). His ambition and goal was to know Christ. Sometimes the last person we get to know is Jesus. Jesus is also saying to us, "For a long time I have been with you all; yet you do not know me . . .? (John 14:9, TEV). Any wonder people have problems when they have no time for Jesus?

How do we get to know Christ? A road sign reads: "Best route to Agawam, Take Exit 49W." The best route to knowing Jesus is a goal of a daily quiet time to study his Word and pray. Like Mildred in chapter 2, we need time to be quiet and get those jumbled thoughts out of our minds.

If a Christian isn't having a quiet time, something is wrong. Their next inning should be to set a goal to do that, such as once or twice a week. But for goodness sake, don't try to encourage people to suddenly set a goal of one hour alone with Jesus each day. It will drive them and others up the wall. Instead, suggest they start with an accomplishable goal, then to improve on it as they go along.

"Take time and trouble to keep yourself spiritually fit. Bodily fitness has a limited value, but spiritual fitness is of unlimited value, for it holds promise both for this present life and for the life to come" (1 Timothy 4:8, Phil.). Jogging time should not exceed quiet time.

People try to fit a quiet time into their schedule and then stop, with this excuse: "I wasn't doing anything. My mind was spinning, thinking about work I had to do. My mind never focused on God. I felt guilty about not working and now feel guilty about not spending time alone with God."

The thought that they must be always doing something squeezes in and crushes some people's walk with Jesus. With no time for Jesus, there is no walking with him—just running and getting out of breath or dropping out for the wrong reason. People not doing *and* being are people problems. Prideful thinking says, "It won't happen without me." Stopping, looking to Jesus, and listening to him sustains the *be* part of life. Our quiet time is the bridge to Paul Vitz's call to such "un-actualized states as contrition and penitence, humility, obedience, and trust in God."

Maybe more people should be considering dropping out (for right reasons) for a time to catch their breath and become spiritually fit. Beatrice, a devoted Christian homemaker, directed several summer church programs. She stopped doing it, saying, "When I was leading, I really wasn't applying Scripture in my life. I've been comparatively inactive in my church this year because God was telling me I really don't know his Word. I was just making decisions off the top of my head and relying too much on methods." Today she's back contributing and serving.

Wesley is minister of Christian education. "My problem," he said, "is being able to spend enough time in the Word. No one ever asks me about my spiritual situation. They're concerned mainly with how many were in Sunday school and how many came to the winter retreat." How concerned are we about other people's daily walk with Jesus? Permanent solutions to people problems happen when Jesus and people grip hands.

The Fulfillment Cycle will be another self-oriented, self-serving device when being used by spiritually unfit people. Quiet time is a must if we are to draw on his resources. Quiet time works best for people who are hungering for his Word and for time alone with him.

"Blessed are those who hunger and thirst for being and doing right, for they will be completely satisfied" (Matthew 5:6, Williams). This hunger and thirst cannot be forced on others. But for a problem solver helping others, *being* and *doing* (words used in our definition of a people problem) are intertwined with spiritual fitness. In *Christian Counter-culture* (Downers Grove, IL: Inter-Varsity, 1978), John R. W. Stott writes: "Such spiritual hunger is a characteristic of all God's people, whose supreme ambition is not material but spiritual." Full, complete satisfaction happens only when God is first.

We must not let the do-mentality make us skip quiet time or make it part of emergency, last-ditch efforts. A commercial airliner developed engine trouble right after take-off. Panicking, a passenger yelled, "We're going down!"

Quickly another passenger blurted, "Do something religious!" Upon landing safely, all the passengers laughed about that "Do something religious" comment. It broke the tension.

Setting a goal to call on God's resources when life is smooth as well as during times of emergency is the only route to full satisfaction and fulfillment. Such a goal helps us avoid many people problems because then our everyday living will be affected the most as we, like Charlie Brown, walk to the mound. "And now just as you trusted Christ to save you, trust him, too, for each day's problems; live in vital union with him" (Colossians 2:6, TLB).

GOALS TO MEET PEOPLE NEEDS

Goals should include also the meeting of people needs. "Have our people learn to give their time in doing good works, to provide for real needs; they should not live useless lives" (Titus 3:14, TEV). Paul was reminded by leaders to "remember the needy in their group . . ." (Galatians 2:10, TEV). "If you refuse to listen to the cry of the poor, your own cry for help will not be heard" (Proverbs 21:13, TEV).

Marion, now retired, is spending two days each week teaching reading to underprivileged teenagers at a local jail. Gladys and Bert are leading the over-sixty-five church group. A middle-aged couple take on caring for their aged aunt rather than putting her in a nursing home right away. A young married couple visits widows two evenings a month. In each case, a specific and short-term goal was set to meet a people need.

How changed are our ambitions? To what extent do we encourage meeting people needs, rather than being at some program or meeting?

Bob said, "Everytime I passed a nursing home, I got convicted. I've changed that. Now I have set aside one evening monthly to visit one." Do our ambitions and accomplishments include meeting a people need that is convicting us?

Frankly, I go crazy thinking of all the needs—handicapped, sick, lonely, troubled—just to name a few. So I boiled it down to one or two things that I can accomplish. Like Bob, we shouldn't be turning a deaf ear to those inner convictions about something.

Emily became widowed when just thirty-five years old. Now, ten years later, Rita confided to her husband, "You know, I've forgotten that Emily [her sister-in-law] is a widow. In my mind, widows are much older. Now I'm just beginning to understand her loneliness." In front of her was a need she had been missing all these years.

What convicted her? "What God the Father considers to be pure and genuine religion is this: to take care of orphans and widows in their suffering . . ." (James 1:27, TEV). Her goal now is to meet one need. In Jesus' view, one person is important.

GOALS HELP SOME

Goals don't make the future clear-cut or life go off like clockwork. At best, goal setting and planning make things somewhat less fuzzy since we never know for sure. "He has set the right time for everything. He has given us a desire to know the future, but never gives us the satisfaction of fully understanding what he does" (Ecclesiastes 3:11, TEV). We would like to know, but we never will. When goal setting and planning cause us to depend on him more—to do more praying and getting to know Jesus more intimately, then God leads and brings about his results. And isn't this what walking with Jesus is all about? We should be planning into the unknown future. "We should make plans—counting on God to direct us" (Proverbs 16:9, TLB). Actual results are in his hands. "We can make our plans, but the final outcome is in God's hands (Proverbs 16:1, TLB). Goals help some, but we must depend on God, not goals.

Bill, a thirty-five-year-old manager, said, "I've tried outthinking, outplanning and outstrategizing God. I've left him out completely. Now I'm trying to rest in God and take one day at a time." Only spiritually-fit people can take one day at a time and leave the future in his hands.

"You know what my goal is this year?" That question from a twenty-nine-year-old assistant pastor had me thinking such things as: get a doctoral degree, a larger church, or maybe even change his career direction. Instead he said: "My goal is to walk with Jesus." Was I floored and humiliated! As a result, on the top of my prayer list I've written goals like: Be faithful; listen to you more; and think more often of Jesus during the day.

None of us knows for sure where we are heading or how we will get there, but we do know who is leading us. As a problem solver, we, along with the others, are helping deal with an unknown future. We and they are going to fail but when we do fail, he is there helping us. "The steps of a good man are directed by the Lord. He delights in each step they take. If they fall, it isn't fatal, for the Lord holds them with his hand" (Psalm 37:23, 24, TLB).

People are creating problems for themselves and others by trying to serve God, relying on their own resources and techniques. They have it all backwards. Instead, people's primary aim should be to get to know him and to experience the firm hold of Jesus' hand.

While we encourage one another, we urge the people we are helping to spend time in the Word; it becomes our primary source of encouragement. "Everything written in the Scriptures was written to teach us, in order that we might have hope through the patience and encouragement which the Scriptures give us" (Rom. 15:4, TEV).

Wendy vacationed with her family and relatives. On her return she tells about it. "I learned we need to be studying his Word daily. I was saying my prayers, yes, but not reading my Bible. I kept saying, 'I'll read my Bible tomorrow.' I never did.

"It was my reactions! The old *me* kept creeping in. Being with people and particularly one's own relatives makes it doubly difficult. There were no confrontations but my reactions weren't right. The divine order is 'Jesus first.' "

Goals aren't the answer, nor do they solve problems. If kept in perspective, they help some. More important, solving people problems hinges on a person's spiritual fitness.

CLIMATE

Climate also influences our sense of fulfillment. Climate is the atmosphere being produced by people's attitudes based on their daily experiences—in the home, factory, office, or church. Climate is either positive or negative. A positive climate generates encouragement and hope. Someone experiencing it might say, "I want to be there. I like my supervisor and I'll be listened to." A negative climate produces just the opposite—unhappy people and unfulfilled needs and most dehumanizing of all, the feeling that "I will not be listened to." Carol, our first example in chapter 1, felt that way. You will remember that she said she bottled up her feelings when no one listened to her ideas.

Studies reveal that a person's supervisor is the key influence on whether climate is positive or negative. Said differently, climate starts at the top. Parents set the family climate; teachers the classroom climate; the chairperson the committee's climate; a choir director the choir's climate. There is pulling or pushing power in climate. A positive climate pulls and attracts. A negative climate pushes people away.

Bob employs six people. He said, "I don't have any real people problems. Is something wrong?"

"No," I replied, "but it's unusual. How do you do it?"

"It's the Lord. It's his attitude in me. It's hard for me to put in words." Bob went on, "I trust my men and try to treat them fairly. They never grumble about wages and I am paying them less than my competitors. I don't have a recruiting problem. People are coming to me looking for work.

"I encourage them and let each one exercise his strengths and capabilities. Oh yes, I'm up at 5:30 A.M. for my quiet time. I pray for my six people."

People want to work for people like Bob. The pulling power of a positive climate is caused by a caring, people-responsible influencer setting the pace. And when he has influenced someone, he rarely knows it. But his workers know.

Roland said, "We love our pastor. He listens. So now I listen to his ideas more. You know, he cares and listens. When we ride in my truck, we really talk. I love him dearly and he is twenty-five years younger than me." Here is an example of a pastor being a positive influencer and quietly fostering a positive climate.

A positive climate pulls so strongly that people who know they are in the wrong job, where personal strengths do not match responsibilities, hesitate to leave. Page said: "I don't want to leave. I love the people here, my supervisor, and our philosophy of ministry. We encourage each other. There's no competition." She decided to stay one more year.

A home fills up with tension when parents' main concern is their children's success (straight A's, for example). The climate turns negative, which pushes teenagers straight out the door. Missing is the warmth and genuineness of loving, caring relationships.

Clyde, president of a Christian organization, said: "I want _____ to be known as a caring organization." Climate does start at the top. His recruiting problem will soon be that he has too many applicants. There is pulling power in a positive climate. Along with prayer, it is one of the most effective recruiting methods.

Forming realistic expectations is important.

Climate is the atmosphere being produced by people's attitudes. People problems fester in a negative climate. Such problems are impossible to solve when climate is negative, whether it is a marriage problem, parent-child problem, or whatever. On the other hand, a positive climate generates encouragement and hope, and these are the fertile grounds for solving people problems.

EXPECTATIONS

Expectations are particularly important since the standard is often stated as: "What they don't know won't hurt them." Expectations are given by telling the pluses and minuses before an experience, rather than letting a person find out for himself.

When people later find out the truth of what was expected of them, they feel deceived by their supervisor. The supervisor in this case has created the people problem.

Why is forming realistic expectations so important? Studies reveal that people's attitudes and effectiveness are favorably affected when expectations are realistic. The opposite is also true, so what a person doesn't know *can* hurt him.

Hospital patients usually recover quicker knowing the full picture. Parents cope better expecting their child to behave like a "terrible two-year-old." Parents can exercise more patience (I know, it's tough!) expecting their nine-year-old to perform when company comes. Remember, you did that too.

We often form unrealistic expectations and hardly bat an eyelash while doing it. Did you ever tell someone something was simple or easy? It may be simple and easy for you, but don't assume it will be for them. For example, you remember the frustrations following those "simple" directions someone gave you through city traffic. Most likely he said, "It's really simple. All you do is . . . ." You rolled up the window and were lost in twelve seconds. It was simple to him but complicated to you. And you felt dumb. Plus the back seat drivers didn't help any. Tension!

Or suppose someone assigns a task to you and tells you, "It's simple. Anyone can do it." Suppose you fail at it. You will most likely not be willing to try again. And even if you do succeed, and are asked to do it again, you may do it only reluctantly.

On the other hand, suppose the same task is assigned and you are told it will most likely be difficult; others have tried and even failed. You are told the pluses and minuses, including problems you may face. You try and then fail. Will you be willing to try again? Most likely you will. And unlike when told it was simple, if you do succeed you'll want to try doing it again. So we should tell the truth, as best we know it, since every situation has pluses and minuses.

Visiting parents of Sunday school students is difficult for me. I get turned off when told, "There's nothing to it." I feel deceived. And double-entry bookkeeping may be simple to you but I still don't understand it!

If college was simple and easy for us, we shouldn't assume our high school senior will see college that way. If teaching is easy for us, we shouldn't tell our substitute teacher it will be simple.

Jesus formed realistic expectations. He taught that his followers would be persecuted, and that they should count the cost. That wasn't negative thinking. It was the truth. We should tell a recruit about people problems on our committee, or in our organization. They will find out anyway within two weeks after starting. A "Let them find out for themselves" attitude deceives and hurts people. What people don't know can hurt them and your relationship with them. We must not cover up the truth.

A problem solver should avoid forming "Oh, it will all turn out OK" expectations unless certain of that. A problem solver must avoid saying "Something good is going to come of this." It may be miles down the road. In the meantime, we must be forming realistic expectations. We know that solving people problems is tough.

RESOURCES

When adequate resources, such as people, money, or equipment are not available, fulfillment and effectiveness decline. For example, when a secretary, whose value and priority is quality work, has a messy typewriter and is asked to produce letters and reports, that person soon feels dissatisfied. Someone volunteering to drive the church bus becomes discouraged spending Saturdays fixing it. Sunday school teachers trying to facilitate discussion in a long, narrow classroom become impatient. Bill hates mowing the lawn with a cranky lawnmower.

Poor equipment and lack of money, while contributing to people problems, are areas outside the purpose of this book. The people resource is what this book is all about. Let us hope equipment and money problems are positively influenced as people problems lessen!

Values and priorities, goals, climate, expectations, and resources are some of the components of the Fulfillment Cycle that affect fulfillment and sense of worth. People with a positive sense of worth can make decisions and feel relatively secure. They feel competent and experience a sense of belonging in their everyday life experiences.

On the other hand, a person who is not fulfilled lacks a sense of worth and so feels guilty about himself for not measuring up. (See Fig. 3.1, Guilt Cycle.) Guilty people feel incompetent. "I'm really not good at anything" attitudes prevail, values and priorities seem unimportant, and goals present a real threat. The result is insecurity and guilt. Guilty people are people problems. They and others know it.

Linus asks, "What's that you're wearing around your neck, Charlie Brown?"

"It's a medical tag . . . lots of people wear them," Charlie says.

"What does it say?" Linus asks.

"Insecure," Charlie answered.

Insecure people are not able to cover it up too long. Attempts at hiding it fail. People soon see it. Insecure people feel guilty.

Secure people are able to make bold decisions. Their goals and priorities reflect sensitivity to people. They feel less pressured by goals and numbers.

FIGURE 3.1

Lorraine, a homemaker, "worked herself to death" in her church four straight years. So she dropped all of her responsibilities for three months. After these three months, she said to Walter, the minister of Christian education, "If there's something I can do, just let me know."

Walter paused, then said, "Yes there is. Would you pray for me and also be the one I can call on to pray about prayer requests I get?" In the face of a recruiting problem, when it was tempting to ask Lorraine to take a "position," Walter made a bold decision. Like the Apostle Paul, Walter's ambitions for himself and others are changed. After doing that for six months, Lorraine also became head of the nursery department. Lorraine says, "Walter's priorities and the example he is setting encourage and affirm me."

The backdrop for solving people problems is built. Values and priorities, goals, climate, expectations, and resources make up this backdrop.

We have already been considering many contributors to people problems. I feel there are three areas that contribute even more. Imagine a tripod being used on a stage to support a backdrop. Each area is represented by one of the legs of the tripod.

Leg one represents the mismatch of capabilities and responsibilities. *Leg two* represents the lack of positive caring supervision, and *Leg three* represents negative relationships. Each leg of a tripod depends on the other two. If one leg breaks or slips, the whole tripod falls. Solving people problems requires that all three legs be positive.

For example, when supervision and relationships (Legs two and three) are positive but the person is not using his capabilities and strengths (Leg one), the person is a people problem. Heavy doses of relationship building and supervision will not solve that problem. Page felt positive about her supervisor and her relationships, but this element (Leg one) was missing. She decided to stay one more year because the climate was so positive.

Or again, if a person is using his capabilities (Leg one) and being supervised (Leg two), but relationships are negative, that is a people problem. So a large crack or a break in one leg causes people problems. In the long run, all three legs must be positive.

The Fulfillment Cycle concept is built on the premise that supervisors don't wear one hat at home and another somewhere else. The principles of problem-solving are universal. Mother doesn't treat her children and her committee members differently. Father doesn't tell a work associate to do something one way and then turn around and act differently when telling his son to wash the car. People are people everywhere. We have created our own people problems by being one person here and another there. Double-standard approaches must be stopped. Most so-called good business practices leave God completely out of the picture. Positive influencers strive to be genuine and, although often self-centered, God's love somehow penetrates and his love influences others positively.

FOUR
GREEN IS GO

Phillip Mack, thirty-two years old, graduated from college with honors. He seemed destined for success—"One who can't miss," as we would say.

Ten years later, he is a failure by all standards. He has succeeded at a few things, but in three different jobs with the same organization he failed miserably. His frustrated and concerned supervisor said, "No one wants to hire him now. They're calling him a job-hopper. And I surely don't know what to do with him."

Using concepts covered in this chapter, his personal strengths and capabilities were pinpointed, and then compared with his key responsibilities in his three jobs. There was little match up; in other words, a mismatch between Phillip's capabilities and what he was expected to do. A leg of the tripod was missing.

Phillip's sense of worth was low because his sense of competence and accomplishment on his jobs was nil. He felt guilty and was told bluntly, "Phillip, you're a failure. You have no successes." In one sense that was true; he had failed. In another sense, it is false, because Phillip himself did not fail. "*You* are not a failure, Phillip," I said. "The failure occurred in the match-up of your capabilities and responsibilities." This concept was foreign to him. Like Carol (chapter 1), so-called constructive criticism from his supervisor, though well intentioned, was like pounding him further into the ground. All he heard was negative things. Using this world's standards, he *was* a failure.

We chatted by his car as he was leaving. He said, "Are you saying *I'm* not a failure?"

I said "yes." A huge burden seemed to lift from his shoulders then and there.

The Phillip Mack story has a positive ending. Prayer teams were set up for him. Four months later, a supervisor rejecting many business "success" standards hired Phillip. Basing the decision on matching the job to Phillip's capabilities made sense. Now, two years later, his new supervisor is saying, "I learned the fallacy of writing a job description without taking a person's capabilities into account. Today my philosophy is 'Fit the job to the person, not the person to the job.' " Amen, I said to myself.

As with Jim Chapman, Phillip Mack and his previous supervisors set goals until they were blue in the face, but that didn't help. Missing was the first step of pinpointing Phillip's capabilities and linking goals to his capabilities.

And like Eugene (chapter 3) it affected his faith in God. He said, "I felt God didn't care about me. He seemed so distant most of the time." Phillip persisted, even though he felt very unfulfilled. Some of his values were being realized, and the fact that his wife was patient helped Phillip. "I don't know what I would have done without her," he kept repeating. Today, Phillip Mack's sense of worth is positive. He is fulfilled and fruitful.

People problems like Phillip's abound. It is easier and more efficient (takes less time) just setting goals and writing job descriptions (starting on the wrong side of the Fulfillment Cycle). It takes less time telling a high school senior what he ought to do rather than helping him pinpoint his strengths and interests. But sooner or later, if there is no match-up, lots of time and money will be spent trying to figure out what was wrong.

Bill, the full-time youth worker (chapter 1) wasn't cutting it even with a job description. One contributing cause of this problem turned out like Phillip Mack's—a mismatch. Neither the committee nor Bill knew Bill's capabilities.

PINPOINTING CAPABILITIES

So how did Phillip Mack pinpoint his capabilities? He first divided his life into four time periods, beginning at age five; then he

"Accept one another, then, for the glory of God, as Christ has accepted you" (Romans 15:7, TEV).

identified two or three positive experiences in each time period. Here is what he came up with:

Time Period I.

In fourth grade, I contributed some major ideas to a class play.

In fifth grade, another guy and I were best at arithmetic. We would help each other figure out difficult math problems.

Time Period II.

I wrestled during practice with varsity wrestlers; I felt good about helping them perfect their techniques. I never won a match.

I "crashed" a planning meeting for a church youth banquet. I came up with the idea for the main skit.

Time Period III.

After being president of the youth group the previous year, I became vice-president my senior year. I enjoyed being advisor and confidant of the president. She trusted my advice.

In college, I had friends who came to me for counsel and advice on spiritual and personal problems.

Time period IV.

Became sort of special assistant to the manager of the produce department in a supermarket. He would ask me to give my opinions and raise questions about decisions he faced. He trusted me.

I enjoyed field training a work associate. I became his friend and confidant. I never pushed him—let him make mistakes as he learned. I loved being more or less his counselor.

Looking back over Phillip's positive experiences, you will notice certain recurring thoughts, such as contributing ideas, counseling, and being an advisor and confidant. In Phillip's three previous job failures, he was required to take charge of several people and make tough organizational decisions. Being a special assistant, for example, to the manager of the produce department is much different from being the one in charge. Phillip's key responsibilities in his three jobs did not require him to contribute ideas, counsel, or be an advisor or confidant; and when he did, he got in trouble with his supervisor. By identifying positive experiences, a person's capabilities keep popping up. Notice how often Phillip contributes ideas. A person tends to keep using his capabilities in his positive experiences.

WHAT IS A POSITIVE EXPERIENCE?

A positive experience is something a person likes and enjoys doing because (1) he is naturally interested in it, (2) he desires to do it, and (3) he does it fairly well (in his opinion).

Positive experiences give a sense of accomplishment and competence, so fulfillment goes up several notches. His sense of worth jumps up too.

Everyone's positive experiences are different and unique to them. No one else knows them, so each person identifies them on

"God has given each of us the ability to do certain things well" (Romans 12:6, TLB).

his own. "It is only a person's own spirit within him that knows all about him" (1 Corinthians 2:11, TEV).

Positive experiences are accomplishments in one's own eyes, not what other people may have felt important. Also they do not have to be earthshaking, but rather, meaningful only to the one who experiences them. These may have occurred at any time—during school, work, at home, or while pursuing a hobby.

A review of a person's positive experiences brings to the surface his capabilities. Each person has capabilities. "God has given each of us the abilities to do certain things well" (Romans 12:6, TLB). "Certain things well" means a person should not try doing everything, but instead concentrate on doing only his particular thing well.

We each have a part to play. "We are all parts of it [Christ's body], and it takes every one of us to make it complete, for we each have different work to do. So we belong to each other, and each needs all the others" (Romans 12:5, TLB). Failure to do our part—those certain things we do well—affects the body of Christ negatively.

Another helpful Scripture is: "Try to have a sane estimate of your capabilities . . ." (Romans 12:3, Phil.). I underscore *your* capabilities.

GREEN IS GO

To help grasp the concept of positive experiences and how people repeat doing things, using their capabilities, we might think of a traffic light. The green represents capabilities. Green is go—foot on the accelerator, and accomplishing something. Green is a welcome sight. The opportunity for people to use their capabilities is also a welcome sight. Green means action, in the eyes of that person.

On the other hand, a yellow light signals a caution, and a red, a stop. Yellow and red represent a person's *limabilities,* identified by reviewing his negative experiences. The word *limability* is coined from the word limit which means "boundary." People feel fenced in by limabilities. A limitation restricts; our foot comes off the accelerator and onto the brakes—we slow down.

When required to use limabilities, a person often procrastinates—has his foot on the brake, stopping rather than starting. Limabilities—yellow or red—is next chapter's topic.

Let us look at other people's positive experiences and pick out their capabilities. People tend to do "their thing" and repeat doing it since it fulfills and satisfies them. God wants fulfilled and satisfied people.

Consider Jim Chapman, our forty-four-year-old teacher. Notice how his positive experiences add up:

CASE 1   JIM CHAPMAN

Time Period I.
   Built model airplanes.
   Customized model cars.

Time Period II.
Was a starting guard on high school football team.
Graduated from officer candidate school.
Took care of a large garden.

Time Period III.
Remodeled kitchen in an old house.
Learned how to tune an engine.
Redecorated an old home. Refinished floors and woodwork.

Time Period IV.
Put up fence around entire yard.
Enjoyed cooking.
Was an assistant coach. Led calisthenics. Liked bandaging and taping injured ankles as a sort of team trainer.

Jim's capabilities include shaping and building, tailoring and modifying, fixing and improving things. He enjoys working with his hands and actually seeing a visible end result, a finished product. His capabilities do not include teaching, so is there any wonder he was so unfulfilled?

Now his goals are tied into his capabilities. Soon he will have his own refinishing business. Jim also asked, "Am I a manager?" This question is asked often since supervision and management are often viewed as the ladder to the top—success. To answer to this question, I consider how someone functions with other people his *personal style. Personal style* is divided into three broad categories:

Category One (by himself). In this category, a person tends to accomplish something mainly by himself, rather than delegating it.

Category Two (through others). The person tends to delegate and assign responsibilities to others.

Category Three (with others). The person's specific accomplishment is combined with others.

To illustrate these categories, let us invade the world of music. The choir director would be a personal style category two, functioning through others. The choir members would be category three, with others, and a soloist, category one, by himself. Putting it very generally, a person whose personal style is category one says: "I'll do it." A category two first says, "Who can we get?" A category three leans toward saying, "Let's all do it together." A category three often loves being a committee member. A category two enjoys chairing and leading a committee. Often a category one resists serving on a committee unless he has a specific task that he himself can do.

Consider another illustration of these categories: Suppose someone decides to build a one-room addition on his home. A personal style category one tends to do it all himself. I'm a category one. So strong are my individualistic tendencies that when a friend volunteered, I did not enjoy his help. As with many other category one people, unsolicited help is often viewed as interference. A category one likes doing it all himself.

A personal style category two tends to function as a general contractor, subletting various parts, orchestrating the entire project. He himself may not drive one nail.

A category three will call his friends, telling them what a good time they will have, and be fulfilled by having his friends at his side hammering away. At the end he will say, "We all did it—teamwork did it." Categories two and three are often part of team efforts. I am not equating cooperativeness and team efforts. We are all expected to be cooperative. I am saying that compared to a category one, a category three will tend to like combined efforts much more.

Someone who prefers making good passes to a team's top scorer is often a category three. A secretary who enjoys collating with another secretary is demonstrating category three tendencies.

A review of Jim's positive experiences puts him into personal style category one. At no point did he delegate to anyone. Only once was he a three—playing football. So while Jim may someday have to manage, he can count on not liking to manage and delegate. Managing is not one of his capabilities.

Phillip Mack's personal style is mainly category one, but he also has category three tendencies (combining with others). For example, he contributed ideas and helped others develop wrestling skills.

Like many other people, Phillip's personal style is not clear-cut so that it falls neatly into one of the three categories. Instead, it may include one, two, or all three categories. One must look closely at positive experiences and then decide. In Phillip's case, as a one, he functioned pretty much in the role of an "assistant to" rather than manager.

Another difference between Jim and Phillip is that Jim liked working with things and Phillip, with people. A *Directory of Occupational Titles* (U.S. Government Printing Office), points out that people function in three broad areas: people, data, or things. Someone who enjoys keeping records and statistics is an example of the classification "data." Without saying Jim dislikes people or data, he is most fulfilled functioning with things such as wood and tools. Phillip likes to function with people rather than data or things.

Positive experiences carry within them what people want to do; capabilities and areas of competence repeat themselves throughout different experiences; the question of "Am I a manager or not?" is answered by the three personal style categories. Positive experiences also answer whether a person prefers functioning with people (a counselor, for example), data (statistician), or working with things, (as a carpenter). People don't necessarily fall neatly into these categories or classifications. But it helps to narrow down a person's area of competence.

It may also be useful to refer to the list of abilities in Appendix C, when helping someone. This list is not complete, but it may help as a guide.

HELPING SOMEONE ELSE PINPOINT HIS GREEN AREAS

Positive experiences are like gold mines. There is a wealth of information underneath that can be dug out. Listing positive experiences may give important clues about a person's strengths. But usually there is much more to dig out.

To help dig out this gold mine of information from positive experiences, one might ask these questions (using Jim's positive experience: remodeling the kitchen):

1. *Tell me how* you remodeled the kitchen.
2. *Give an example of* building a cabinet.

To further pinpoint his personal style, ask a question about his role.

3. *How did you view your role* while remodeling the kitchen?

People answer this role question dozens of ways such as, facilitator, encourager, helper, organizer, promoter, initiator, motivator, information resource, counselor, one of the team, teacher, catalyst, communicator, designer, problem solver, director, enabler, manager, and overseer. If unclear about what someone means after explaining his role, one might ask him to clarify it: "You mentioned your role was catalyst. What did you mean by that?" A person might answer, "I was the one who got it started. It wouldn't have happened if I hadn't been there." This tells how he saw himself functioning as a catalyst.

David asked Fred to write out his positive experiences; then they got together and Fred gave out more detailed information as David asked the above three questions about each positive experience. In quotes are a few of Fred's nuggets that David dug up:

CASE 2   FRED BAILEY

Time Period I.

Played sandlot baseball. "*I put together our team. I played and coached. Role? I decided who played and in what position, then made out the batting order. I was the coach and manager.*"

Printed a neighborhood newspaper. "*I recruited my brother and a neighbor girl to write it and print it. Then I paid other kids to sell it. Role? I had my own little business—director I guess.*"

Time Period II.

President of church youth group. "*Loved to run and organize things. I gave out assignments, followed up to see that they did them. Liked getting them excited. Role? Motivator.*"

Entered all-school track meet. "*I never won anything, but liked to encourage others, to help them improve and develop. Role? Unofficial coach.*"

Time Period III.

Recruited students for intramural football team. "*Loved to diagram plays and strategies. Would schedule practices. Role? I held the team together. Coached and was the quarterback.*"

Recruiting, interviewing and training people on my first job.

Time Period IV.

Did all the landscaping for the first house we bought. "Hired
an artist to design it, then I sublet a lot of it. I recruited five friends
and one Saturday they rolled out 1000 rolls of sod. I directed
it—didn't touch a piece of sod all day. Role? General contractor
and supervisor."

Formed side business selling industrial cleaning products. "I
recruited eight sales people. Helped each one lay out his
marketing strategy. Role? Supervisor and trainer."

Fred's personal style category is two, in the role of supervisor
and motivator. He enjoys delegating. His other capabilities
include recruiting, supervision, training, and motivating. His
people—data—things classification leans toward people in
situations that include sales marketing.

During positive experiences people tend to lose themselves,
becoming engrossed or immersed in something that fulfills them.
Fred said, "When I'm working out plays and strategies with a
team I've recruited, the adrenaline is really flowing."

Someone describing a positive experience such as acting
says, "It was so fulfilling, immersing myself into that role. I hardly
noticed the audience."

Someone who enjoys writing offers: "I sort of get into my own
world, almost oblivious to noises and people." Time flies when
people like what they are doing.

Charlotte said, "I'm not sure what knowing my capabilities
will accomplish but I want to find out what I'm good at, and find
out how to go about being satisfied."

A trusted friend helped her by asking the three questions and
listening to her talk about her positive experiences. Notice the
things she wrote down and talked about:

CASE 3   CHARLOTTE SHOCKLEY

Time Period I.

In grammar school I won an award for designing school logo.
Taught kids archery at a children's camp. "I planned and
organized it by myself. Role? Organizer and teacher of skills."

Time Period II.

Elected president of high school senior service club. "A
committee and I set up the day. I enjoyed chairing the meeting.

Loved to follow-up on a project, not waste time. Made sure everyone was informed and knew what to do. Role? Initiator, planner, and organizer."

Designed and made door signs. "Each had to be hand-spaced. All customized."

Made all the paintings for our first apartment. "They were all my designs. Love to blend colors together."

Time Period III.

Worked for a company in personnel department. "I set up file systems. Kept all the records neat, accurate, and up to date. Role? More or less an administrator. I did what they asked me to do."

In charge of the department budget for XYZ company. "I liked recording figures neatly, balancing figures—all the detail involved. Role? Budget supervisor or maybe budget administrator."

Time Period IV.

Achieved high level of competency in calligraphy.

Set up a community instructional program for young parents. "I organized it, listened to their suggestions, scheduled it, sent out invitations that I designed and made. Role? In charge, the organizer."

Keeping our checkbook and compiling our income tax returns.

Charlotte's personal style category is mainly one and some two; her personal style role is organizer and administrator. Her other capabilities include creating, designing and drawing, organizing and administrating, and keeping financial records. Charlotte likes to work with figures and projects as well as doing things with her hands.

After making this evaluation, Charlotte's friend commented, "After all these years, I never knew this about you." That is a typical comment, even from parents looking at their twenty-five-year-old son or daughter's positive experiences. We think we know, yet so often we really don't. Assumptions cause people problems! Assuming someone else's willingness often fails. People are usually willing to do things that use their capabilities.

Dolores Swanberg has jumped from job to job, never really

happy about her job experiences. She said, "People keep telling me I have so much talent. But what should I be doing?" Jeanette, a work associate, encouraged her to pinpoint her capabilities. So here we go again!

CASE 4   DOLORES SWANBERG

Time Period I.

I colored very exactly in coloring books. "I would color for hours. I wanted it to look perfect and beautiful. I loved to create, make something out of nothing."

I would make little cards for people to make them happy. "I'm very conscious of colors and how they blend together. Role? Sort of a cheering agent—telling through cards I liked them."

Time Period II.

Wrote small books with drawings for school history class. "Would first read and vicariously be a person living there; for example in Egypt or Holland. I'd write to create a tone and mood."

In school I drew pictures for decorations.

Time Period III.

I taught myself sewing and needlework. "I would make sure it was done right and properly—everything straight and proper. I felt creative to be able to take something flat and ugly and make it into something beautiful. Role? Creator. Designer."

Decorated my apartment. "Continually balanced furniture style, pictures, lighting, and drapes. It all fits perfectly. Role? The designer."

Time Period IV.

Entertaining creatively for friends. "I love to do ethnic dinners, do something special to have right music, food, lighting, aura. I serve them. They don't do anything. Role? Creator of an atmosphere. A comforter to help my friends relax."

Organized product promotions for my company. "I designed the brochure. Would set up display area and create the right atmosphere. Role? A visualizer—one who pictured the display area in my mind at the start. So I really was the creator of it."

Jeanette and Dolores pulled out these capabilities from Dolores' positive experiences: size up, create and visualize, design, draw, and write. She also enjoyed building relationships with people. She functions mainly with things, and some with people. She often said, "I like seeing that visible end result." Her personal style category is mainly one, and her personal style role is creative designer.

Her present job is mainly administrating and organizing projects. Jeanette helped her see this and this helped her understand her previous job dissatisfaction. Changing her responsibilities to fit the job to the person has brought a higher level of fulfillment.

Michael's track record in staff turnover is poor. While he is able to recruit quality people, his staff complain about getting no supervision. "He's never around, always going someplace," as one staffer said.

Michael turned up these positive experiences which surprised his supervisor but not his staff. They said, "Yes, that's what he does."

CASE 5   MICHAEL FIPPS

Time Period I.

Friends and I built a dirt race track. I played announcer. "I just loved hollering off the play by play—let my imagination run wild. Role? Inspirer and communicator."

Played little league baseball. "Role? Team member—do my part well."

Time Period II.

Had lead in high school drama production. "I loved the total exhilaration of being on stage. Acting is a big challenge to me. Role? The director would ask me for ideas. I also helped the other actors in their parts. Was sort of assistant coordinator of the performance."

Went on a speaking tour for a missions organization.

Time Period III.

In college, helped coordinate senior class drama production. "The director didn't have much time, so I stepped in with the director's approval. I was gung ho to pull it off. Role? Not the director, because I hate telling people what to do. More the coordinator, I let them create their own parts—I made suggestions."

Part of a Christian comedy team.

Time Period IV.

Gave commencement address at high school from which I graduated. "I loved preparing for that speech, plus I enjoy the total satisfaction I get being up front."

Was main speaker at a church weekend retreat. "I even got them to act out some Bible characters. I sort of suggested it—then coordinated it. They loved it. I did too."

Any wonder Michael never supervised his staff? He got his fulfillment up front, on stage, before audiences. When he did supervise, it ended up a mini-speech. He gravitated in that direction; the internal pull to do what satisfies is strong. For example, Michael's last positive experience finds him going ahead and doing his thing—coordinating a drama production. In this case, he could do it; in another situation it may have gotten him in trouble; someone may have stopped him. Much like Phillip Mack getting into trouble with his supervisor when he kept contributing ideas, counseling, advising, and being a confidant. I am not advocating, "Do your own thing," but only suggesting that every person has strong tendencies to exercise his capabilities. Recognizing these tendencies in ourselves and others helps explain why people do some things and don't do other things.

While speaking, Michael's personal style category is one. When performing or in the role of a performance coordinator, his personal style category is mainly two and three. His people—data—things classification is people—people in the sense of audiences and drama productions.

These examples show why people do something once or twice and then stop and don't follow up; or why someone "goes hard" six months or so (because it is new or different) and then starts becoming less and less effective. One key reason is mismatch. That leg of the tripod is missing. It explains also why people don't follow up.

LISTEN, LISTEN, LISTEN

The biggest challenge facing someone helping another person is first to accept what they are saying. It sounds easy, but listening and being objective is hard work. After helping eight people discover their capabilities, Jim said, "I'm just learning how important it is just to accept what they are saying. I keep trying to transpose and project my experiences and definitions on them." How true.

Like Jim, we project ourselves on others—our values, our experiences, our terminology, rather than first accepting what they are saying. "Accept one another, then, for the glory of God, as Christ has accepted you" (Rom. 15:7, TEV). First accepting people, who they are and what they say, is our biggest challenge. Usually we first try to change them to conform to our standards!

Besides the problem of projecting ourselves, there is the tendency to use counseling techniques that look for the reasons a person did something. For example, we ask, "Why do you feel this way toward Jean?" While asking *why* is useful in counseling, we should stick to asking *how* a person did something. This is not to demean counseling principles and techniques. It is only to point out that the purposes of counseling and pinpointing capabilities are different.

To project less and listen more objectively, one person says, "I think of myself as an empty container. The other person fills this container with information. I don't have to ask why; instead I ask those three questions. Doing this requires concentration and listening to what the person is saying. I write as they talk; sometimes we record it. Then we sift through the container of information, looking for recurring ideas. It is hard work."

One side benefit of listening carefully when someone is telling about his positive experiences is reflected in Katherine's comment, "You're the first person in my life who has ever listened to me like this and at least tried to understand me, who first accepted me and what I was saying. Now we can make changes and improvements based on my strengths. Now I'm willing—before I wasn't."

Sandra expressed a second side benefit. "I felt fulfilled and better about myself recalling my accomplishments. The questions helped me see how I really do things."

So in this setting to pinpoint capabilities we should relax and enjoy what the person is saying. Any possible change or correction can be done at other times.

There must be a high level of trust between people if this concept is to work effectively. If a person feels he will be exploited or made fun of when capabilities are known, he will get hurt. So whether in the home, office, or church, a positive climate where people come first is a must. People lose interest if goals are idolized, or worse yet, if goals are not tied in with interests and capabilities. Linking capabilities to individual and group goals is exciting.

Thirty-five people in one church pinpointed each other's capabilities. Then several ministry programs, such as visitation, evangelism, discipleship, teaching, building things, maintenance, and music were set up. People with capabilities in those areas became part of a group. For example, those with the capability of visitation were part of the visitation group. Each group met to plan and set goals. Leadership asked each group, "What is your vision for this area of visitation?" The pastor's enthusiastic reaction was, "Each group took the meeting away from us." He meant they had many ideas and each wanted to pitch in. He said, "They're motivated to follow up. All we are doing is coordinating and harnessing them. They want to because they're exercising their capabilities."

Fitting responsibilities to the person nips many potential people problems in the bud. This church understands now that starting on the right side of the fulfillment cycle works. Starting on the left side (goals first) is backwards and counterproductive.

Planning is starting with what people want to do and going clockwise around the fulfillment cycle. Goals emerge out of people's ideas and capabilities. They occur usually in a positive, supportive, trusting climate.

In summary, each person has capabilities. No one is neglected since God wants us to be satisfied in our service to him. Whether a person enjoys people, data, or things, it is all done to serve God and man. For example, a Christian auto mechanic (things) serves God and man, the car owner. The mechanic's medium, unlike a counselor, is engines and tools, but counselors need cars and mechanics need counselors. We need each other.

In Appendix A is a three-step process designed to help individuals discover their capabilities.

FIVE
YELLOW AND RED ARE
SLOW DOWN AND STOP

Charlie Brown and Lucy are sitting against a tree pondering the future. Lucy asks, "You really liked that little red-haired girl, didn't you, Chuck? Which would you rather do, hit a home run with the bases loaded or marry the little red-haired girl?"

"Why couldn't I do both?" Charlie asks.

Lucy answers, "We live in a real world, Chuck!"

The real world comes in positive *and* negative experiences. The traffic light is often yellow or red; we wish it would stay green, but that is wishful thinking. Every responsible person must be doing things he dislikes doing. Clara said she coped with things she disliked doing. That is how it usually is when away from green and into doing yellow and red things.

"I realize I have to do these things I dislike," Clara added. "They are essential and necessary, so I do them—no, I cope with them. But I don't exactly feel as though I have accomplished anything." As the green light is capabilities, the yellow and red lights are a person's limabilities.

We don't procrastinate, of course, but we have observed others, for example, putting off straightening out the garage, trimming the hedge, or cleaning the living room. We have seen others put off writing a letter to their church missionary. Who of us hasn't started something and never finished it—making a dress, or supervising adequately those seven people who report to us? Many of us have unfinished tasks piling up around us and if we do start, down deep inside we are hoping for a distraction such as a phone call or some excuse not to do it. Or do we do some things sporadically—only when we really feel like doing them or are up to it?

Join the rest of us. We are part of the human race. These never-started and half-finished tasks are important clues to our limabilities. Solving people problems in a way that puts people first is to recognize that all people have strengths (capabilities) as well as limitations (limabilities). This is the real world. Knowing what a person does not want to do is often as important as knowing what he wants to do.

To pinpoint limabilities, a person looks back on his life and lists his negative experiences, the opposite of his positive experiences.

WHAT IS A NEGATIVE EXPERIENCE?

A negative experience is generally something a person dislikes and does not enjoy doing because he: (1) has little or no interest in it; (2) has little or no desire to do it; or (3) does not do it very well (in his opinion).

Negative experiences give off little feeling of accomplishment, as Clara said. Jim said, "When using my limabilities, I get no feeling of accomplishment. But at the end I do, saying to myself, 'I'm sure glad to get that over with.'" So when a task takes time, a person's attitude sours toward that task. To him, it is dissatisfying and distasteful. A sense of accomplishment when it is finished helps some, but not much.

The net result of such an experience is that people will tend to avoid, rather than repeat (as in positive experiences), doing unfulfilling things. Such tasks often go unfinished. Or when they are done, they are not done very well, or they take three times longer than expected, causing people problems to surface.

The person then feels guilty—he is not measuring up to his and others' standards. Guilty people feel indecisive and insecure; their sense of worth, negative.

Jim Chapman, for example, the forty-four-year-old former teacher, reviews his negative experiences:

The real world comes in positive and negative experiences.

Speaking in front of an audience at a sports award banquet. "I felt uneasy and nervous. I even got angry at the head coach (I was assistant coach). He told me it would be simple and easy. It wasn't for me."

Presiding over a committee. "I don't like telling people what they should be doing. I hate to delegate. I'd rather do it myself."

Organizing a church fund-raising project for our young people. "It was a worthy project but I hated being in charge. The pressure was almost unbearable. I hardly slept the night before a committee meeting."

Teaching math to high schoolers. "I hated having to discipline. And I felt uncomfortable in front of them. I had no confidence."

During graduate school, I had to present an oral report. "I felt uneasy and unsure of myself."

Some of Jim's limabilities include speaking, teaching, organizing, and chairing committee meetings. He dislikes being in front of people as well as delegating.

Any wonder he is unfulfilled teaching, even with a master's degree? The match-up was negative. He was using mainly limabilities; he disliked going to work in the morning. His day dragged, because people don't look forward to unpleasant things.

Jim's capabilities included shaping and building, fixing and working with his hands. His personal style category is one. Looking at his positive experiences reveals that he did not delegate even one task. His negative experiences ooze with dislike for category two (through others) functions. Since he is a category one, he also dislikes category three things. Notice he said, "I'd rather do it myself."

Negative experiences are the other side of positive experiences, so what is not a capability is a limability. Some people locate their limabilities saying, "What is not a capability is automatically a limability." That is true, but I find most people want to see for themselves, so they go ahead and identify their negative experiences (see Appendix B) and then add other limabilities not picked up in their negative experiences. For example, it is safe to say that some of Jim's other limabilities include promoting, selling, counseling, researching, writing, to name a few. Whatever is not a capability is a limability. Jim also agreed. He said, "What I want to do is work with my hands and see a visible end result. I hate all that other stuff."

From chapter 4, you will recall that Charlotte's capabilities included creating, designing and drawing, organizing and administering, and keeping financial records. Her personal style category is mainly one and some two, in a role of organizer and administrator.

Let's take a look at some of her negative experiences.

CASE 3   CHARLOTTE SHOCKLEY

Learning to knit. "It was so boring. And if I lost my count, I'd get frustrated."

Working as a salesperson in a department store. "Hated
having to look busy, even when nothing to do. They made me be
aggressive by approaching everyone who walked in and asking
if I could help them. I don't like selling."

As a college junior, she assisted in a church youth group. "I
was supposed to be thirty minutes early and I had to strike up a
conversation with newcomers. I disliked not knowing anyone. I
felt pressure from the leader to jump right in with the kids. I quit
after the first semester."

Worked full time for a church with senior high group. "The goal
was to build strong relationships with the kids. I never was
much for small talk and a lot of one-on-one stuff. Never got into
going to the socials Saturday nights. One objective was to
make some kind of contact during the week, so I had to call twelve
people that were my responsibility on Thursday nights. I
dreaded Thursday nights."

Being promoted to office manager. "I didn't like giving away
my duties (which I enjoyed) and being put in a supervisory
position. I felt frustrated not having a specific job to work on.
Felt as if I wasn't accomplishing much."

Charlotte's limabilities include knitting, selling, contacting
people, and building relationships. Another is personal style
category two (delegating). Other limabilities could be added—to
name a few—speaking, singing, and working directly with
people (from her positive experiences her people-data-things
classification was mainly figures and projects). Charlotte loves
people and has a serving heart. She just feels more fulfilled and
has a sense of accomplishment working with figures and
projects.

In chapter 4 we talked about Michael Fipps. Since we may
feel like predicting some of his limabilities let us list his negative
experiences briefly.

CASE 5   MICHAEL FIPPS

*Working with figures, the legal aspects of being an office
manager.*

Confronting people about their responsibilities.

Office administration.

Delegating and asking people to do something.

Working in a factory; operated a drill press. It was dissatisfying doing the same thing all day.

Supervising my staff, particularly sitting down and training them. "It's so tedious and hard."

Studying at college. "It was too confining. I never saw the point of my major, business administration. I was more interested in speaking and dramatics. I always procrastinated, studied at the last minute."

Working on my car motor.

Trying to fix our TV, "felt humiliated when my neighbor had to do it. Seemed simple to him."

Michael's limabilities include supervising and training, delegating, administration, fixing and repairing. Data and things frustrate him. Other limabilities could be added: visiting, designing, drawing, cleaning, maintaining, counseling, operating machines, selling, and researching.

All people have limabilities. Isolating limabilities helps answer the "Why don't they do it?" question. People tend to avoid doing something unfulfilling, so they procrastinate. Michael Fipps avoided supervising, since that is one of his limabilities. People who dislike cleaning and dusting will procrastinate. Procrastination causes people problems.

WHAT IS YELLOW, WHAT IS RED?

The real world means not only positive and negative experiences where real people have both capabilities and limabilities. The real world also means that most jobs and tasks require people to use both their capabilities and limabilities. In other words, there is no perfect job. As Pat said, "As a homemaker, there are things I want to do (using capabilities) and things I have to do (using limabilities). Want to and have to go together."

The fact that there is no perfect job is illustrated by the traffic light. But let us, in our minds, turn it upside down. Starting with people first is an upside down approach! Now the green light is on top.

Since there is no perfect job, it is my view that about 40 percent of what someone does will mean using his capabilities, his "greens." Dropping down, the yellow light represents

People first is an upside down approach.

yellow limabilities—things a person may do fairly well, but not want to do much of it. About 20 percent of what someone does may require using yellow limabilities, as we will see in a moment.

At the bottom, the red light represents red limabilities — things people find dissatisfying yet must do. Forty percent of what someone does may require using his red limabilities.

I call this the 40/20/40 concept to give a rough picture of real life. One person said, "The top (green) 40 percent is what I want to do a lot, the middle (yellow) 20 percent is what I want to do a little, and the lower 40 percent (red) is what I do not want to do at all." As responsible drivers can't avoid yellow and red signals, so responsible people-problem solving can't avoid yellow and red limabilities.

Scripture points out that avoiding or ducking unpleasant things is irresponsible. "Don't always be trying to get out of doing your duty, even when it's unpleasant" (Ecclesiastes 8:2, 3, TLB). "Do not be proud, but be willing to associate with people of low position" (Romans 12:16, NIV). (The footnote in the NIV reads "or willing to do menial work.") We must not duck our responsibility. Meeting people needs may be something unpleasant but it is still our responsibility.

People should be willing to reach across social, color, and economic barriers to demonstrate compassion (goals that meet people needs). The answer to people problems is not in patronizing, parading your good deeds, but in serving and influencing people—silently and positively. And we should do it even if it means using limabilities. No task or responsibility that we take on is "perfect."

People cannot be ignored just because we prefer data and/or things rather than people. Scripture is clear: "I tell you the truth, anyone who gives you a cup of water in my name because you belong to Christ will certainly not lose his reward" (Mark 9:41, TEV).

On the other hand, someone who loves people (top 40 percent) but hates paperwork and administrative responsibilities (lower 40 percent) is shirking his responsibilities. A pastor whose capabilities include speaking should think twice before ducking visitation with his people (he may even feel guilty about not visiting) because visiting is not his thing. Rationalizing, he may even crowd his schedule full of speaking to have excuses not to visit. Meanwhile, his people long to see him, and the pastor wonders why people are responding less and less to his leadership.

While doing evaluation and feedback interviews with people, I discovered a very important concept. If a person is using his capabilities and is fulfilled enough, he is more apt to try doing (even though it is tough) and even repeat doing what he doesn't like to do if surrounded by accepting, caring people. Fulfillment goes a long way toward solving people problems.

Jerry's capabilities include contacting, visiting, encouraging, assisting, helping, befriending, and building relationships. At the same time, he pinpointed his limabilities—administration, supervision, completing reports, and telephone contacting. He

was using 10 percent of his capabilities on his job, so he was not
fulfilled enough. He was 10/20/70 rather than 40/20/40. He and
his supervisor changed his responsibilities to include more use
of his capabilities. (Remember: fit the job to the person, not the
person to the job!)

Two years later he said, "Dick, you know how much I detest
office work. In my view, it's so non-people. But I'm doing that
much better now, since Fred [his supervisor] and I redesigned my
job. My attitude toward my limabilities is changing too. For
some reason, I can put up with them now. I don't do them that
well, but I'm at least doing them. And I'm supervising three
people. I'm now feeling more productive. And Fred has been so
understanding. He has his faults but nowhere else could I get
the supervision and training that I needed."

When Jerry's fulfillment jumped, his willingness to do
unpleasant things also jumped. Then I saw time and time again
how people using more and more of their capabilities soon
were also using more of their limabilities.

Real life consists of adjusting and balancing so that a person
is adequately fulfilled. There is nothing magical about 40 percent.
If 60 percent of a person's responsibilities use capabilities, that
is fine. The percentages are only to illustrate the concept of
fulfillment and that there is no perfect job.

SO WHAT IS YELLOW?

Yellow limabilities are things a person may enjoy doing briefly,
and may even do fairly well. The key word is *briefly.* Too much
of yellow limabilities creates dissatisfaction. One way to pinpoint
yellow limabilities is to look for things that don't repeat in
positive experiences. Six years ago, I listed my positive
experiences.

Time Period I.
   *Learning to drive truck; practicing shifting to do it without
grinding the gears.*
   Gave valedictory speech in eighth grade.
   *As high school student council president, I liked stirring up
things, asking the tough questions. I liked it when kids called me
to talk over their problems.*

Time Period II.

In college, was elected president of ASCE. Shook up status quo bringing in controversial speakers.

As president, took over a floundering church youth group. Particularly liked running meetings, speaking, and emceeing a banquet.

Instructor in school for new sales people. Loved teaching and leading discussions.

Time Period III.

Troubleshooter for my company and problem solver with executives.

Instructor in management school for managers and executives.

Introduced and implemented a new in-company supervisory program. I liked supervising and training new consultants.

Time Period IV.

Put an addition on our home; built furniture.

Directed a training conference, after four others by other directors had failed.

Did an in-company management seminar on my own.

I enjoyed putting the addition on our home, even though building things is a yellow limability. A little is OK, but too much of it and I'm dissatisfied. At one point, I thought I would help my brother build houses. The first day was OK, the second began to drag, and by Wednesday, I had had it. I learned "my thing" is not eight hours a day of building. I like it, but to do it all the time would be unfulfilling. A careful review of my positive experiences tells a clear story. Take away speaking, teaching, troubleshooting, and problem-solving, and my wife has a people problem on her hands! And I do too.

Another of my yellow limabilities is supervising people. I'm a category one. I have not supervised anyone for six years, and unlike a category two, who is fulfilled supervising, I don't miss it a lick. When I did it, I felt I did it fairly well, but other things fulfill me more.

Another yellow is building furniture. It would be crazy for me to go into the furniture making business. After six months, I'd go crazy, but as a hobby, it would be fine.

Yellow is caution. It does not mean a total stop. That is, a person enjoys something for a while, but he should be cautious. To enjoy something once or twice or for a little while might fool us and lead us into jumping into something where we would have to do it all the time. I, for instance, should avoid being in the furniture business.

We can see that people have a few capabilities but many more limabilities. Using limabilities seems contradictory to God's plan that people be satisfied. On the other hand, using limabilities is consistent with his injunction to do unpleasant tasks, or even so-called menial tasks. We shall bring these seemingly inconsistent concepts about using limabilities to the forefront now and consider how to deal (cope?) with limabilities.

DEALING WITH LIMABILITIES

Being able to deal with limabilities depends on a person's spiritual fitness. "For apart from me you can do nothing at all" (John 15:5, Phil.). As branches, we depend on the vine. If a person is skipping his daily Bible study and prayer time, that person is not spiritually fit. So he is (a branch) hanging on by a tiny thread through which very little spiritual resource flows from God. When using a limability, a thread-Christian often goes around proving to others he can do what he dislikes doing, mechanically, or loudly going through the motions. Missing is the mellowness and fruitfulness of Christ.

On the other hand, someone more firmly attached to the vine is capable of receiving more of his resources. Speaking only for myself, I need an extra measure of God's inner enabling when using my limabilities. And God does step in and help. So, while I also need to be abiding in Christ while using my capabilities, it is even more important when using my limabilities. If my attitude makes me dependent on him more, I should be more fruitful than if hanging by a thread.

This concept brings together the seeming inconsistencies in the concept of using both capabilities *and* limabilities. If fulfilled enough and if abiding in Christ (someone *experiencing* the presence of Jesus), a person can be fruitful in either case.

Abiding is the key. A pastor pinpointed Steve's capabilities. I asked, "Is he studying the Word and praying?" The pastor said he wasn't. It took nine months before Steve was "on his own" and into the Word each day. It took hours and hours of the pastor's time. Afterwards, God moved in beautiful and unexplainable ways and Steve, with a Ph.D. degree, has begun a new career. It all started with a pastor caring about one person.

There are three ways to help you and others deal with limabilities:

1. Accept your limabilities. Don't underestimate the difficulty in doing this. For example, it was hard for me to accept that I am not a speaker and entertainer—a performance-oriented person who motivates and leaves people laughing in the aisles—rather than speaker and teacher. I speak, yes, but when I try to entertain, I feel terrible inside and superficial. It is not me. I also had dreams of making big money on the business speaking circuit so I could reduce my fees to Christian organizations. Those sound like good motives, but I was off base. I was ignoring the real me. Not only was I not accepting my limabilities, worse yet, I spent tons of time gearing up for it. All wasted.

It takes a special, caring supervisor to accept other people's limabilities. So often supervisors jump in without first considering the person's real feelings. One of Natalie's limabilities is speaking. Before, during, and after a speaking engagement, she is a nervous wreck. In her own mind, she does not speak well.

After observing her speak once, her boss said, "You did it so well. That was tremendous." Natalie then burst out in tears saying, "But I don't, I don't."

Maybe she did it fairly well that time, but Natalie feels she does not speak well. If only her boss had listened first, rather than complimenting her. Sometimes encouragers and motivators go overboard when capabilities and limabilities are not known, since like Natalie's boss they are acting without knowing how a person really feels when doing something.

Supervision, as I said, is one of my limabilities. Accepting this fact was like releasing a burden from my shoulders. Now I don't have to downgrade my accomplishments and capabilities because I don't have six or eight people reporting to me. As one person said to me, "Dick, you can concentrate on becoming more competent in who you are [green] rather than in who you

are not [yellow and red]." So when limabilities are accepted,
guilt is removed for not measuring up to other people's standards
of success.

Right after I helped Don uncover his capabilities, he asked, "Am
I a salesman?"

I said, "No," and I wanted to know the reason for his question.

"I've been on a sales job now for four weeks but I'm finding
it difficult to call on people. I don't like to close." Selling is one of
his limabilities. He also asked, "I've presented Christ to 136
people and only one has received Christ. What's wrong—aren't
we all evangelists? What they are teaching me about selling
and evangelism seems about the same."

His capabilities included cleaning, maintaining, visiting,
making friends, and building relationships. Don was trying to use
a set presentation as he evangelized and, in his view, was
failing miserably. And he was! He felt guilty too.

I replied, "We're all evangelists, but I'd suggest using a
different approach, capitalizing more on making friends [one of
his strengths] and building relationships." He accepted this
and today is a better evangelist, influencing many to commit their
lives to Christ. When he accepted his limabilities, guilt was
removed, and now he is doing a better job of evangelizing.

I'm not primarily an evangelist and I have accepted that.
Now that I know this, I think I do better at sharing Christ with
others. I have stopped comparing myself with others and
feeling inferior and guilty about my "evangelistic efforts." Now I
literally give my Bible to people and have them read Scripture.
I suggest, rather than confront. I sow a few seeds here and there.
Removing guilt had a lot to do with it.

A lady said, "I'm not a verbal witness or an evangelist. All I can
do is invite people to church."

I said, "That's evangelism." Her guilt feelings seemed to
evaporate when I said, "How I wish our churches had more
evangelists like you." In her mind, she was not measuring up.
Her guilt was removed. The pastor says that by accepting her
new role as "inviter," she is pointing many people to their church.
And by herself she led two people to Christ last year.

One of my wife's capabilities is homemaking, but one of her
limabilities is sewing. Until the traffic light concept dawned and
developed in my mind, I felt every housewife should sew,

including my wife. After all, I thought, since my mother used to sew the holes in my socks, my wife should too. Sparks would fly when I'd put on a sock with holes.

I wonder how many husbands are imposing their mothers' standards on their wives rather than first finding out and accepting their spouses' green, yellow, and red areas. I wonder how many wives are doing the same thing to their husbands. Accepting people is easy to say but difficult to put into practice.

2. Form Realistic Expectations. In other words, we shouldn't try talking ourselves and others into liking something that is dissatisfying. If a person dislikes record keeping and one day happens to feel like doing it, that should not signal long-term feelings. For example, sometimes I like doing a few hours of red light things just for a change of pace. But those occasions happen when everything is going right, so it doesn't happen very often.

Also, we should form realistic expectations for others by letting them know when we will be "redding" it. Remember, in doing so we will tend to be somewhat less fruitful. The look on Lucy's face made Linus say to Charlie Brown, "Don't go near Lucy today. She's in one of her super crabby moods. When she's like this, everybody should be warned to stay away from her."

A few moments later, Charlie asks, "What are you doing?"

Linus answers, "Setting out flares!"

I let my wife and others know when I am doing accounting and record keeping. At tax time, they need a whole supply of flares. During such times, my attitude varies from bad to very bad. I even spout off to my wife, get angry at her just because the figures don't balance. Of course, she had nothing to do with it. Even though I ask God for his help, and ask others to pray, doing my red light things for extended periods is hard, tough work. Like many others, I am often a disagreeable person at such times; not very Christlike.

Jill coined this phrase: Agreeable experiences (green), agreeable people, disagreeable experiences (red), disagreeable people. When using a limability some of us see red and become angry, particularly when down emotionally.

My wife bought some dress material and was at the sewing machine and needle all day. It was a hot, humid New England day.

Around four o'clock, she was exasperated. She felt the sewing didn't come out well. Having formed that realistic expectation, I could accept her feelings and did not say, "I told you so!" At other times, I have been insensitive and said the wrong thing, which started an argument.

When we form realistic expectations, we don't end up blaming ourselves and others. I have stopped kicking myself for not taking more accounting. Knowing more about it may help some, but the fact remains that bookkeeping is one of my reds. I don't blame my wife for not liking to sew. I have accepted it as one of her reds.

3. Exercise Self-Discipline. We play all sorts of mental games to come up with excuses not to do something.

For example, one of my reds, as I said, is calling on people and house-to-house canvassing. Our Sunday school decided to canvass a neighborhood from two to four on Sunday afternoon to hand out information about our church and Sunday school. Doing this may be simple and easy for you, but it is one of my strong reds. Two days before this I thought, "Maybe it will rain so I won't have to go. Perhaps I'll catch a cold—certainly I wouldn't want to spread my disease; I think we should invite someone for Sunday dinner—certainly I will be needed to entertain them for the afternoon." I was doing everything to avoid it.

Then I said, "This is part of your responsibility. One week ago you made a commitment to do it, so pull the pacifier out of your mouth and *do* it." So I did—I chose to do it. We can *choose* to take on or avoid reds.

Writing about 1 Corinthians 13 in *Love Within Limits* (Grand Rapids: Eerdmans, 1978), Lewis B. Smedes describes suffering as "the experience of anything we want very much not to experience. The key here is the phrase 'very much' " (p. 1). Love, in the Scriptures, is "long-suffering." Most of us want very much to avoid doing red things. Smedes really hits the nail on the head in saying, "The paradox of long-suffering is that we choose to suffer long . . . we have to make a decision for what we do not want, choose to live indefinitely with what we hate. This is the paradox that makes long-suffering a creative art of living."

Accepting my dislike for contacting and canvassing is not enough. I have a choice. And when I choose to do something to serve and glorify God, realizing my inability to do something on my own, I must abide in Christ, and his divine resources. Then people see me more as a positive influencer. Using limabilities can become a point of growth in our daily walk with Jesus.

Dr. Johnson's comment about my brother's Sunday school class verifies that while we may not feel qualified, God uses committed people. When faced with a limabilities task, self-discipline shoves aside excuses such as, "It's too hot," or "It's too cold," "I really don't feel up to it" (we never do when facing a limability-using task), or "Let someone else do it."

A pastor's capabilities included speaking and promoting. As the church grew to more than 200 members, he was visiting his people regularly, but then he stopped visiting as other responsibilties crowded in on him. Then growth stopped.

He admitted, "When I stopped visiting, my illustrations became lifeless and second-hand." Today, he's back visiting and has accepted it as a challenge and point of growth. His elder board is supportive and encouraging too. This pastor chose to meet people needs and be people-responsible. He admits, "I really don't like to visit, but I'd be remiss if I didn't."

Bob, convicted about not visiting nursing homes, was functioning in a red area. This didn't stop him from responding to the need. He admits, "It's tough. Compared to other things, I feel I accomplish less visiting. Yet I want to do it, and with God's help, I am."

My guiding verses are: "For God has said, 'I will never leave you; I will never abandon you.' Let us be bold, then, and say, 'The Lord is my helper, I will not be afraid' " (Hebrews 13:5, 6, TEV). Nervous, yes, but not afraid.

You may be thinking, "Can't someone be hired to do the red things?" Yes, and that is often what is done in secular business, where money tends to be more available. Even there, however, this traffic light concept holds true. But remember, typical business methods and decisions are 180 degrees different from volunteer settings. I can hire someone to do my bookkeeping, but I've chosen to do it myself, no matter how unpleasant. Perhaps the pastor can hire someone to visit, but he chose to do it himself. A homemaker may dislike cooking, but she has to do it. Students may dislike studying, but choose to do it. In volunteer settings, there are many things that must be done when people really don't want to. We choose whether or not to do them. It takes self-discipline to minimize the procrastination problem. Here are four ways that will help in learning self-discipline:

Do it right away. Doing anything mechanical is limabilities-using. It took me three months to replace the trailer hitch—a forty-five-minute job. It showed up on my weekly list of things to do week after week.

One way to get something like this done is to do it immediately. There is a saying: "One way to make an easy job difficult is to keep putting it off." Tasks accumulate, and correspondence, papers and undarned socks pile up. As Lillian said, "Planning is the art of putting off until tomorrow what you have no intention of doing today." Ouch! I'm guilty!

Again, God's Word is to the point: "So when you talk to God and vow to him that you will do something, don't delay in doing it. . . . Keep your promise to him. It is far better not to say you'll do something than to say you will and then not do it" (Ecclesiastes 5:4, 5, TLB).

After returning from a trip and before opening my mail, I do three limability-using things right away. First, I return all my material to its right file; second, I make out my expense account, and third, do the billing.

I also try to answer all correspondence (red area) within twenty-four hours. Otherwise, it just piles up. Doing it right away helps.

Complete it. Since people are easily distracted from red areas, commit yourself to completing jobs rather than feeling guilty about half-finished projects lying around.

Alex dislikes fund-raising and soliciting his personal support, so he plans what he calls an "intensive effort." He takes one day each week and concentrates all his energies in that one area. That way, he completes it. When I'm doing a follow-up, I make sure I finish it before going on to something I like doing better, or jumping from task to task. If I don't, it will never get done! It takes self-discipline and people around me who understand. "Finishing is better than starting!" (Ecclesiastes 7:8, TLB). "The wise man will find a time and a way to do what he says" (Ecclesiastes 8:5, TLB). Completing something 75 percent rather than 25 percent of the time is improvement. At least we can turn back more often and say, "I'm glad that it's over with!"

Pace by Switching. We should alternate fulfilling and unfulfilling tasks. For example, if we like to counsel but dislike writing, we should plan to write before or after counseling, in anticipation of something fulfilling or, better yet, after something fulfilling.

Speaking at a church retreat is a fulfilling experience for me. It carries over and motivates me for several days. I can draw on that fulfillment and plan to do red things the days afterward.

Plan Plus. People get behind by underestimating how long it takes to do something. For example, someone tells us it takes twenty minutes to drive downtown. It actually takes thirty-five minutes. Or we think, "I'll knock out these three letters in thirty minutes." One hour later we might finish.

Even when we function in our green areas, we often underestimate. We should either start sooner or schedule more time. *Plan plus* by adding a comfortable margin to the time you think it will take to do something.

This really hits hardest when we are doing something major in our red area. It often takes two to three times longer than we at first estimate, so the plus factor is even longer. Working against us is the inclination to procrastinate, and by definition a negative experience is something we feel we don't do very well. So if we try to do a job well, it will take much longer.

I set a deadline for writing this manuscript. Writing is one of my limabilities. I had finished five of eleven chapters by the deadline. Will I ever learn! Will we ever learn!

So we must allow ourselves enough time. If we finish sooner, fine. But if something is important and needs to be done right the first time, we should *plan plus*—add a single plus when "greening" it, and add two or three plusses when "redding" it. Yes, it takes discipline to do this.

SIX
APPLYING THE TRAFFIC LIGHT CONCEPT

The traffic light concept stands in front of us. By watching for green, yellow, and red signals, many (not all) questions about people are answered. Here are some examples:

"Why doesn't someone volunteer to head up the church's fiftieth anniversary celebration?" Most likely, no one on the anniversary committee feels he has this capability. The signals are red.

"Why doesn't she ever straighten out the front room or ever bake my favorite cookies?" The answer? Most likely these tasks are limabilities-using.

"Why is his bedroom so messy?" Most likely, arranging and straightening out are his limabilities. (On the other side, isn't it interesting how neatness fanatics also give other people fits.)

"I can't understand why he keeps doing that. Every night when Bill comes home from work he tinkers with the car. Last night he fixed the neighbor's lawn mower. Why doesn't he do what I want?" Those signals suggest two reasons: He may not be fulfilled enough at work, or fixing things is one of his capabilities. In either case, fixing and repairing seem to be his thing.

"Why is Shirley always [in my case it's never!] trimming the hedge?" It's her thing.

"Why is Sandra always painting murals, rather than doing housework?" Painting is her thing.

Let me sound a loud note of caution: The traffic light concept answers questions about people, but by no means does it answer all of them. Only God understands people completely. Our understanding of ourselves and others is limited, imperfect, and incomplete. Looking through the traffic light raises our level of people understanding from 35 percent to perhaps 55 percent. It is never 100 percent.

We have imperfect understanding for two reasons. One, people are God's creation, not man's design to figure out. Most likely a perfect understanding of each other would mean relying on methods and techniques rather than upon God.

Second, if someone were understood totally, other people would tend to put him into slots or boxes. While no one really wants to be labeled or slotted, people drift toward slot approaches such as when trying to find someone both willing and qualified.

Greg is on the church nominating committee and asks, "Why don't people come in neat packages so we could identify their strengths, limitations, and weaknesses and then put them in slot X? It would be so much simpler."

Eleanor said, "I don't think anyone, including me, wants to be labeled and put in a box or slot."

So without putting people into slots and also without perfect understanding of people, our aim now is either to avoid or to solve people problems. The traffic light concept is one tool among many other people-problem solving tools. Also, we should keep in mind the three questions from chapter 1:

1. What is God trying to accomplish *in that person?*
2. What is God trying to accomplish *through you* in that person?
3. What is God trying to accomplish *in you* because of that person?

Problem solvers are quiet positive influencers—serving, helping, and coming alongside someone else. Let us make sure our advice is coming from a caring heart. People who don't care pepper too much advice at others, which leaves no room for God to get near them.

EDUCATIONAL CHOICES

George's parents want him to go to a liberal arts college. Now a senior in high school, George has little interest in college.

"He's always messing up our driveway with old cars and grease," his father says. "Grades? Mostly C's," his mother chips in.

George looked back on his positive experiences and also ranked them number one (most fulfilling), number two (a little less fulfilling), etc. Often this evaluation points out capabilities more clearly. George's number one positive experience is working on his car.

Notice the rest of George's positive experiences and the order in which he ranked them (in parentheses):

Time Period I.
   (9) Serving as hall monitor in school.
   (10) Doing math problems quickly.

Time Period II.
   (5) Working on my bike, fixing it.
   (6) Building racetrack for AFX cars.
   (1) Working on my car.

Time Period III.
   (3) Having a tag (garage) sale. "I love buying something cheap, fixing it and then selling it at a profit."
   (8) Buying things at auctions.
   (7) Working in a machine shop.

Time Period IV.
   (4) Building balsa wood airplanes and rockets.
   (2) Learning about combustion engines.

George's capabilities are pointing him toward a technical school rather than a liberal arts college because, obviously, he would rather fix cars than study history. If he went to a liberal arts college, since realistic expectations improve performance, George should form the realistic expectation that he wasn't going to like liberal arts college very much. We can almost see his frustration in a philosophy or English class. A B grade would be excellent for George. He isn't dumb. His interests and capabilities just don't match up with liberal arts.

The other side of the coin is that philosophy and English majors would be just as frustrated grappling with something mechanical. They too would look pretty dumb in that area and George would appear the smart one.

If George goes to a liberal arts college, his parents and friends need to encourage and affirm him. George will probably feel guilty because he will seldom measure up to his friends' A's and B's. George, knowing this about himself, should feel good about his C's and be thrilled to death with an occasional A or B. If his parents expect him to make the dean's list, George will most likely quit.

In order that George be fulfilled enough at college, his parents should expect him to develop a side business fixing clunkers on campus. Then he will be more apt to do what he doesn't want to do—study philosophy and English, or whatever.

We can imagine his reluctance to be on the deacons' board of his church ten years from now. He would likely do it if a sensitive chairperson understood him. In any event, he would volunteer to fix the old Sunday school bus and keep it running.

Charlene completed two years of college, majoring in counseling and social work. Her goal up to now, and reflected in her major, is to get into direct people work. She said, "After all, isn't that the most Christian thing to do?"

Now Charlene hates college. "I don't want to go back and waste your money," she said to her parents. Notice Charlene's positive experiences:

Time Period I.
  (7) Learned songs, acting out parts, and sang.
  (8) Played in the snow, acting out fairy queen fantasies.

Time Period II.
  (4) Performed in grade school play. Had one of the leads.
  (5) Learned to play the guitar, wrote songs and sang them in church.

Time Period III.
  (2) Had her own singing group.
  (3) Created a folk mass.

Time Period IV.
  (6) Sang weekends at a local restaurant.
  (1) Sang solos. "I write my own songs."

Applying the traffic light concept and accepting people is one of life's biggest challenges.

Any wonder Charlene hates college? While in college, she stopped singing, writing songs, and acting because, in her words, "I felt I ought to do something more Christian—like counseling." To a large extent, she went unfulfilled for two years. Rather than being a 40/20/40 on the capabilities-limabilities scale, she was a 5/5/90. Her sense of worth was negative, and she lost all confidence in herself. She was right in the middle of the Guilt Cycle saying, "I'm not good at anything. I've lost my sense of purpose, so why set goals?"

She switched her major to dramatics. Now she is enjoying college. But it took a special and mature twenty-year-old to do

this. She said: "Most of all, I want a serving heart." Any
wonder doors are opening for her in what she feels is a crowded
field? Understanding parents were affirming and encouraging.
Her future is unknown, but she knows where she is going.

David felt guilty about quitting college after two years. His grades
were a few C's, many D's and some F's. *"I'm* no good," he kept
saying. "And how will my college record look on my resumé?
I'll never get a job."

After reviewing his positive experiences, David saw he
had no interest or desire to study, understand, and compre-
hend—capabilities that were essential to an engineering major.

"So it's not me," he said. "But what should I do?" He and
five friends prayed, while David looked for opportunities that used
his capabilities. He found work that matched his capabilities
with key responsibilities. He doesn't feel inferior without a
college degree. Today he is serving God in what others would
consider a lowly secular occupation. He is fulfilled and fruitful, and
very active in his local church. David is one who is not letting
the world squeeze him into its mold.

WHEN HOMEMAKING IS "HAVE TO," NOT "WANT TO"

In chapter 2, Maureen admitted quietly, "I just don't like
housework, or even taking care of my family for that matter"
(quietly because in many circles it is unacceptable for mothers
and wives to admit it). She added, "I don't like cooking, baking,
washing, or hanging out clothes. I dislike taking care of our kids,
shopping, being schedule coordinator, and taxi driver—
taking the kids here, picking them up there. Entertaining?
Now that's where Herb and I really go round and round. He wants
to but I don't."

Maureen is not saying she hates her husband and kids. In a
nutshell, she is saying: "I do not like being a homemaker." To
put it in Maureen's words, "I can't stand being everyone's slave!"

This problem is triply difficult to solve when Herb projects
and imposes his mother's standards on Maureen. His mother
loved being a homemaker, and Herb just can't fathom any

woman, particularly his wife, not *doing* and *being* the same way. As a kid he remembers the smell of cookies when he came home from school, and all he is experiencing now are empty cookie jars and too many TV dinners. Projecting our own standards and imposing them on other people keeps raising its ugly head. Accepting people is life's biggest challenge. And the hardest place to accept people is in our own homes. Models and roles have been erected by writers and experts whose sole aim is to build models, rather than to accept people. Roles and models emerge out of a person's capabilities, going clockwise around the Fulfillment Cycle, not shoving people into some uncomfortable role or model.

In such a situation, cold wars develop, and the home climate turns negative, and relationships sour. As Eleanor said in chapter 1, "He just doesn't understand. It's like hitting my head against the wall talking to him. The problem is communication."

Yes, the problem is communication; however, we should take it one step further. Are each other's capabilities and limabilities pinpointed? Most likely no. Just as in a business, we suffer from the problem of fitting the person to the job (homemaking) rather than the job to the person.

In his own mind, Herb had a job description (role model) written for Maureen when he married her. Genuine commitments were made on both sides. Maureen felt she would like homemaking. Herb felt he would be a good breadwinner. Occasionally, things work out, but when they don't, people problems break out.

Homemaking is an ability like any other ability, such as speaking, teaching, designing, and fixing. If anyone doubts this, listen to a husband being homemaker while his wife is away for three weeks. "Drying kids' hair, running the dishwasher, taking them to school, church meetings, helping with homework, a trip to the doctor, preparing meals, bugging them about piano and flute practice, phone calls, money for this and that. . . ." Homemaking should not be relegated to a number two position. It is important and takes loads of time. Since homemaking is important and time consuming, what happens when it is a "have to," a red limability, say, for a wife and mother?

One of Lillian's limabilities is homemaking. Lillian's capabilities include setting up systems, administering, initiating projects, contacting people to explain a program, and then convincing them to take action. Her personal style is category one in the role of representative representing a program and telling people about it.

Lillian has one child. She and her husband want two more children. After pinpointing her capabilities, her first reaction was "So that's why housework is so frustrating! I feel so cooped up being in the house all day." Together they turned to the three ways of dealing with limabilities (last chapter): accepting them, forming realistic expectations, and exercising self-discipline. Then they searched out opportunities for Lillian to be out of the house more; Bill agreed to babysit occasionally. They are budgeting money each week for a baby sitter when Bill can't do it. Their search led to Lillian's volunteering to canvass the area near her church. She is also a representative for a small firm where she can set her own schedule.

Is it working out perfectly? Of course not. But now that Lillian is getting some fulfillment, her attitude about homemaking is better, since her guilt for not liking homemaking is removed.

On a scale of one-low, five-average, and ten-high, Vivian's level of fulfillment as a homemaker is three. Her capabilities do not include homemaking—yet a positive experience for her was being mother of two children. She ranked it number four. Her capabilities include teaching, encouraging, befriending, and building relationships. A yellow limability is taking care of children.

Her husband says, "Vivian is always teaching Rebecca. She never picks up around the house. Sometimes it looks like a tornado hit the inside of our house."

Now Vivian is teaching a neighborhood Bible study, and substitute teaching in elementary school. Her husband is saying, "The house is beginning to look better too." A simple adjustment, a profound result.

Homemaking carries with it varied responsibilities. Seldom does one person's capabilities embrace all a homemaker has to do, so the 40/20/40 concept applies here too. Most homemakers will want to do some things (Lillian was an exception) and dislike doing other things.

HUSBAND-WIFE RELATIONSHIPS

I'm not suggesting that this method is the solution to all marriage problems. I am only suggesting that the traffic-light concept is another possible tool. And if one partner's heart is insensitive and hard, nothing will work for very long.

"Why doesn't he ever grow up?" Pam asked. "He's always going to the gym to play basketball, or getting excited when someone mentions softball. He should be studying. To get anywhere, he must have his master's degree." Examining closely we can see four of his eleven positive experiences:

Played little league baseball; made all-star team.
Drummed up neighborhood scrimmages; would practice and practice basketball dribbling and shooting.
Became a good basketball player; "It's my major sport; I lettered every year of high school. Role? I wasn't captain, but I took charge because I wanted to win; if guys didn't hustle I'd challenge them. I demanded they give 100 percent—I was."
Camp counselor. "Loved teaching them to play basketball. Role? I psyched them up, motivated my team of guys. Would say, 'Give everything you've got. Do it until it hurts.' "

Pam's reaction was, "I could have told you that" when she found out that her husband's personal style category is three and personal style role is team inspirer.

Nevertheless, a review of Barry's positive experiences confirmed her thoughts and she later agreed that she was wrong to equate her husband's love for sports with immaturity. Things are ironing out in their relationship now that she knows her husband shouldn't be pursuing a master's degree in business administration. Her brother is a successful manager for a large corporation (projection again!).

The answer to "Why is he (or she) always . . " is often answered by looking at positive and negative experiences. Ralph enjoys cooking. His wife asks, "Why is he always in my kitchen?" To solve that problem, he now cooks (a green) for two youth groups and prepares supper in their home one evening a week. He doesn't want to be a full-time cook. A minor adjustment produced profound results.

Carol lamented, "He's a mad scientist. He's always in the basement fixing radios or building stereos. He's always got a soldering iron in his hand." They decided to separate. A review of each other's positive and negative experiences revealed she was in the right job and he mismatched.

He is now in the computer field, doing what he should. He spends less time in his basement. Since being back together again, Carol says, "Now we do things together occasionally. He's a different person!"

When a spouse is unfulfilled, people problems break out fast. Fuses shorten, and minor irritants become major disasters between people. Listing positive and negative experiences and then talking about them together is often a means of rebuilding communication. Hard hearts make solutions impossible because it takes every ounce of God's love and grace to admit wrong expectations in the first place, and then allow the other spouse to be fulfilled.

CHANGING RESPONSIBILITIES AND CAREERS

Karen's education is geared to secretarial functions. Her capabilities include designing and doing layout, hand/finger dexterity such as sewing, and contacting people and presenting ideas. She likes PR functions.

After ten months as secretary, her boss is saying, "Her work is slipping fast; she has so much talent but what's wrong?"

Secretarial functions turn out to be Karen's yellow limability. Rather than having her leave the company, the boss changed her responsibilities. Now Karen writes the company's press releases, handles their house organ, and is beginning to do PR work in their industry and local community. She still spends 50 percent of her time doing secretarial work and is now doing well at it.

Her job description and responsibilities were brought in line with her capabilities and so prevented an unnecessary termination.

Robert is thirty-six, and has been running a drill press for twelve years. He feels God is calling him into the pastoral ministry. Notice what he gave as his positive experiences:

Time Period I.
Chosen to take part in several school plays.
Coached a church softball team. "*I enjoyed the contact with kids, talking over school problems and problems with parents. I never took sides. Got them to think about their parents' side. Got into their shoes. Role? More a counselor than coach.*"

Time Period II.
Secretary of Sunday school.
Church elder. "*Enjoyed calling on people, relating to them, visiting, talking about everyday things.*"

Time Period III.
Taught high school Sunday school classes.
Preached at Sunday worship service. "*I'm more a teacher than a preacher.*"

Time Period IV.
Went with high school youth group to _____ to work with poor people. "*We did work projects. Enjoyed visiting with those people.*"
Preached at a gospel mission.

Robert's capabilities include speaking, teaching, counseling, encouraging, visiting, and making friends. His limabilities include recruiting, organizing, selling, and promoting.

By having his capabilities pointed out, Robert had a better grip on his strengths. Robert said, "I suspected these results, but seeing it on paper is confirming." He decided to go to seminary—not because he knew his green area, but because he felt God's call. A discussion of the 40/20/40 concept helped.

You are thinking, "Suppose public speaking didn't pop up as a capability. What should someone like Robert decide to do?"

In Robert's case, with his other capabilities, such as visiting and counseling, he would be fulfilled even though speaking is not a green, so he should continue considering the ministry. But I would suggest a qualification. He should pastor a church where speaking is required once weekly rather than three or four times weekly. Here, as in other situations, the 40/20/40 concept applies. The match-up must be positive enough for Robert, or any pastor, to be fulfilled.

When public speaking is a limability, and using the pastoral ministry as the example, pastoral ministers should avoid situations where speaking is a time-consuming responsibility.

Glenn has been with his Christian missionary organization seven years. He is being considered for director of a field office, requiring him to recruit, supervise, train, and run the day-to-day operations. Six people would report to him. Already on a comparatively low salary, he would get a $3,000 annual raise.

His capabilities include creating and writing, photography, taking and developing pictures, recording and keeping track of statistics and ratios. His personal style category is one and his people-data-things classification is mainly data and some things.

This job would be an obvious mismatch. The director responsibilities require a personal style category two in the role of supervisor. His limabilities include recruiting, supervision, training, and making day-to-day decisions. The traffic light ratios would be 10/20/70.

But the decision isn't as cut and dried as it sounds. Since starting in his organization his dream is the director's job. Besides, peer pressure is strong since many of his peers are now directors. They make more money too.

He decided to stay in his present job. He said, "The more I think about this, the more I realize God is not calling me to a position but to be his person today, wherever that may be. I can see now how I'd really struggle in that job. Sure, the prestige and recognition would be nice, but it would soon wear thin and then I'd be dissatisfied." This decision took four months to make, but it was a good one.

Many pressures squeeze in on people. Often, fulfillment and fruitfulness are pushed aside and other success standards take over. Glen didn't let that happen to him.

Myron is twenty-six and works full-time for a Christian organization. He said, "I'd just like to know my strengths and capabilities."

Time Period I.
Built toy airplanes, boats, and cars.
Experimented and built things out of wood.

Time Period II.
Built two rafts on our pond.
Built a tree house.

Time Period III.
Paid cash for my first car.
Made it through four years of college.

Time Period IV.
Worked on a summer mission project overseas rebuilding
houses and ministering to people.
Worked for a building contractor 3 1/2 years.

Notice that Myron finished college. He said, "What a struggle and hassle. Everyone expected me to make the dean's list. I never did."

Earlier in this chapter, we discussed George, who considered a liberal arts college although a technical school seemed more suitable. Myron, although "perfectly equipped for carpentry," is proof that college studies can be successful. He said, "I really went to college to get into the Bible, and to get more background in history. It took tons of discipline, and I felt like quitting college at least once a month."

Myron got his fulfillment at college working for the building contractor, the way George fixed old clunkers on campus to achieve fulfillment.

Today Myron's job is church youth work. What a mismatch! But listen to Myron: "You know, I'm not that fulfilled and satisfied now, but I've made a two-year commitment and I'm keeping it. Now that I understand myself better, I'm going to do more building on the side. Then in two years, I'll go into carpentry full time and do youth work part time as a volunteer." Myron is an abider. He knows he is not doing as well as other youth workers, but he is not quitting. He wants to fulfill his commitment. Decision making isn't clear-cut. It would have been easy for Myron to quit, but he loves young people. His goal to meet people needs through youth work is mapped out for the next several years.

Myron's experience points out that each person needs to sort out for himself what is right to do. Knowing capabilities and limabilities does not make decision making clear-cut and automatic. It does, however, give an additional dimension to the whole process. Myron decided to wait two years before linking up more closely his goals and capabilities. I respect and applaud that decision.

Like many people whose personal style is category one, Myron asked "Should I ever take a supervisory job?"

This question is complex, since supervisory responsibilities often carry with them increased compensation, so that a person may be forced into making a decision for financial reasons, such as to pay off college expenses, or some high medical bills.

Putting good financial considerations aside, a category one should supervise no more than three people. He should go into it with his eyes wide open, since he is using a yellow or red limability. Although starting out like a whirlwind, he will most likely put off supervising over the long pull. While his supervising trails off, he will tend to do more fulfilling things.

To fill the supervisory gap, many category one "supervisors" recruit a supervisor to be one of the three reporting to him.

Don is a category one. He feels he should have at least six people reporting to him to have a strong power and authority base in his company. Now he has two people reporting to him, and they are complaining about not being supervised!

After several weeks, Don made a decision. He says, "After looking at who I am and my personal strengths and limitations, I've decided to risk it. I'm going to do a better job with the two people reporting to me now." The politics in his company are thick and he is going against this world's road to the top. He adds, "I've decided not to take the power trip." In a new way, Don is putting his future in God's hands.

In William's organization, responsibilities are often rotated. He is eyeing a job that matches his strengths. One of his organization's requirements is first to gain experience in two other jobs, both of which are mismatches. He is going ahead and gaining that experience, knowing ahead of time he will be unfulfilled. In the meantime, he is making sure he gets at least partial fulfillment off the job.

In today's society, it is difficult to go against the grain. Financial realities and other people's "success" expectations press down hard on us. People problems are minimized if we form realistic expectations.

SCREENING

Screening people in volunteer situations is a tough, tough task. Compared to the relatively large recruiting pool in business and industry, the market, or number of available people, in Christian volunteer settings is small. This is true whether recruiting someone to be pastor, youth worker, Sunday school teacher, deacon, or the person whose turn it is to mow the lawn. The pool of people willing to consider doing something often means "grabbing a warm body" or taking whoever is available. Church directories, pored over, frayed and marked up by frustrated nominating committees, are often the norm. So few to do so much! Organizations often try vainly to compete at salary levels below industry.

But wait a minute! Aren't recruiters looking for self-starters—those who will show initiative, be aggressive, be motivated, and willing to work? While it is not always possible, taking time to pinpoint capabilities helps locate self-starters and avoids many people problems later on.

After hiring two youth workers who each stayed less than two years, one pastor said, "I've quit taking shortcuts and making assumptions. To me, selection is one of the keys. Let's face it. Taking a few more hours to find out a person's capabilities avoids headaches and frustrations later on. I've spent endless hours with these two youth workers trying to fit a square peg into a round hole. A few more hours invested during screening saves hundreds of hours later on."

So next time, the pastor, elders' board, and Christian education committee narrowed down their choice to two people: Betty and Joan. Both are youth ministries graduates and have made a favorable impression on people and committees interviewing them—particularly Betty. "She's so enthusiastic and vivacious. The high school kids fell in love with her," they commented.

But to avoid assumptions and shortcuts, the pastor pinpointed their capabilities. He used the "match-up checklist" (See Fig. 6.1 and Fig. 6.2). The results are clear. Joan's responsibilities match up quite well (it's never perfect) with her capabilities and she should be fulfilled enough to use her limabilities, which are teaching and counseling.

Matchup Checklist for JOAN CARPENTER

Capabilities:

Plan projects.

Organize committees and assign responsibilities, oversee.

Take interest in and build relationships.

Excite, inspire.

Personal style category is mainly two; Personal style role is spark plug/organizer.

Classification is people and projects.

Six key responsibilities:

Matchup?*

Plan and coordinate weekend programs—socials and Sunday night programs.

0	5	10
very little	pretty good	very high

Teach Wednesday night Bible study.

Organize two major weekend retreats.

Observe high school programs and activities

Promote youth programs. Motivate youth to invite other youth.

Counsel with youth.

Overall, the matchup is:

*To what extent do responsibilities match up with capabilities? Check appropriate rating from 0 to 10.

FIGURE 6.1

Matchup Checklist for BETTY STEVENSON

Capabilities:

Imagine and conceive.

Memorize and rehearse.

Sing.

Perform, portray.

Personal style category: three;

Personal style role: performer

Classification is people, but in sense of audiences, being on stage.

Six key responsibilities: *Matchup?**

Responsibility	0	5	10

Plan and coordinate weekend programs — Socials and Sunday night program. — ✓ at 0 (very little)

very little / pretty good / very high

Teach Wednesday night Bible study. — ✓ at 0

Organize two major weekend retreats. — ✓ near 1

Observe high school programs and activities — ✓ near 3

Promote youth programs. Motivate youth to invite other youth. — ✓ near 4

Counsel with youth. — ✓ near 3

Overall, the matchup is: — ✓ near 2

*To what extent do responsibilities match up with capabilities? Check appropriate rating from 0 to 10.

FIGURE 6.2

This pastor said, "I invested six additional hours surfacing their capabilities. But as I listened to each one tell me about her positive experiences, I said to myself, 'We would have been wrong a third time if we had chosen Betty.' Our first impressions were wrong. We were guilty of trying to decide based primarily on appearance and enthusiasm."

Arnold, a supervisor, said, "Our selection is based on whether or not a person is aggressive, well-dressed, and educated. It's mainly observation and a lot of selling—no attempt at matching. Those people are turned over to me to be supervised and trained. After six months they quit."

Why don't people do what the job description says, even though they are being paid to do it? One reason is, like Betty Stevenson, their responsibilities don't match up with capabilities.

Most screening practices rely on what can be known about past experiences, including education, or they place a lot of weight on personal appearance and how the person comes across. The interviewer is looking for successes; so the alert interviewee tries to parade out his successes. So often both lose since success and what fulfills the person are often different. This success orientation is right out of the books on business. Interviewers should be going beyond a person's past successful experiences and pinpointing capabilities.

For proof, talk to Joan Carpenter. She loves her work. For further proof, listen to Betty Stevenson, who said, "When the pastor pointed out my capabilities, I saw why I wasn't the person for that job. His insights gave the direction I was lacking. Today, I'm in a different field. I believe I've found my niche."

So even though the recruiting pool is shallow, the traffic light applies and even more so. One pastor said, "Since we have so few to select from, it's only more reason to be sure we have the right person. We want to keep him as long as possible."

Responsible positive influencers notice all the needs "out there" and all the work that needs to be done inside an organization to run and maintain it. There will always be too much to do, but leaders who influence positively screen people carefully.

Another screening tool is the *Screening Summary* (See Fig. 6.3), which is designed to pull everything together and evaluate the overall potential of a person.

SCREENING SUMMARY*

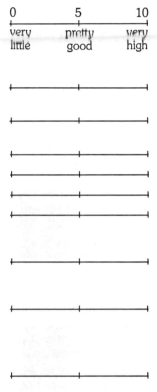

	0	5	10
To what extent:			
1. Is person's philosophy and methodology consistent with the organization's?	very little	pretty good	very high
2. Do personal strengths, capabilities, and interests match responsibilities?			
3. Do past experiences (including education) match responsibilities?			
4. Is the person willing to function cooperatively with other people?			
5. Is person willing to be supervised?			
6. Is person willing to plan?			
7. Is person willing to follow through?			
8. Are you and/or person's supervisor committed to invest time and resources in this person?			
9. Will your (or others') personal feelings toward the person affect how well they will do?			
Summarizing:			
10. Do overall qualifications meet what you are really looking for in a person to do well in these responsibilities?			

*At the end of the screening process, review all your notes and information; then summarize by checking (x) appropriate rating from 0 to 10.

FIGURE 6.3

"Afterwards he [Jesus] went up into the hills and summoned certain ones he chose, inviting them to come and join him there; and they did. Then he selected twelve of them . . ." (Mark 3:13, 14, TLB). Debra said, "I want to be known as a willing worker." Let us help each other be willing workers. Jesus set the example. He selected twelve.

EXPECT SOME RESISTANCE

Solving people problems using the traffic light concept is different and although you see its value, the person you are helping may not. Three mind-sets often stop people from accepting and applying their green, yellow, and red.

1. People downplay their capabilities. "Oh, is that all there is?" some react. There are at least two reasons for this:

a. The "Anyone can do it" syndrome. One of Jon's capabilities is fixing and repairing. Looking at a TV set he said, "Can't anyone do that?" That's an honest feeling. A mechanic may say, "There's nothing to fixing the carburetor." A cook says, "There is nothing to putting on a church dinner. Just do this, this, and this—anybody with half a brain could do it." Many of us with up to 100 percent of our brains wouldn't do half as well as these people, even if we tried. I'm all thumbs around a carburetor. It is easy to downplay capabilities. Others fix and repair things, but not everyone. Others speak, but not everyone. Others are writers, but not everyone. Jon is wrong—not everyone can fix and repair a TV. When a person discovers his capabilities, he immediately thinks of "all the others" who do that. It is a natural reaction. (Remember when you bought a red Toyota, or had your house painted a certain color? All of a sudden you saw all those other red Toyotas or barn red houses.)

But unlike cars and houses, people are unique. While others do have one of your capabilities, only you have that unique cluster of capabilities and limabilities. There is no second edition. We are like snowflakes—all different. Each person is God's unique, not-to-be-repeated creation. People are unique when doing almost anything. Each does it differently, even when trained similarly. Each person does something his own way, adding his personal touch.

Every person is God's unique, not-to-be-repeated creation.

For example, cooks following the same recipe turn out different-tasting cookies. Counselors following similar concepts and methods counsel differently.

When people look around and notice others with a similar capability, they should think of and accept their uniqueness, rather than downplay their capabilities. An accepting, affirming, positive influencer helps people accept their uniqueness.

b. "I've never really accomplished anything." This comment is even more prevalent. It is an honest feeling, although not accurate. Carol is thirty-eight and the mother of four children. Three years ago she committed her life to Jesus. During a seminar at her church she said, "I don't have any positive experiences. I'm embarrassed." We talked. She kept saying, "I've never accomplished anything." Then she added, "Compared to _____ , I haven't created much of a splash." Like many people she felt she never led anything, or won a race, or was a person others flocked to. She said, "All I can do is cook and a few things like that."

Picking up on "a few things like that," we reviewed what a positive experience is and that it is not success, but what brings fulfillment to a person. The upshot of this conversation was like many others. Carol was playing the comparison game— looking at others and always ending up second best or last. She too was smack in the middle of the guilt cycle. By the way, if you need someone who loves to organize a church supper, Carol is the person.

Karen said about her positive experiences: "Mine look so simple." Saying this is another way people downplay their capabilities and accomplishments. Behind that "mine look so simple" statement was a tutor/teacher and an enabling helper. She is one of those quiet positive influencers who is loving and caring behind the scenes. Both men and women sometimes downplay their capabilities. Meeting this resistance requires patience.

2. People rank some capabilities more important than others.

Subtly and quietly, people erect a hierarchy of abilities—some capabilities are ranked high on the "totem pole," others ranked low. For example, an x has been placed indicating how most people would rank the importance of the jobs mentioned below:

Job	High	Low
Manager	x	
Laborer		x
Teacher	x	
Homemaker		x
Someone who thinks	x	
Someone using his hands		x
People classification	x	
Data/things classification		x

Job	High	Low
Director: administrator	x	
Custodian		x
College degree	x	
Technical school degree		x
Boss	x	
Secretary		x

Would anyone dare to say a carpenter doesn't think? Does a drill press operator not think? Yet it is easy to look down on people based on the importance we attach to their capabilities. Some people even feel working with people is ten cuts above working with things. Or how about someone who can do only detail work? Often that person is put into the category of one doing flunky work. He is at the bottom of the low end of the totem pole. Under their breath some managers say they put up with such people. Did anyone ever try to handle a project when someone didn't do the detail work? Ranking capabilities should stop. It complicates work relationships and causes people problems. When people look down on other people at the lower end of the pole, the lower people's sense of worth is affected negatively.

Roland is a college graduate. He just loves what he's doing now—driving a city bus. It is his number one positive experience. He gives six hours weekly to church projects.

But Roland is uneasy. He said, "When I tell people I'm a bus driver, they look at me kind of funny." People are looking down on him because he is considered as one of the bottom guys. His uneasy feelings are real. God's view is entirely different from man's view of people. God has no totem pole or pecking order. Jesus didn't promise box seats or any special privileges to James and John (Mark 10:35-45). He had to remind the Twelve what was essential—a serving attitude. In God's sight, the totem pole is horizontal. We have equal value. People have different responsibilities because we have different capabilities. God gives abilities to all of us. He doesn't give preferential treatment because someone is a category two and someone else just a category one.

The real fly in the ointment is society's tendency to pay and reward the high ones on the totem pole so much more than the low ones. If each person is fulfilled and fruitful and so using his capabilities, that is God's will. But in most organizations, the pay disparity between number one, be it president or director, and the workers is far too large. People are often forced upward to other positions for financial reasons, often resulting in a mismatch. I have trouble understanding why a custodian serving Jesus makes so much less than the principal who is also serving Jesus. Both are matched up and fruitful. I wonder what Jesus would tell us to do?

I have raised an issue with which I'm struggling. I don't have answers. Down deep, I feel we Christians have also been squeezed in by the world's compensation system. Our response to such issues affects our capacity to solve people problems in real world situations. If in God's view people have equal value, how do compensation philosophies in Christian organizations reflect that?

3. People looking for one forty-hour-a-week job. As we solve people problems and help people use their capabilities, the system stares us in the face again. It is standard practice for a person to have one job. Says who? Why can't a person have two or three jobs during those forty or so hours? Let us look at Joe's positive experiences and see how this works out.

Time Period I.
  (2) Tinkered with lawn mower engine, getting it to run smoothly.
  (9) Built and operated dark room for photography.

Time Period II.
  (8) Set up electronics shop in basement; experimented a lot. Built and repaired things for myself and friends.
  (7) Owned a tow truck; operated my own auto salvage business; did free-lance mechanic work.

Time Period III.
  (1) Bought a used motorcycle and fixed it up.
  (3) Re-machined discarded tape reel and used it for my stereo.

Time Period IV.
  (6) Directed a youth choir.
  (4) Directed and produced a major concert.
  (5) Taught private piano lessons.

Today, Joe has three jobs: fixing electronic equipment, tutoring people to play piano, and directing a large church choir. He spreads this out over a forty-five-hour work week. The one forty-hour-a-week job is often treated as a sacred cow and becomes the norm for everyone. Starting with people first and going clockwise around the Fulfillment Cycle requires new and creative approaches.

As leg one of the tripod has unfolded, it is clear there is no perfect job or situation. Green, yellow, and red are a part of real life.
  The 40/20/40 concept hits hardest at people practicing what I call shielding—the "don't give it to me" syndrome. Like a medieval knight, a shielder gets behind his shield of capabilties and says, "No, you mow the lawn; no, you go visit. It's not one of my strengths." Reality means being fulfilled enough to enable someone to do things they don't want to do but must.
  The 40/20/40 concept also reminds us it is OK for a person to like what he is doing. Christians often feel that doing God's will is synonymous with hating one's work or having to exercise severe self-discipline all the time. Self-discipline helps people do "red" things. But that concept should not be carried to extremes. We need to help each other strike a balance in doing our green, yellow, and red tasks.

SEVEN
SUPERVISION—
WHERE IS THE *IF?*

TODAY'S SUPERVISORY PRACTICES

Today's no-time-for-the-people life-style produces several
different kinds of supervisory practices—two common and one
rather uncommon. The two most common practices are
negative supervision and *conditional supervision.* Both practices
miss the essence of the more uncommon kind—*positive
supervision,* which helps and builds up people. Some definitions
are in order:

1. Negative supervision: Little supervision or supervision that
discourages people. Neither the Fulfillment Cycle nor someone's
personal fulfillment enters the supervisor's mind. Families
break up or people leave organizations and committees. People
problems abound.

An example of negative supervision was Carol's (chapter 1)
supervisor whose methods produced a negative climate and
whose constant criticism discouraged her.

Another example is a supervisor's attitudes that shut the
door to the need for supervision. "If I have to supervise him,"
Charles says, "I don't think I have got the right person for the
job." Charles is equating the need for supervision with weak
people.

Attitudes like these spawn people problems. Negative
supervisors do not go even the first mile with people.

2. Conditional supervision: Emphasis is on results and reaching goals. People are means to an end and often are made to feel forced to do something or be a certain type of person. The Fulfillment Cycle may enter the picture, but only as a second thought. Since goals come first, someone's personal fulfillment is also a second thought.

One example was Linda. "As I look back now," Linda recalled, "everything I did was for a reason. If my assistant performed, I'd smile; if the kids sang well, I'd clap. I had my hidden agenda, my standard of excellence, and if I didn't like someone, I couldn't wait for him to stumble and fail. At that point I had never experienced Christ's love in my heart. Our reward is from him, not from how well others do. I wonder," Linda pondered, "how many leaders have themselves experienced God's love?"

"I don't know," I answered. I thought: where is the IF? Linda's comment "If they perform," started me thinking.

Conditional supervision is close to the real thing. It goes the first mile, then stops abruptly.

3. Positive supervision: People and people problems are seen in clockwise motion around the Fulfillment Cycle. Goals (conditions and expectations) are linked up with capabilities, limabilities, and priorities. Someone's personal fulfillment is of first concern. People are treated as coequals. Bob and Sandy are an example. "We really miss Bob," Sandy said about Bob, who was transferred to another city a year ago. "The first of the year I'd share my last year's positive and negative experiences, talk about my values, and then set some goals. Then he did the same with me. He really wanted my opinions. I miss Bob. He cared." Positive supervision means that each goes the second mile for the other, helping and developing each other.

I don't expect anyone to fully agree with these three definitions. They are obviously oversimplifications of something complex. But they help us see how we either ignite people, to influence positively, or pour water on someone's initial enthusiasm, and so influence negatively.

Assumptions about people's willingness in the absence of capabilities and limabilities cause people problems. Down deep many of us wish people would react to our requests for action the way automatic doors swing open as we approach our favorite grocery store, or the way new recruits are supposed to react to a drill sergeant's commands. This is especially so among families where rules and conditions control and unconditional love is a second thought or not present at all.

Like the psalmist, we struggle: "I will try to walk a blameless path, but how I need your help, especially in my own home, where I long to act as I should" (Psalm 101:2, TLB). In the home and elsewhere, we need to remember that people, unlike machines, care how they are treated.

Positive supervision takes place in a climate where people function as equals. Whoever is in charge serves willingly, not grudgingly. Each learns from the other. Father learns from daughter, president from clerk, teachers from pupils, supervisor from truck drivers, experienced from inexperienced. Preferential treatment is eliminated. Ability hierarchies are leveled. "What can you do for me?" attitudes are replaced by "How can I help you?" attitudes. "What can I learn from that person?" is asked before "What can I teach that person?" "People learn from one another, just as iron sharpens iron" (Proverbs 27:17, TEV).

A discussion of people-first approaches to supervision is often viewed with skepticism or outright rejection. It triggers comments like, "We've got work to do" or "Nothing would ever get done." In a moment, we'll see how the "We've got work to do" mentality affects people.

WHAT IS NEGATIVE SUPERVISION?

Negative supervision is either total absence of supervision or supervision that turns people off. It pushes people into third place, behind paper (weekly reports, *Time* magazine, and the daily newspaper) and program (built around quality, professionalism, well-known speakers, and statistics). Notice the people problems which it causes.

Richard Blackford is twenty-nine and serves as staff counselor to emotionally disturbed people. His salary for doing this is what his friends voluntarily give him. After six weeks of work, he said, "I have no one to talk to and listen to me. I am already feeling drained. My supervisor is five years younger than I, but that makes no difference; I wish he had just one hour a week for me, but I guess he doesn't. Others say he sees his job more as paper pushing and program promoting. I feel pushed aside and unimportant."

A strong and independent-looking regional manager for a Christian organization admits, "I wish someone would come by and ask me what I think I should be accomplishing next year, ask me tough questions to force me to think through what I'm doing and what I should be doing. I develop tunnel vision too easily. I'm feeling separated from my organization. Does anyone really care about me?"

Bob Brickhouse has completed one year on staff with a Christian organization. "The first year was fine," Bob confided. "We had seminars to train us to use procedure and resource manuals, which helped a lot. I'd see my supervisor occasionally. Now I'm in a town twenty miles away with my office in my home. All of a sudden I feel cut off. My supervisor's main concern is first-year people, as I was last year. Something is missing. Is it too much for me to expect him to show more concern for me? Some people tell me I need to grow up, or it's all part of God's testing and training for something down the road. Is loneliness the price I must pay to be doing his will? I'm frustrated and confused."

"I feel like there's a person of ability inside me," a librarian said, "but no one ever brought her out. I don't know how."

A grade school principal put it succinctly: "I wish I had more contact with my supervisor."

One could almost feel the pain from her parent's hammering blows as Kate Rosen told her story. "I'm adopted. As a teenager, my adoptive mother told me my real father had a history of mental illness. She kept telling me, 'See what I mean? You're getting just like your father. You sound like you may be having mental problems.' I felt crushed when she said this.

Negative supervision **turns people off—does not "go the first mile."**

Today I still have trouble accepting people. I've been hurt by my mother's negativism. I just don't know where I'd be today without my husband [an example of positive supervision]. He accepts me and loves me. I'd be afraid to reveal the real me in our church. I don't think they would understand. They're so advice-prone."

As I was consulting with a church group, a gentle, heavy-set craftsman said to me, "We have lots of church members who are lonely, even though they are faithful to the church program. We've encouraged people to be spectators of our quality church program. My wife feels lonely here. Once over-involved, we've both retreated into the choir. We still feel something is lacking in our lives and in our church.''

The net effect of negative supervision is loneliness. People begin to feel they don't belong. Their sense of worth drops, so they are less fulfilled and become less fruitful. They backtrack, dig in, and try to stick it out by themselves for a while. But willingness fades, negative attitudes set in, and hard hearts replace sensitivity, gentleness, and willingness.

Drop-outs take many forms. Some do nothing or as little as possible. Some do something visible to show others they are still active and somewhat involved. Some become smug: "I'll listen for a change." Some resort to a favorite of the over-forty crowd: "Let the younger ones take over now." Then there is the "survival of the fittest" syndrome. These ooze with "The few good ones make it somehow, but the majority are too weak."

A compounding negative net effect takes place in the next place of service for these people. Whether it be a new church or a new organization, their attitude will be: "I'm never going to get that involved again or let that happen again."

The sour taste of a former bitter experience lingers. Only extra-special positive supervision will turn around such negativism. Think, for example, of people leaving churches with negative attitudes and how that affects their next church. Leaders who supervise negatively influence negatively.

"OK, OK, that's enough examples and talk about negative supervision," you're saying. "What's the solution? Positive supervision?"

For years I've struggled with the biblical concept of unconditional love and how it fits in with supervision. "This love of which I speak is slow to lose patience—it looks for a way of being constructive" (1 Corinthians 13:4, Phil.). As I look around, so much supervision I see is businesslike and conditional. It lacks the constructive dimension. Are we looking for ways to be constructive with people? Sometimes. But there is a larger question: "Is conditional loving the same as positive supervision?" I believe it isn't.

A LOOK AT CONDITIONAL SUPERVISION

Rather than loving unconditionally, well-intentioned love in real life seems to be more conditional than unconditional. In other

words, _if_ you do this (your job description, meet your goals,
fulfill your spouse models, make excellent grades, or mow the
lawn by four o'clock) and so meet the conditions, you will be
rewarded (compensation, position, title, a private office, a larger
office, bigger desks, use of company or family automobile, a
new couch, my acceptance of you—in other words, I'll get off
your case and maybe even hug you). Conditions and carrots
are dangled before people. Let's call it what it is—it is loving
conditionally. I am not saying these practices are wrong per se.
I am only asking whether or not we are striving to be
unconditionally loving as we supervise. Can a supervisor really
love unconditionally?

Expectations placed on people are often conditional and
based on proven track records and success standards. Good
intentioned supervisors (parents, managers, and presidents)
are letting the world system "squeeze them into its mold" rather
than starting with the mind of Christ and also looking out for
the interests of others, or asking, "What would Jesus do?"

Negative and conditional supervision seldom starts with
people. Any wonder people are not _doing_ and _being_ what is
expected (our definition of a people problem)? Paper and
programs are king. Supervisors fail to identify a person's
capabilities and limabilities. They even ignore sorting through
someone's values. "No time" is the usual excuse. Today's
no-time-for-people life-style steamrollers over people.

SEVEN CONDITIONAL SUPERVISORY PRACTICES

It would be easy to jump right into positive supervision and
leapfrog what may seem controversial—conditional supervision.
But we need to stir our thinking by observing both negative
and conditional supervision.

Because we are human, the "old self" creeps in. As the
Apostle Paul said, "I don't do what I would like to do, but instead I
do what I hate" (Romans 7:15, TEV). Before we know it, our
supervision becomes negative or conditional. Standards, rules,
agendas, and clocks become our comfort blanket. We forget
Jesus laid down, rather than rules, a principle, "to love others as I
have loved you." While we would like to love more and be
more unconditional, we often slip back to conditions. And we do
need conditions for orderliness. But what comes first—the

person or his "good behavior?" Do we tend to look more favorably on on-timers or late-comers? What is king, conditional supervision or positive and more unconditional supervision?

Here are seven negative or conditional supervisory practices. Perhaps no one will agree or disagree with all of them. They are one way for us to examine how we supervise. Some of these seven are good, some very bad; in either case, relying on them causes people problems.

1. Managing-by-memo. "If they know what to do, or what I'm thinking" a supervisor says, "it will solve the communication problem." In such settings, everything is "reduced to writing." Paper is king and carefully worded memos and kitchens with blackboards are vehicles to make sure things happen correctly. So people are kept at arm's length. Supervisors spend more time with paper, pencils, chalk, and dictating machines than with people. Efficiency is high, but people effectiveness is low.

Off-shoots of managing-by-memo are ever enlarging procedure and resource manuals. Since it is put in writing, supervisors rationalize, employees should know what to do, so systems and charts abound. Church communication bulletins get larger and more frequent. Memos and manuals are necessary, but they are not a substitute for positive supervision.

2. Managing-by-job-description. Here everyone has a job description. Most are already too long and too detailed. "It would take two people to do my job," one staff worker said. Scope, responsibilities, accountabilities, and authority are supposed to be clearly spelled out.

Job descriptions are so complete that few read them! In fact, they scare people away, because they are so long and complicated. I've seen three-page job descriptions for volunteers already working forty hours weekly. Any wonder they have a recruiting problem?

People are expected to do what the job description says and fit into the slot. After all, supervisors and committees say, "This is what we are hiring him to do, so he'd better do it." And no one would dare tinker with finely honed job descriptions. When job descriptions are king, people are slaves and the means to an

Conditional supervision **slows people down—goes the "first mile" and then stops.**

end. The "program" calls for everyone to have a job description This philosophy hits families too. Many parents make out to-do lists for their kids, then leave to do what they consider more important things.

Job descriptions and lists are needed, but they are not substitutes for one-on-one positive supervision. Positive supervisors keep job descriptions to one page and insist that they reflect directly a person's desires, interests, and capabilities.

Positive supervisors know that job descriptions must be changed and updated occasionally, since no one has a clear crystal ball into the future. People and their attitudes change. Job descriptions and lists of things to do must mirror real-life people in real-world situations. The six key responsibilities from the *Match-Up Checklist* (Fig. 6.2) ought to be at the heart of a job description.

3. Managing-by-encouragement. Superficiality reigns where comments such as "Great job, wonderful presentation" prevail. Everything is tip-top and positive, even though it is about to tip over.

Encouragement is particularly thick and syrupy if the encourager has either dumped (delegated things he doesn't want to do) on someone or assigns a responsibility without taking into account his interests, capabilities, and limabilities. Having dumped, he urges people on and compliments them even when they are doing poorly. Supervisors who rely on encouragement keep people at arm's length. They even resort to public pronouncements such as "I know Jeanette will do a tremendous job." Recognition is high on their list of motivators, but the person being encouraged isn't fooled. Inside, he knows when he isn't doing something well or feels he has been dumped on, and he becomes insecure.

Lyle's comments (from chapter 1) were: "You get lots of pats on the back, so-called encouragement, which I interpret as pretty shallow. All I get is 'Great job, Lyle, keep it up'—pat, pat, pat."

After losing another ballgame, for the umpteenth time, Charlie Brown tells Lucy, "Ask our players to line up to shake hands with the other team and say 'nice game.' "

Lucy blares out to her teammates, "OK, team, it's hypocrite time."

Sincere, genuine encouragement is part of, not a substitute for, positive supervision. Encouragement that influences positively takes into account capabilities and limabilities.

4. Managing-by-meetings. The weekly staff meeting, monthly committee meeting, quarterly teachers' meeting syndrome, and annual conference, or retreat, by this method are substituted for individual one-on-one times. It even hits families who insist that family supper is at six o'clock, period. Or the way for a couple to solve a serious dispute is "take the day off, hire a babysitter, and let's hammer things out."

Meetings are king, usually dominated by one person who

runs them with one eye on the agenda and the other on the clock. The precision and organization are scary.

Supervisors often use meetings to motivate people. One pastor says, "In every committee meeting we make assignments to everyone, then ask them to report at the next meeting. In that way we make sure things get done." I felt depressed after listening to him. I said to myself, "People's motivation is to avoid being embarrassed. His supervision is an example of conditional love in action."

Meetings are important and necessary to communicate and make decisions. But "managing-by-meetings" is a poor substitute for positive supervision where each person is important.

5. *Managing-by-quality.* While I was consulting with a church group, a chairperson said to me, "I make sure only quality and top-notch people are on my committee, those who've proven themselves reliable. You see, they're people I can count on. In that way, I don't have to check up on people between meetings. If I have to check up, I don't want them on my committee."

I asked, "Suppose you couldn't get top-notch people. What would you do?"

Pausing for a moment, he replied emphatically, "I don't know, I've never had that problem. Deadwood I don't need—I'm not going to carry deadwood."

"Deadwood—what a way to look at people!" I said to myself. This person has a total preoccupation with proven track records and success. I kept thinking of people who serve on committees and boards whom he would call deadwood.

I thought of parents who see one of their children as deadwood, one who doesn't "live up to" his parents' high standards as child number two, whose grades are at C level, when child number one whizzed through with straight A's. I thought of Little Leaguers whose coach and parents think only of winning rather than coming alongside the clumsy child who can't field or hit. Quality, excellence, winning, and profession-alism is king. Anything else and all others are viewed as deadwood.

Contrast Mr. Deadwood's attitude with Mrs. Realistic's attitude. "I looked at my committee," she said, "and asked, 'Why are they there?' But then I realized there must be a reason and that God knows. So prayerfully I tried looking at my committee as equals—not as people holding us back or putting the kibosh on things. I couldn't hide behind the excuse, 'I had nothing to do with them being on the committee.' I had a responsibility to see them as needy people. Isn't that what the Body of Christ is all about?"

A church moderator asked me, "What do you do with a seventy-seven-year-old lady whose capability is singing but whose voice is beginning to crack?" I replied, "I'd rather listen to a not-so-perfect seventy-seven-year-old cracked singer who is faithful and devoted to Jesus than a professional, perfect forty-year-old singing to impress and hear the applause." Some of us not yet seventy-seven years old forget we too will be old someday. Any wonder people want to start letting younger people take over? This church moderator's only concern was, "What will the viewers think?"

Selecting reliable people is a good practice. But in volunteer situations, we often have to start with what the nominating committee gives us, or people who sign up, or who volunteer. To want reliable people so the supervisor won't have to check up on them or feel a bit uncomfortable if his performance includes mistakes is another form of conditional supervision.

I make mistakes in front of people. I love listening to people who are depending on Jesus, both professionals and "nonprofessionals."

6. *Managing-by-training.* Annette works for a publishing firm. She shared her capabilities and limabilities with her new supervisor, Sheila Newsoup. Ann tells about it.

"She asked me to instruct teachers in a new teaching method, but math is the most difficult subject for me. She insisted I was belittling myself. If I could consult successfully, as she had heard, I could teach math to teachers. Nothing I said made any difference.

"She sent me to a one-week workshop to train me in math. It was a nightmare. Others literally whizzed through math. I didn't even know what questions to ask. Soon I was the silent, dumb member of the class. I was miserable.

"When I told Sheila about all of this she said teasingly that I

was just chicken—to be a sport, to go home and stop worrying."
People want training, but training geared to who they are. The
most effective training is tied in with capabilities and interests.

Training often places accountability totally on the supervisee, with the rationalization, "She's trained. She now knows
what to do." The benefits of training done in lieu of positive
one-on-one supervision are short-lived.

Parents send their offspring away to be educated often to
"get them out of our hair" or to allow the parent "to do God's
will." After listening to a missionary's well-educated
twenty-six-year-old son say, with tears coming down his cheeks,
"I never really had a dad. I really don't know him," I had to
wonder about how people-responsible some are, especially to
their own household.

Training and education have their place when they build up
strengths, but they are not a substitute for positive supervision.

7. *Managing-by-insistence.* Supervisees ask for help and
one-on-one supervision. A wife wants some time alone with her
husband; a six-year-old does attention-getting things, asking
for his parent's time. Older people want visitors. People in jail want
to see concerned people. Teachers ask for more time with the
principal.

After much pleading for supervision by his staff, a supervisor
says, "OK, I will, but on my terms" or "If that's what they want I'll
give it to them." The supervisor does it unwillingly and
grudgingly because others are insisting on it. It is done as part of
a program and at times most convenient to the supervisor.

One day Clarence gathered his six staff people and had them
write their own job descriptions. Afterward he said, "Now they
should know what to do, plus it ought to keep them quiet."

Dick and others like him said, "We're being supervised now,
but it's his agenda. He focuses in on results and goals. He hardly
asks about me. I feel like a piece of machinery. Now I wish we
had never asked for supervision."

One-on-one supervision often turns into a mechanical
process. The president of a Christian organization said, "When I
was with another Christian organization, my supervisor and I
set annual goals and reviewed them every quarter. I felt reduced

to a file folder. It was done hurriedly, routinely, and with little sensitivity. We never prayed or even exchanged prayer needs. In no way will I install that system here."

Managing-by-insistence takes many forms. It often turns into a mechanistic system. It is done by supervisors who feel they "have to" rather than by those who function willingly. It is close to the real thing—positive supervision. Like counterfeit money, it looks real, but under closer examination, you see it isn't.

Negative and conditional supervision overlap. The conditional "if" is the by-word: *If* you (or they) do what I expect, I'll reward you.

Conditional supervision goes one mile, then stops. Our human nature agrees with conditional supervision. It at least goes one mile. A success-oriented world likes its emphasis on efficiency, results, and goal-attainment.

But in Jesus' kingdom, one mile is not enough. Jesus' love and gentleness seldom penetrate conditional barriers. Conditional supervisors often come across hard and domineering to people. So although this kind of supervision sounds good and even looks good on paper, it doesn't go far enough.

POSITIVE SUPERVISION

Positive supervision includes memos, scribbled messages on envelopes and blackboards, manuals, job descriptions, encouragement, meetings, quality control, training, and even one-on-one planning in one form or another. But positive supervision goes beyond just results and efficiency tactics. Its aim is to help and to build up individuals. It rejects the success-oriented definition of management—"getting others to do things" where the emphasis is on *getting the job done* through any means. In such settings, results are first and people last. People are the means, not the end. Deadwood is tossed into the trash; winners are applauded.

Instead positive supervision is helping and building up or developing people—all kinds of people. "Do not forget to do good and to help one another, because these are the sacrifices that please God" (Hebrews 13:16, TEV). "Instead, we should all please our brothers for their own good, in order to build them up in the faith" (Romans 15:2, TEV).

With *positive supervision* people feel like equal partners with others and respond willingly—"go the second mile."

Positive supervision aims at balancing people and program. In any given situation, people come first. Positive supervision produces people growth, including what is often overlooked—their spiritual walk and growth. The Apostle Paul saw results as growth in his followers' walk with Jesus. He wrote: ". . . And aren't you the result of my work for the Lord? Even if others do not accept me as an apostle, surely you do! Because of your life in the Lord you yourselves are proof of the fact that I am an apostle" (1 Corinthians 9:1, 2, TEV).

"Should I be considering a field position rather than remaining in this home office position?" Ron asked.

"What is happening to you spiritually?" was my first question.

"It's been going downhill for two years," Ron replied. Ron is ripe for a change.

When the seventy returned after Jesus had sent them out two by two, he said, "But don't be glad because the evil spirits obey you; rather be glad because your names are written in heaven" (Luke 10:20, TEV). Jesus did not minimize their accomplishments but said their earthly success was relative— more important was their relationship to God, the spiritual dimension.

Even people doing well can become people problems, parading their accomplishments, turning people off, and in the process they dry up spiritually. Positive supervisors come alongside all kinds of people in order to gently, quietly, and sensitively talk about spiritual fitness. One goal of positive influencers is to be concerned about a person's walk with Jesus. Here are some self-evaluation questions:

To what extent am I concerned about other people's spiritual growth—People like my spouse? the Sunday school class? the committee chairperson I really don't like? other committee members?

Can I naturally and comfortably discuss spiritual things with others?

Do I let programs, paper, and results be king rather than first helping and building others up in their faith?

When I look at people, how often do I ask, "What's my role in helping them spiritually?"

Is my love unconditional often enough?

Helping people means rising above conditional supervisory tactics. It is unconditional—it means doing things that don't count in man's eyes, but count in God's eyes. It is doing things in the face of opposition, going against accepted standards, and doing things that seem crazy, such as attaching no conditions to other people's response to our good deeds. Jesus said, "No! Love your enemies and do good to them; lend and expect nothing back" (Luke 6:35, TEV).

"But Lord," you and I cry out, "not even a 'thank you?' "

Yes, Jesus would say, not even a "thank you." To you and me, he is repeating what he told the seventy, "Rather be glad because your names are written in heaven."

I recall once having a chip on my shoulder because "they" didn't even say thank you. After volunteering to do something for someone, I see myself in my office wondering, "Was it worth it?" It is wrong to even ask that question because my main role is to do good and to develop people, and to do it unconditionally—no strings attached. Sometimes results are seen, but most often, not. For example, helping others grow spiritually is an invisible long-term process. Many positive influencers contribute to one person's growth, and as we said in chapter 1, positive influencers hardly know they have influenced.

IT IS OUR CHOICE

We have a choice whether or not to strive toward supervising unconditionally. Since we are human, our best efforts often fail, and we revert to selfish tactics. It is like the choice of whether to use one's limabilities. We don't want to, but must. Positive supervisors say yes to the choice and give up their right to themselves. It is our decision, not something based on someone else's performance. "And he said to them all, 'If anyone wants to come with me, he must forget himself, take up his cross every day, and follow me' " (Luke 9:23, TEV). To be a positive supervisor or not is our choice.

Unlike conditional supervision, where the condition is placed on others, positive supervision places the condition on you and me. God's conditions are daily surrender of self and cross-bearing.

But God never forces us. We choose. And to do this, positive supervisors must have a disciple (personal, intimate, and growing) relationship to Jesus. Notice also the condition stated in John 14:15, "If you love me, you will obey my commandments" (TEV). Helping others means giving up my selfish rights. Hebrews 13:16 ends with the words, "because these are sacrifices that please God" (TEV).

HELPING OTHERS MEANS SACRIFICE

To sacrifice sometimes means to give up something of value, such as a favorite TV program. Why is positive supervision considered, in the context of doing good, helping, and building up people in the faith, a sacrifice? There are three reasons.

1. People take time. Often they take more time than we have. We may say, "You're telling me!" People stay longer and schedules go awry. One of my wife's responsibilities was recruiting church greeters. One lady couldn't because of a problem with her right hand. That led my wife to over an hour of listening to her explanation.

People come to my office for three hours (the plan). Five or six hours later they leave. Someone drops in for a "few minutes." Two hours later he leaves. Someone waits in the car after Sunday morning services while the spouse is doing good and helping one person.

While not always possible, positive supervisors willingly strive to make people their agenda rather than schedules, or cleaning up unorganized desk drawers. They don't edge people to doorways. They are genuine, caring people. And solving people problems unconditionally takes time. It would be easier to spout out pearls of wisdom, then leave, or nudge them out. Instead it means turning off the TV, putting down your pencil, or listening when you would rather be playing tennis.

2. Helping doesn't come naturally. Helping and developing people is a sacrifice in that a positive supervisor often has to *temper his capabilities and limabilities tendencies.* In other words, he must do things that don't come naturally, or give up things he prefers to do.

For example, consider the way people first tell or ask others to do something. Telling and asking in themselves are OK, if done caringly and gently. But the situation may call for someone to temper his natural tendency.

For example, the Apostle Paul often told people to do things, yet when writing to Philemon, he put the brakes on his natural tendencies. "For this reason, I could be bold enough, as your brother in Christ, to order you to do what should be done. But because I love you, I make a request instead. . . . However, I do not want to force you to help me; rather I would like for you to do it of your own free will" (Philemon 8, 9, 14, TEV). J. B. Phillips translation expresses verse 14, "But I would do nothing without consulting you first. . . ." God's love changes me when I'm moldable.

Paul wrote, "Which do you prefer? Shall I come to you with a whip, or in the spirit of love and gentleness?" (1 Corinthians 4:21, TEV). Paul seemed willing to go either way—telling or asking—forcefully or gently. If given a choice, in any age bracket people prefer love and gentleness over whips and yelling.

When supervisors first listen, ask questions, learn about, and accept another's feelings, research indicates the following benefits: fewer arguments, greater mutual understanding, and supervisees felt motivated and both expressed more positive feelings toward each other.

Someone must steer people to decisions, yet not become a ramrod. There are always exceptions. "I must tell them what to do and not do," said the director of a downtown rescue mission. "I'm doing it for their own good." Someone must take charge and tell others—yet he must not be obnoxious. Our style, and how we decide things with people, need constant adjustment. There is no one right way. But given a choice, supervisors who lean toward asking rather than telling are most effective.

Tellers, like the Apostle Paul, find this practice difficult. Tellers love to tell and talk at every turn. It is a sacrifice when a teller puts "tongue in check."

But on the other hand, sometimes the askers ought to tell. Fred's personal style category is one, and one of his capabilities is counseling. He enjoys asking questions and drawing out a counselee's thoughts and feelings. He is supervising two people. His employees say, "I wish he would quit asking questions and affirming us all the time. Once in a while I wish he would evaluate us—tell us what we're doing wrong so we could improve ourselves. We never seem to make any decisions."

Myles is a personal style category three. He loves committees and making decisions with others. He is an asker. After his second child was born, his wife experienced depression and indecision to the point of being unable to decide what to wear. Myles said, "That was rough, telling her what to wear. I felt awkward, unnatural. But I saw I had to, for my wife's own good."

The role of a positive supervisor is to help and build up people. Myles was doing just that. He loved and cared enough to temper his natural tendencies, and to do it willingly. "Be shepherds of the flock that God gave you, and look after it willingly, as God wants you to, and not unwillingly. Do your work, not for mere pay, but from a real desire to serve" (1 Peter 5:2-3, TEV). Whether someone first asks or tells depends on the immediate situation facing him. Positive supervisors think first, not last, about whether it is best to tell or ask.

3. Sacrifice includes taking your place in the Body of Christ.
Four years ago, a Christian field supervisor hit me hard with this question, "Dick, you talk a lot about what supervisors should do, but what should supervisees do?"

That sent me scrambling to God's Word. There it was—right in front of me—the very next verse. "Obey your leaders and follow their orders. . . . If you obey them, they will do their work gladly; if not, they will do it with sadness, and that would be of no help to you" (Hebrews 13:17, TEV).

Cooperative efforts mean both supervisor and supervisee have to hold up their end of the responsibility toward a common purpose and goal. Teamwork and cooperative efforts mean willingness on both sides.

It is easy to talk about cooperation and teamwork. For example, I find many people asking for supervision. Yet when they get a supervisor, they continue on their own merry way.

"Can you get across to my people," a pastor says, "that they all are not chiefs?" Talk about teamwork is cheap, but sacrificial submission is costly. It is another matter to actually obey, or submit to, others, particularly that person with whom we don't see eye-to-eye.

Several pastors were talking about how they weren't accountable to anyone—no authority figure over them. Upon further questioning, all but one admitted having a supervisor.

I quoted Hebrew 13:17 and we talked about their role as supervisee with their supervisor. But instead, they hit me with, "Dick you must deal with political realities. Those people [supervisors] are there because of politics. Besides, most of them were never successful." I shuddered.

The world around us is not essentially political, although that dimension is often present. Instead, the practical reality is that we are needy people so we need each other. Whether at the top or bottom, loneliness strikes and often the loneliness of someone at the top is self-inflicted.

Unconditional lovers do not first attach success tags to their supervisors. And if we are really honest, many so-called successes are highly questionable. We have all stubbed our toes at times. Some of us more often than others perhaps.

Everyone is a supervisee to someone and everyone needs a supervisor. Positive supervision occurs when helping and development are a two-way street, as with Bob and Sandy, who were mentioned earlier in this chapter. I love hearing about fathers learning from daughters who also willingly help them find a lost notebook, husbands who help and learn from their wives, and vice versa, committee chairpersons who help and learn from a new committee member, committees that first listen to people and their needs before finalizing a program.

In volunteer situations, cooperation cannot be forced, for very long at least. "I tried cranking up my enthusiasm," a pastor says, talking about what led to his resignation by "mutual consent." "I wanted them to see I was behind the program. I admit pushing and cajoling people to do things they didn't want to do. Thirty-five people said they would do it, but the first night only eight showed up."

"Why did you do this?" I asked.

"I thought this was my role, to run and control the program, push it, make it succeed," he answered.

Pushing seldom works. Cranked up enthusiasm is paper thin. People see right through it. Instead, cooperation happens when authority is viewed in terms of the credibility of the relationships. Credible, believable people help and develop each other. Cooperation happens somehow.

Someone said to me, "I have no right to hold someone else accountable unless we have a positive, genuine relationship." Job description authority soon disappears when this attitude is maintained.

Taking our place in the Body of Christ requires submission and sacrifice. It means doing our part in the helping, developing process, sometimes being the helper, sometimes the one receiving help. Cooperation often means giving up a pet idea. That is tough to do with the right spirit.

Someone has said: the message of the Sermon on the Mount is doing what is *not* our duty. Helping and developing people is going beyond, to the two-mile point. It is rising above this world's "If you scratch my back, I'll scratch yours" mentality. Authority based on experience, power, titles, position, seniority, or who dresses best, soon crumbles. "I earned it; I deserve it" attitudes fade away when saints realize it is by sheer grace that any of us are where we are.

EIGHT
POSITIVE SUPERVISION
IN ACTION

"Our organization is growing," Anita Bennett says. "What our people need most is to know someone is in charge and in control. You can work independently for just so long. There is a lot of growth potential in this job, but it is tough to get there without supervision."

Fred Carpenter put it this way: "Without pressure from the outside, I never seem to use my limabilities. I get bored so quickly with no challenge. I'd like to be challenged occasionally by someone."

"After we enlist people," Bob admitted, "we run away from them."

Tommy (chapter 1) is angered by his father's negative supervision. At the beginning of chapter 7, Richard Blackford and people "strong and independent looking" are reaching out for help. We all need a supervisor.

OUR MODEL IS JESUS

Jesus is our only positive-supervision-in-action model. His ministry was growing; his popularity on the upbeat (Mark 3:9). Perhaps his life-style was getting to be a hassle. Rather than consider programs and paper and better communication

techniques first, he did something completely out of phase
with today's "bigger is better" mentality. He put his stock in twelve
people, and of those twelve, three in particular—Peter, James,
and John. "Afterwards he went up into the hills and summoned
certain ones he chose, inviting them to come and join him
there. . . . Then he selected twelve of them to be his regular
companions and to go out to preach and cast out demons"
(Mark 3:13-15, TLB).

Note that Jesus invited—not pressured, pushed or coerced.
Apparently they responded willingly.

He selected twelve. The criteria he used aren't mentioned.
Many scholars agree that Jesus knew a lot more about them than
we at first think. The scholars also conclude the Twelve's
primary qualification was teachableness.

Did he know their capabilities and limabilities? I don't know.
I want to believe he did, however! "If he knows the number of
hairs in our head," one person suggested, "he most certainly
knew their capabilities and limabilities."

"Right," I agreed immediately, but with nothing to back up
my assertion. What we know for sure is that Jesus selected some,
did not select others, and that the Twelve responded to Jesus.

These Twelve became his regular companions—his close
associates, not subordinates (I hate that word). They were his
priority. He spent time with them, forming an intimate
teacher-disciple relationship. It seems his main goal was their
personal, spiritual development, their spiritual fitness, so they
would be fruitful. "My Father's glory is shown by your bearing
much fruit; and in this way you become my disciples" (John 15:8,
TEV). Fruitfulness and fulfillment go hand-in-hand, as
discussed in chapter 2. Jesus wanted his disciples to be fruitful.

Unfulfilled people are unfruitful, their sense of worth,
negative. The result is often indecision and slothfulness. Positive
supervisors must constantly keep an eye on their own and
others' fulfillment, since fulfilled people are more productive.
Decisiveness includes someone taking charge.

JESUS TAKES CHARGE

Notice how Jesus made decisions and took charge at the
beginning of his ministry. He first decided to "go with the

twelve," which was a tough choice. The night before this decision, he spent the entire night praying (Luke 6:12), an example of good recruiting methods and of drawing on God's resources. Does our strategy include enough prayer?

Near the end of Jesus' ministry he "took charge." His mission was clearly in focus as he and his followers approached Jerusalem just before his death. "Jesus and his disciples were now on the road going up to Jerusalem. Jesus was going ahead of the disciples, who were filled with alarm; the people who followed behind were afraid. Once again Jesus took the twelve disciples aside and spoke of things that were going to happen to him" (Mark 10:32, TEV). "Once again" suggests that Jesus met often with the Twelve.

Shortly afterwards, James and John asked Jesus who would sit on his left and right when Jesus sits on his throne. Jesus reminded the Twelve not to function like rulers with power and leaders with complete authority. "This, however, is not the way it is among you. If one of you wants to be great, he must be the servant of the rest" (Mark 10:43, TEV).

Jesus turned tables over in the temple and also on man's conditional supervisory tactics. Positive supervisors are to serve, not strive for power, authority, and positions. To ask a thirty-three-year-old, "Where do you want your Christian power base in five years?" (mentioned in chapter 1) is appalling. Unconditional love is "doing and being" in ways that don't count in man's eyes.

Jesus "went on ahead." But then he recognized fear in his "regular companions." He made a decision—even though his schedule would be upset and he would get to Jerusalem during five o'clock rush hour traffic! Since his Twelve were his priority and agenda, he stopped and spent time with them. Why? He was helping to build twelve people. He consistently concentrated on them rather than on the larger masses of people.

"I just dreaded our committee meetings," Janice said. "The only time we spent together was haggling over problems. Our meetings went three, even four hours."

"We would spend thirty seconds praying at the beginning and end. We didn't know each other as persons."

Al, the committee chairman, was frustrated too. He took

charge and in three months they made a bold decision to have as the agenda one major item and two minor items. All other matters would be decided out of committee. Also, during the first thirty minutes prayer needs were expressed and prayed about immediately.

"Now I look forward to our meetings," Janice says. "More is getting done and morale is up 100 percent. But Al led us through the process. It all started by taking thirty minutes to see how Jesus functioned, and then applying that to our own situation."

Jesus' positive-supervision-in-action model turns up "conditions" so that unconditional love and positive supervision fit together:

> *Put people before program.*
> *Concentrated on a few people rather than large numbers.*
> *Where possible, selected people for responsibilities.*
> *Spent time with regular companions. Took them aside.*
> *Made decisions about people and strategies, but also prayed*
> *"all night long."*

But it is easy to forget people and what got us to the place of responsibility. If something is working, we stop doing it! Programs squeeze out people. "I began picking up rumblings here and there," Pastor Carely related, "like not seeing Harry at the hospital, or a late church newsletter. It sounded like small stuff, but it was adding up. On top of that, I felt tension from the newer church members. We were subtly communicating to them that 'It's the Christian thing' to be directly involved in the church right away. They were resisting it and were saying, 'Don't tell me where and when I ought to be serving Jesus.'"

Pastor Carely agonized over what to do. Unlike four years before, his church was packed on Sunday mornings—speaking was a limability, too. He felt tension increasing, so he had to do something. Note how Pastor Carely took charge.

"I gathered twenty trusted people together and shared my thoughts. Quickly Phil, the florist, observed, 'The problem, Pastor, is the sheer number of relationships. You are spread too thin. We have been growing these past four years.'

"The light dawned." Pastor Carely smiled. "The sheer

number of relationships—that was it. People, new and old, were not feeling cared for, as they had before. In our growth, I missed that. In that meeting we were asking ourselves: 'How can we have the same quality of caring as before? What new ways can we do this?' Mutual concern for the problem sparked many new ideas.

"I learned two things," Pastor Carely said. "One, we couldn't push people to serve our church; instead, they wanted us to appreciate every avenue of help and service. One member, for instance, felt his Christian mission was helping underprivileged kids through a community agency. Since that wasn't directly church connected, he felt snubbed by us. Second, I had failed to concentrate on a few people, like Jesus did. Phil the florist put his finger on the nub of the matter. And I found I had to take charge and make some tough decisions. It has been a plus experience for me."

"I meet individually with the chairperson of each church committee," Pastor Ersinger, a positive supervisor, says. "We share thoughts from our devotional life and exchange prayer requests as well as discuss his committee. But it's spiritual and personal first, before church business.

"Through these five people," he went on, "I touch fifty lives, since ten people are on each committee. So it is critical to know them and to be with them. The Lord has given me these people, just as the Lord had his disciples. I must initiate the relationship, and I found out they really wanted this kind of relationship with me. Two of them openly admitted being lonely people. So my philosophy is seeing them as people first, rather than first exploiting them as workers in the church." Positive supervisors initiate the building of relationships.

Companions are people with whom we want to be. We might look at those we supervise, or our spouses, children, committee members, Sunday school friends, pupils, work associates, and staff. Are they our regular companions? Do we want to be with them? Do we fellowship with them willingly and unconditionally, before seeing them as workers who wash dishes, clean their rooms, or give reports at meetings?

Positive supervisors serve, influencing positively. They love. Jesus is their only model. Paul wrote: "Let love make you serve one another" (Gal. 5:13, TEV). "Let us be concerned for one

another, to help one another to show love and do good"
(Hebrews 10:24, TEV). We look to Jesus as model, we come to
Jesus for direction and teaching. Jesus' invitation stands: "Come
unto me . . . learn from me, because I am gentle and humble in
spirit" (Matt. 11:28, 29, TEV).

What is our attitude today? Do we want to learn or do we say
flippantly, "I've got so much to learn" and then go our merry
way?

Suppose we were some of the Twelve chosen by Jesus. How
would we have felt? Worthy or unworthy? Independent or
dependent?

Positive supervisors must check their attitude often.
"Unworthy and dependent" are obvious responses to the last
questions, but so often we forget people care how they are
treated, and that we must initiate the building of relationships. It
takes a gentle and humble spirit to learn from Jesus.

Moving up the questions 2,000 years, we might ask ourselves
now: How do we feel—worthy or unworthy? Independent or
dependent? Our answers will indicate the extent to which we are
teachable. For example, how often do we specifically ask for
his Holy Spirit and mean it? Positive supervisors are learning
constantly.

A POSITIVE SUPERVISOR IS AN ENABLING COACH

A high school coach functions with volunteers—players who
are there to be helped and built up. A coach spots capabilities and
positions players to maximize their capabilities, holds practices,
and makes out the lineup. He often asks players what position
they prefer to play.

A caring coach respects each player. In turn, they respect him.
He often is much more than a coach, rising above what he is
paid to do. He is often father-confessor, counselor, one who
helps someone decide such things as which college to go to.
He has unique opportunities to influence positively or negatively.

A high school coach is seldom known nationally. He often
goes unnoticed except by those who know him. His coaching
enables his players to do something. He can turn a gangling
six-foot sophomore into an above-average first baseman. The
coach is practical—he trains on the field and in game

The Good Shepherd knows his sheep (John 10:27). He knows them by name (John 10:3).

conditions. He takes charge—he decides, helps, and builds up.

Unlike professional sports, there are no contracts in high school athletics. Trust prevails, not the fine print of contract conditions. They don't even have written job descriptions!

My high school basketball coach never yelled. When he talked, we listened. He didn't have to cut many players during tryouts. We were such a small school virtually everyone who came out for basketball made the team. But we knew he cared about us. His heart was in our town. He aspired to nothing more than to help us excel. He was a quiet positive influencer who supervised positively.

For supervision to be unconditional, supervisors, like

coaches, must first spot the capabilities and limabilities of their supervisees—their regular companions. The conditions, or expectations, goals, or standards are based on what people want to do. By definition, positive experiences are things people are naturally interested in doing, desire to do, and things they do fairly well.

The dictionary defines *enable* as (1) make one able to do something and (2) make practical or easy. High school coaches enable by their attitude and by fostering a positive climate so players can approach their coach about almost anything. Players want to give 110 percent for the coach and the team. The coach does his best to position people. His training is practical, since players are positively matched up with their capabilities. Winning isn't everything—one person is. Stars and bench-warmers are viewed equally.

As with my high school coach, positive supervisors work with and through people as they are—family, relatives, students, and committees. Enabling coaches try to link up goals to capabilities and values. These goals become conditions, but they are conditions set and mutually agreed on in the light of people, going clockwise around the Fulfillment Cycle. Just trying to spot capabilities and interests, starting with people first, appeals to the people being supervised.

On the other hand, conditional supervisors go one-quarter or even one-half turn around the Fulfillment Cycle, but go counter-clockwise, looking first to goals and priorities. They go one mile. They skip the second mile—which is taking time to find out a person's traffic light, his capabilities and limabilities. They aren't coaches, since their player-decisions are made in complete ignorance of what people do well.

Such coaches have to resort to dark, conditional tactics, with emphasis on getting others to do things, always yelling or telling first, working up a lather of enthusiasm that is paper-thin. They even have to entice with title promises or advancement opportunities.

We have defined a people problem as that which occurs when someone is not *doing* and *being* what is expected. How that expectation is formed—by supervisors and regular companions—is the key to understanding its solution. For the expectation to be realistic and unconditional, it must depend on each other's capabilities and limabilities. Otherwise, expectations for each other are wrong; so people conclude there is a people problem, when in fact there isn't.

Parents are enabling coaches. For example, when parents take the traffic light (capabilities and limabilities) into account, they see that just because one child happens to clean his room well, that doesn't mean all will. By accepting the person, and then expecting less (yes, I mean that) in a yellow or red area, a people problem can be avoided. Positive supervisors have to temper their tendencies to "project on others." Rather than yelling, parents and offspring can discuss how to keep the room less messy, but not necessarily perfectly clean and organized. Now the expectation is realistic. It takes every ounce of self-discipline and God's grace to love unconditionally. Some do this—others just talk about doing it.

The basic assumption is that people tend to do a capability fairly well, in their opinion, and a limability not so well. But be careful, because a capability does not measure competence—only that the person has that capability. Further training and positive supervision can improve this competence. For example, a person may have the capability of selling but not up to the supervisor's standards. Training and supervision can improve the level of competency. Another example would be someone, who may love to cook. Further training should move up his or her level of competency.

Jim Chapman's wife is now more unconditionally loving. She can now help him and build him up in his areas of capability (making and building things), and when he speaks or teaches (limabilities) she doesn't expect him to do it as well. A people problem is avoided by having more realistic expectations.

Charlie Warren is chairman of the Christian education committee. As co-leaders of their Sunday school department, one loyal, faithful couple in their early fifties were causing problems. They were not keeping pace with new teaching concepts. They bucked new ideas, and teacher morale in their department dropped fast.

Charlie talked to the pastor. They decided that Charlie should try pinpointing their interests and capabilities. One Saturday morning he found out that this couple wanted to spearhead a puppet ministry.

While on vacation a month later, they happened (God always surprises us) to run into a couple already in a puppet ministry. The upshot is that this couple volunteered to give up their Sunday school job for the puppet ministry.

"It all happened so naturally," Charlie said. "I really didn't do a thing except draw them out while they discussed their positive experiences." A people problem solved, quietly. Only a few knew this was happening.

"As Sunday school superintendent," Betty Ratelle says, "I try to make things run smoothly without being obvious." Positive influencers lead quietly. Jesus' first concern was people, as when he stayed two more days after talking to the Samaritan woman. "So when the Samaritans came to him, they begged him to stay with them, and Jesus stayed there two days" (John 4:40, TEV). Jesus often took his disciples aside away from the crowds. His strategy was people. Charlie Warren put people into his agenda. A one-hour visit turned into three hours. He went the third mile! He is an enabling coach, trying to make things run smoothly without being obvious.

George's capabilities include singing. "I hate speaking and teaching," he says. His pastor asked him to lead morning devotions at a church retreat. Agreeing, he decided to sing his devotions. Let me tell you, he moved us all. It was beautiful. Pastor is an unconditional lover. Devotions don't have to be read.

Enabling coaches are like a ship's rudder. Unseen, unnoticed, and perhaps even unappreciated, they steer and give direction.

Take away the rudder of positive supervision and soon people start jumping overboard because of the negative climate, tension, and competition. The result is often a high turnover rate, but even more significant, the compounding negative on top of negative effect. Hurt people soon turn into insensitive people who often drop out of sight. Negative and conditional supervision in action causes negative reactions.

The enabling coach functions from the principles of unconditional love, not tested techniques. An enabling coach often feels helpless—absolutely helpless—techniqueless. Often he really doesn't know the answers or have answers. But he doesn't always have to. Unlike the ship's captain, he doesn't know another's port destiny and God's call for another person. God is captain of that person's life. Positive supervisors must avoid being amateur palm readers or playing futurist with someone else's life.

Let us assume now we have a handle on someone's capabilities and limabilities. At least we have a general idea, based on his positive and negative experiences. Our initial job description should expect us to accept what he says, to listen, and while advice is needed, to give it only after hearing out the other person. "A person's thoughts are like a deep well, but someone with insight can draw them out" (Proverbs 20:5, TEV).

Drawing someone out doesn't mean asking questions all the time, but questions are a good way to avoid hoof-in-mouth disease (opening your mouth and putting your foot in it). Jesus asked many questions.

What questions should we ask in helping another person make a decision? It may be a parent with a teenager, a daughter with her parent, an uncle with nephew, president with vice-presidents, counselor with counselee. Our aim is to help them be fulfilled and fruitful. Our role is to be that of an enabling coach.

1. *Where is your heart?* This question gets to the nub of a person's aspirations. In addition to asking "Where is your heart?" I follow with "When you're alone and thinking about what you really want to do, what do you see yourself doing?" Other questions might be: "Is your heart in Christian or secular work? Church or parachurch? Home missions or foreign missions? With older or younger people? Why not a business and make money to give to others? What about being a Christian in a secular business organization? Have you considered working with the Sunday school or on the missions board?" The answers to these questions may vary widely.

"My heart is with high school teenagers," one college senior replied. "The final product is a high schooler committing his life to Jesus and seeing him grow." Larry said, "My real desire is working in the inner city."

"My heart is in construction work," says Paul Johnson. "But I've got a second heart pull—teaching Sunday school." Today

he is positively influencing others as a construction worker.
Although he is using a limability, he teaches a young couple's
class. A positive supervisor stays close to Paul as he teaches.
Since he doesn't do it very well, he needs encouragement. The
key to his teaching is visitation. He sees each couple in their
home once a year. He has told his class that teaching is a limability
for him. He prays for his class—they are his regular companions.

He is also a regular companion of the Sunday school
superintendent, who meets with him quarterly to evaluate
progress and set goals. As they got to know each other, each
helped the other pinpoint his capabilities. So each formed
realistic expectations of the other based on knowing each
other's strengths and limitations. The Sunday school teacher
doesn't expect Paul to be a whiz at teaching. Neither does his
class. Paul is an example of unconditional positive supervision in
action.

"Where is your heart?" a father asked his son. "I want to write,
express my thoughts, and work for a publishing firm." Today,
he's in his second year of college headed in that direction.

"My heart is to have my own business," I said seven years
ago, "and have my office in our home." To me, that was
opportunity linked to capabilities and values. Our heart
answers represent our real desires. If we get those desires out of
our minds and tell them to God, he says he will respond.
"Delight yourself in the Lord and he will give you the desires of
your heart" (Psalm 37:4, NIV).

God doesn't snap to attention and grant our desires
immediately or automatically. We have to be patient. We cry
out with Peter, "Lord, why can't I follow now? . . . .I am ready to
die for you" (John 13:37, TEV). For our own testing and good,
God allows our time-tested, well-researched approaches to fail.
Timetables go awry. An enabling coach cannot just tell others.
While he would love to be able to give specific direction, like a
ship's captain, he realizes he must let God move in that
person's life and not himself try to become a hero to someone.
That is sometimes a helpless feeling. So when we help
someone, we may begin seeing God move immediately or a year
or two later. And when God does move, we sometimes hardly
recognize that he is leading!

So an enabling coach often asks:

*What is God trying to accomplish in that person? Most likely we
don't know specifically. It is God's timing, not man's timetables.
   What is God trying to accomplish through us in that person?
Sometimes God has to push us back and out of the way, so he has
room to work with him. The nudge hurts, particularly our pride.
   What is God trying to accomplish in us because of that
person? To have more patience and self-control? Usually I
have to ask, "Am I really trusting God or my advice to him?" Also,
"Am I encouraging him to trust God or me?"*

A person's heart's desire tends to reflect his capabilities and
what fulfills him. Expressing desires without knowing capabilities
and limabilities is risky because it doesn't allow for proper
comparisons between desire and capabilities. When desires
reflect capabilities, it affirms a person. For example, Jim
Chapman, the forty-four-year-old former teacher, wanted to be in
the refinishing business, a career that reflected his capabilities.

Heart's desires also reflect a person's values. "One of my
values is developing people," says Greg. "I know my personal
style category is one, but my heart is in helping people
grow—spiritually, mentally, and emotionally."

Jason is also a personal style category one. He supervises four
people. Paul is a personal style category two—a supervisor
and decision maker. "What do I do to keep him?" Jason asked.
"He'll soon pass me up in our organization."

"What's your role?" I asked.

"To develop him in his area of capabilities," Jason replied.
So Jason did just that. "I can hardly hold him down," Jason said
excitedly one year later. "He's now one rung above me, but
am I proud of him! You know, Dick, if I had been trying to be
competitive, this could not have happened. Trying to keep Paul
at his old job would have stifled him. What a fulfilling experience
to see him develop!" Jason's values also include helping
people grow, even potential competitors. That is an example of
realistic goals and expectations (conditions) set unconditionally.

The inner tug of God on a person's heart should be expressed
and written down to capture those fleeting moments when
thoughts flash through the mind. Then we should pray about
them.

A husband had an inner urge to go to Europe on a unique missionary assignment. He didn't share this with anyone for several months. He finally told his wife. It was news to her! Four months later, while driving along the highway, she too suddenly wanted to go to Europe, with no urging or persuading by either one. Instead, each was sensitive to God's direct dealing in the other's life. Each stepped aside, letting God intercede— giving him elbow room—rather than trying to be God's word to each other.

2. What are your interests? Closely tied in with the heart and the inner tugs are a person's interests. Sometimes interests match up with capabilities. At other times they don't. Quality professional organizations that administer interest tests tell people at the outset that there *may be* a good match of interests and capabilities, but not necessarily so. For example, I remember wanting to learn oil painting in my twenties. It was a pipe dream, totally unrealistic in view of my capabilities. And I've never done it.

Charlene (chapter 6), who switched her college major from counseling and social work to dramatics, listed these interests: music, Bible study, reading, hiking, concerts, craft shows, art festivals, and museums. An enabling coach and friend helped her pinpoint her capabilities; among her limabilities were counseling and overseeing.

When asked by her friend, "Where is your heart?" and "What are your aspirations?" she wrote down three possibilities: (1) Have a coffee house and counseling ministry to kids where I'd sing and play and have other Christian musicians come in and play. Then have counseling available during the day. (2) I'd love to have my own craft shop. (3) I would like to sing and make my own records, to perform in big and small places, to be able to share my music with others.

These aspirations, call them goals if you wish, are consistent with her capabilities and interests. That is positive supervision in action. Charlene doesn't have to be motivated—she wants to move ahead. She is already fulfilled and fruitful.

Charlene and her friend agreed to meet monthly. They decided next time each will share his values (Fig. 2.2), and then they will help each other realize them more. Each is helping the other;

each is developing and learning—quiet teamwork in action!

Their goals and standards for each other are unconditional, since these are individual matters and emerge from one's own heart and mind. First accepting each other's thoughts and ideas enables realistic goal refinement.

With this approach, people try to do too much, so an enabling coach comes invisibly alongside to harness things and remind the other person to concentrate on one or two areas, rather than trying to do everything at once.

Remember from chapter 5 the discussion of four ways to exercise self-discipline, the *plan plus* idea. We need to *plan plus* since people tend to underestimate how long it takes to do something.

Thomas Trustly heads the church trustee board. The board's first planning meeting included an expression of possible spiritual goals, in line with their main purpose—building each other up in the faith. Suggested spiritual goals included a deeper spiritual life, to be more faithful, a closer walk with Jesus, better verbal witness, better silent witness, to pray more, to be a better spouse and parent, a better daily quiet time, and to make a prayer commitment to two or three others on the committee as each feels led. As one veteran committee member said, "More work will get done if we start with what's really important. Why didn't we do this twenty years ago?"

They also decided to help each other pinpoint capabilities and limabilities at the next meeting and try to match up the committee goals to what individuals wanted to do. Each person's assignment was to list his positive and negative experiences.

At the next committee meeting, in groups of three, they shared positive and negative experiences and surfaced capabilities and limabilities. Each also wrote down his heart aspirations and interests.

Five of the ten had interests and capabilities that fell outside the trustee board functions. For example, Peter's capabilities are mainly teaching and visitation. He also has a Sunday school class, so the committee expects much less from Peter, and knows when he shows up for church workday, it's pure love. The committee has encouraged him to concentrate on teaching and to be an idea contributor and the committee prayer warrior. Peter loves it. He says, "It's taken the pressure and guilt away. I wouldn't miss a committee meeting for anything."

Twice each year, Thomas meets with people on his committee individually—or with two or three at a time. They are his regular companions. They share, plan, exchange ideas and get to know each other. He said, "Much to my surprise, each one wants to write his goals. Sarah came up with the idea of green goals (capabilities using) and red goals (limabilities using). Each of us had red goals and we're seeing how each is trying to accomplish too much. So the need is to chop down rather than challenge, push, or ask them to do more."

Thomas and I discussed his role as chairman, which is to be an enabling coach, a rudder helping others be realistic and not to become discouraged when goals are not reached. We discussed *plan plus* and its application to green goals and red goals. Then he said, "I can't wait to share this idea with them. Three are somewhat discouraged, feeling they haven't done enough. We tend to underestimate how long it takes. Now I see why I've had to chop down expectations."

Thomas ended our discussion by saying, "After asking one of the committee a question, just being a good listener to him is a lot of help. Sometimes people just want to unwind. If they have a problem, when they get through talking about it, they've usually figured it out for themselves. I don't have to say anything. Sometimes people just need a sounding board—somebody to listen."

Affirming him, I agreed saying, "Supervisors don't need to have all the answers. People don't want whiz kids—they want a fellow human being who cares." We can always follow up and get answers.

Notice what happened as Thomas Trustly supervised positively. Five people problems were avoided, since realistic expectations were set for five people functioning in their red areas. If group goals had been jammed down their throats, to be done by everyone, just think of the negative ramifications and the ripple effect. It was similar to what happened to the pastor whose excitement turned into disappointment when everyone's commitment was to visit one, just one, church member monthly. The commitment sounded like a good decision, and was made with good intentions, but it was going counterclockwise around the Fulfillment Cycle. Chairmen like Thomas, who see their role as enabling coaches helping others develop spiritually and grow in responsibilities, foster a positive climate.

There are two major reasons why committee members don't follow through, leaving chairmen holding the bag, and why Sunday school teachers don't go to teachers' meetings. One reason is negative or conditional supervision. The second reason is that people don't know each other's capabilities and limabilities.

If a program is more important than one person, don't start doing it. We have a choice. Jesus is our only model. We must choose to be examples of people willingly serving him and others, not numbers and trends. After all, God is the one causing growth. "Under Christ's control the whole body is nourished and held together by its joints and ligaments, and it grows as God wants it to grow" (Colossians 2:19, TEV).

Here is how another pastor supervises positively: "I meet weekly with one leader at 7 A.M. for breakfast to discuss his church responsibilities. I spend the first five minutes or so sharing a thought or two from my devotional life. Invariably the leader says, 'You know, that reminds me of something that's been a problem in my life.' We'll talk about it, then pray about it immediately. In the days ahead I may ask him about it to see if he's overcoming the problem. Then we discuss his church responsibilities."

Julie Hollander's capabilities include supervising and training, particularly one-on-one. Her church was without a pastor for two years. She volunteered (when people see a chance to use their capabilities, they often volunteer) to be administrator and coordinator. She was soon supervising positively.

"What I like doing most is meeting one-on-one with the committee heads," Julie says. Here are questions she asks:

What are your plans?
What would you like to see happen this year?
What are your interests?
How can I help you?
What can I pray about with you?
What do you expect of me?

"I particularly remember meeting with a recently retired couple in charge of our over-sixty-five program," she adds. "Here are questions I asked them."

What needs are being met? What needs are not being met?
How can the church help meet those needs? How can
Sunday school or our teenage group help?

"It was amazing how much they all appreciated talking about their needs and plans," Julie related. "We marked their green, yellow, and red goals. One shared how he hated running the committee meeting. On his committee was Harry, who liked that responsibility, so he did it. As a result, the committee chairman did better meeting preparation and follow-up. And now he looks forward to committee meetings."

Unconditional supervision affects recruitment. Jesus didn't press people or sell them, as we already noted. Instead, they willingly followed him after he called them.

When recruiters ask people to take responsibilities in light of their reds, yellows, and greens rather than asking blindly in ignorance of people's strengths and limitations, they are able to recruit unconditionally. People hate being sold or pressed into doing something. Remember the saying: If you have to sell the solution, you've got the wrong solution.

People (recruiters and recruits) indicate the preferred method of recruitment is open-ended. One recruiter uses what he calls a ten-day approach. He says, "If I don't know their green, yellow, and red, I'll admit it at the outset. Then I say, 'I'm not trying to pressure you, but would you think and pray about it? Ask yourself, "Do I have the time, and second, do I feel God would want me to do it at this time?" I'll pray and would you pray. Perhaps God will say no on both accounts. Could I get back to you in ten days?' "

He adds, "If I know a person has capabilities in that area, I'll avoid exploiting that. If it's a limability, we'll discuss that too. In either case, I use the 'ten-day approach.' "

Helen took on being chairperson of her church weekend retreat. She loves her forty-hour-a-week job and she knows her capabilities and limabilities.

At the end of the retreat she said, "Organizing is one of my limabilities. Everyone knows it, but everyone has been so helpful. They know I tend to be bossy. A few times they've had to put up with my controlling nature. But I love these people so much.

"I've had four people praying for me," she said quietly. "I feel God is mellowing me through this whole process. When I use my limabilities, I must really depend on God. You know what, if they ask me to do it again, I will." Behind the scenes is an enabling coach—her pastor. There is pulling power in a positive climate. Style starts at the top with the pastor. Style flows to other co-partners like Helen. In turn, her style affected the entire retreat. Positive supervision in action. It affects recruitment and willingness.

When capabilities and limabilities aren't known, one positive supervisor has his volunteers write goals, then he has them mark each goal green, yellow or red. "It's a second-best approach," he admits, "but it helps. For example, when Ben and I got together, all five of his goals were red goals, close to 0/0/100 [compared to the 40/20/40 concept discussed earlier]. First, we reduced his responsibilities and set goals in two areas. Then I helped him come up with some green goals in other volunteer things he really wanted to do.

"We've communicated this about Ben to the other volunteers, so there's no peer pressure. It's fun to see this evolve. Each knows the others' green, yellow, and red goals. Each is trying to help the others reach their goals."

An enabling coach uses the 40/20/40 concept. Goals always include doses of green, pinches of yellow, and some red. But in any situation (parents, teenagers, roommates, office peers), people being sold on doing something they don't want to do feel dumped on. Worse yet, they resent having to use a limability.

To illustrate what often happens, Ralph and several other lay people in the church pinpointed their capabilities and limabilities. Ralph is Sunday school superintendent and found out he is functioning in a strong red area. As we talked, guilt from not measuring up was removed when he realized it wasn't his problem, since he was functioning in a red area.

As we talked, he seemed to have renewed enthusiasm to do a

better job. We discussed ways to perform his tasks in the light of its being a limability. He agreed to ask three people to pray for a more positive attitude and about his tendencies to procrastinate. We prayed together.

Then in popped a member of the church staff. "Ralph, you're doing a great job; you're improving every Sunday. We want you to be our Sunday school superintendent next year. Great job, great job."

I became speechless and frustrated. Here was a totally insensitive person using only encouragement and motivation. Without knowing it, he was trying to jam a square peg into a round hole. Ralph looked at me dumbfounded. I left.

I thought, "people first" seems for some to be an upside-down concept. Accepting people and who they are is one of our biggest challenges. I felt sorry for the staff person whose responsibilities are so large that people come last. He didn't know Ralph's green, yellow, and red areas. His supervision was conditional. I felt sorry for Ralph. I felt sorry for both of them, because a relationship was breaking down.

On the way home, I thought: "Think of parents selling their offspring on doing something major in an area that's a red. I wonder how many people are being supervised by encouragement and meetings only? I wonder how many people today are making an effort to integrate the concept of unconditional love when they see someone." I also thought, "How quick we are to hang up impossible standards for other people, like expecting *them* to be Christ-like all the time, or to be automatically willing to do something *I* think is simple, yet for them might be difficult because it's a red."

Arriving home and closing the garage door, I mumbled to myself, "Any wonder Jesus selected the Twelve; of the Twelve three, Peter, James, and John, who got more of his time? Any wonder he had to tell us about going after one of the one hundred missing?" Jesus concentrated on a few people. Bigger isn't necessarily better. Positive supervision is being willing to sacrifice.

Then I sat down and reread John 10. My heart warmed. Jesus led the sheep, he knew them by name, and the sheep knew his voice. Thomas Trustly, our trustee chairman, is following Jesus' model. He is no longer under the bondage of

Positive supervision in action

goals-first approaches. I recall someone saying, "I'd rather not go to our annual conference if I don't make my goals. I have to fake it when asked, 'How is it going?' I fabricate an answer like 'Great, just great.' It hurts inside."

All people are supervisors. All people choose to supervise negatively, conditionally, or positively. The *if* of positive supervision hits both supervisor and supervisee. We are all in the same boat.

Carol, our first example from chapter 1, has a supervisor who wears too many hats. He isn't concentrating—working long hours, yes, but supervising negatively.

Sue's husband Carl (chapter 1) hasn't changed much since

receiving Jesus. He is ignoring God's inner tug to go into farming, so relationships are sour. Sue is supervising positively but Carl isn't submitting, to God or to Sue. He is ignoring Hebrews 13:17.

Jennifer (chapter 1) chafed under her parents' rules and regulations. Their conditional supervision drove her into a shaky, quick marriage. She submitted to her parents, but it was a one-way street. She felt they never listened to her.

Brad and Marilyn (chapter 1), the married couple who have breakfast together each Sunday morning to discuss next week's plans, are supervising each other positively. Brad confided, "Now we're even having devotions together twice a week."

Where is the *if?* When a supervisor's *if* is the choice to willingly pick up his cross daily, the *if* is in the right place. *If* is in the wrong place when it is first pointed at supervisee's grade level or whether a goal is reached.

"Then Jesus turned around and when he saw them following him spoke to them, 'What do you want?' he said" (John 1:38, Phil.). Is Jesus' question one of your first questions to your regular companions?

Positive supervision is neither hand holding nor "do your own thing." It means being mutually responsible and accountable to each other.

TEN QUALITIES OF GOOD SUPERVISION

Good supervision centers around the supervisor himself experiencing the reality of Christ's presence in his life. He is having daily devotions, has a prayer list, and prays daily for those he supervises. Decision-making is preceded by prayer for wisdom (James 1:5) and the mind of Christ (Philippians 2:5).

1. Accountable. He respects and trusts his supervisor. Strives to cooperate with that person and help meet his or her goals. Understands his job responsibilities and accompanying problems; modifies goals and priorities to mesh with overall organization goals. Keeps lines of communication open.

2. People Responsible. He is deeply committed to those he supervises. His heart is with them—they are priority. Is available, approachable, and open. Willingly discusses their needs and problems. Keeps confidences.

3. Develops People. He supervises to develop the whole person. Delegates important tasks as well as someone-has-to-do-it tasks. Strives to fit responsibilities to person's capabilities and strengths. Tailors training to person's strengths. Periodically plans and reviews, primarily one-on-one, and in the real-life situations demonstrates but more often observes and then critiques immediately afterwards.

4. Servant Authority. He has authority because he accepts people, serving and helping them. Clearly understands authority is not a direct result of office, position, or title. Downplays by constantly reminding himself, "I'm here to help people. They don't work for me." Never resorts to "do it, that's what we're paying you for" mentality.

5. Tactful. He never belittles or ridicules publicly. Gives deserved praise and affirmation. When he asks for advice or an opinion, he isn't secretly looking for approval and affirmation. Listens with an open mind. Does not argue.

6. Always Follows Up. If he cannot do as promised or agreed on, immediately informs those most affected. If he delegates during a meeting, he follows up immediately afterwards to discuss and tie down expectations.

7. Influences by Example. He adheres to the same standards expected of his staff. Personal priorities and values are being realized—living a balanced life-style. He is disciplined—prepares well. Has an appropriate and fitting personal appearance; does not dress to impress and out-class others, nor to draw attention to himself. He is not trying to lead by number of hours worked or "I'm doing it; so can you" attitude.

8. Makes Decisions. He realizes he must take charge in an attitude of servanthood. He initiates, causes the right things to happen. He understands that many decisions are unpopular and must at times say "No." He knows he is often the person in the middle—between the ones supervised and his boss. He does not avoid or duck people problems.

9. *Is Fair.* He does not play favorites or show partiality. He includes everyone he supervises in what is going on. He listens to both inexperienced and experienced people. He never betrays a confidence. Whenever possible, he includes those he supervises in problem-solving.

10. *Builds Positive Climate.* He fosters a caring, helping atmosphere. He downplays whatever would be competition-causing divisiveness or win-loss situations. He does not try to outperform those he supervises. He is open, and admits failures. He constantly strives for quality, within situational constraints. He builds relationships around respect and trust for each other. He is open to new ideas. He says "we" not "I."

A DOZEN THINGS TO DO
WHEN YOU'RE NOT BEING SUPERVISED

1. *Take the initiative.* Find someone you respect and trust and, as much as possible, become accountable to him. Establish regular times to meet together to plan, review, and evaluate.

2. *Take the initiative.* Get into a small group—share your problem and become accountable to them or to one person in the group.

3. *Take the initiative.* Write your goals and priorities. Schedule your time wisely. In the meantime, include talking out loud to God about your goals. Talk to him as if he were actually with you. Share your need—ask him for someone to be your supervisor.

4. *Listen to the advice that naturally comes your way, no matter from whom it comes.* Thank them, digest it, and if it is no good, forget it.

5. *Take advantage of seminars and meetings.* Look for practical ideas to meet your needs. Downplay the fact that you aren't being supervised. Act responsibly.

6. *Develop yourself.* Set up a reading development program that you would find interesting and practical. Schedule regular times to study. Take notes. Tell someone about it.

7. *Look for something with which your supervisor may help you.* Pray about how to approach him. Have no hidden agenda. Be open and sensitive. Be considerate of his time. Afterwards express your appreciation in some special way.

8. *List all the things you could do (not give advice) to make your supervisor's job less difficult.* Start with little things. Encourage him occasionally. Ask him how things are going. Do something for him that is not in your job description.

9. *Follow up well on assignments from him.* Volunteer to do something extra. Read Colossians 3:23 every day.

10. *Ask yourself:*
   Do I pray for him? Do I really want God's best for him or do I secretly want him to fail?
   Do I really want to be supervised? And by him? Am I playing games—really enjoying not being supervised and getting a secret pleasure from complaining about it?
   Am I expecting too much supervision? Could I modify my expectations?
   Have I been insensitive to his job pressures? Should I take one hour, get away and really try to understand his situation? Have I been too selfish, thinking only of my needs?
   Have I completely forgotten to look for my supervisor's good points and been mired down by noticing only his failures and weaknesses?
   Am I overlooking that he is God's creation?
   Do I believe change begins with me?

11. *Share your concern with one trusted friend.* Establish a thirty-day prayer covenant to pray about this daily. Each week,

tell your prayer partner about positive things you are doing for your supervisor.

12.   If you still feel no change forthcoming, realize it takes two to fight as well as to function together constructively. If your needs are acute enough, consider relocating, but only as a last resort, after having done everything possible on your part (Romans 12:18).

NINE
TAKING THE NEGATIVE OUT
OF EVALUATION—REALITIES

"We, I mean myself and all of us, don't follow up. Nothing seems to get done. What's the matter? Here we are a group of seven supposedly committed people and only three show up. What's wrong?"

Sandra Schoolford, Sunday school superintendent, is meeting with six Sunday school department heads—nursery, kindergarten, primary, junior, senior, and adult. At the March meeting they decided the aim of the April meeting would be an evaluation of the past year and then a decision about the summer program. The April meeting is starting. Sandra senses uneasiness: "I must confess I have a sense of uneasiness tonight. Am I the only one?" There was silence.

"I'm not looking forward to this evaluation," Bill says, head down. "As I look at what we were supposed to accomplish, and what we actually did accomplish, I for one didn't do much. I never seemed to get started."

"The same old problem," Greta adds. "Follow-up. Our plans never got off the ground. Why? Why?" She is angry at herself.

Concerns like "We don't know each other," "We hardly ever pray together or for each other," "No one ever asks me how things are going," "I don't know what's going on in other departments," and "I don't look forward to these meetings" surfaced the real problem—lack of accountability to each other.

"The solution is supervision," Bill says. "Let's list why more individualized planning and evaluation would solve our problem."

At a flip chart Sandra lists their reasons:

— *Build a positive, working relationship*
— *Can discuss our spiritual needs; know how to pray better for each other.*
— *Build expectations so we know what to do.*
— *Facilitates self-evaluation.*
— *Fosters teamwork.*
— *Shows the importance of the job to the supervisee.*
— *Can discuss each other's strengths and limitations.*
— *Giving individualized attention is encouraging.*
— *It says you value their opinions and need them.*
— *Improves communication.*
— *Ripple effect—through one influence many.*
— *Mutual teaching and learning.*
— *A bridge between ideas and implementation.*

They concluded: There is no way to evaluate specifically without one-on-one planning. "Group planning and evaluation has its place," Frank says, "but plans must get to the doers—those of us who will do the work."

Negative and conditional supervisors like goals (particularly group goal setting) because it makes evaluation easier and more clear cut. They can also keep people at arm's length and not get too involved with just one or two lives. But as Frank just said, planning and evaluation must get to the doers. That means people-first approaches to planning and evaluation. Positive supervisors like Sandra Schoolford see positive supervision as a "bridge between ideas and implementation."

Let's face it, goals scare many people. Group goals are impersonal. Leader-imposed goals dispose of people. One good way to keep volunteers away is continually to emphasize "We've got to do more. We've got to become bigger." Goals exist for individual people, not people for goals. Changing attitudes positively requires a personal touch.

So to evaluate, planning—group and one-on-one—must be taking place. Here are some examples of evaluation. Most businesses do it poorly too. Notice there is lots of counterclockwise motion around the Fulfillment Cycle.

Lowell sells paper products for his company. In all but two of his twenty-five years, he has met the sales quota (which he had no say in) set for him. "Did I feel boxed in!" Lowell says. "They called me into the office, closed the door, and in five minutes laid out the options—create a new inside position (limabilities using) or give me time to find something else with another company. I chose the former, knowing full well I'd do the latter."

"All the while, I felt my hands were tied" and then he adds, "they seemed so unconcerned about me—my goals, my values, my future. It was so cut-and dried. It was like me against them, and they were the enemy. What really hurts is that previous to this, no one had ever expressed dissatisfaction with my work. What a shock!"

No one-on-one planning and evaluation was taking place. Did they evaluate? Yes, but the wrong way. Negative and conditional supervisors never start evaluation with the person (doers) themselves. That's wrong.

"I wish pastor would evaluate me. I have been on staff three years, and his main concern is staff meetings and bringing me up to date about complaints and problems in my area. I really don't know where I stand with him."

"When I get a call from the boss I think two things: Oh no, I did something wrong or he has something to give me to do. You see, that's the only time we get together other than staff meetings. I hate going into his office."

Tellthem, Inc. is a large national corporation with a staff of forty-five people. They have five levels of people. Three senior people make up level one. Level five people are the newest (one to four years). Level four, three, and two people are more experienced. "How do you evaluate someone at level five?" I asked.

A senior partner revealed: "At salary review time, we three partners get together and evaluate him, then we bring in a level four person to include in our discussion; then we bring in a level three and two person for their thoughts. Then a level four person presents it to 'level five.' You see, by this time he won't know who said what and we make sure he's told in such a way that he can't pinpoint who said it." I gulped.

"Is there any input from level five?" I asked. He replied, "No."

Talk about steamrolling over people! Then I thought of hundreds of organizations whose evaluation is like Tellthem, Inc. For example, school systems where administrators evaluate with no input from the supervisee. Teachers whose semiannual evaluation is being observed by a veteran administrator in one class, then while walking down the corridor, dodging students, are told what they did wrong. No previous one-on-one planning provides a benchmark or standard. Little concern is shown for how the person views his performance. It is a one-shot, one-way, no-win deal.

Negative and conditional supervision sees evaluation as a one-way street. To do so is unthinkable, untenable, and dehumanizing. It turns evaluators into judges who pronounce sentences. It lowers people to peons. Parents who "tell only" are just as guilty. It is easy to forget a seven-year-old has a mind. And certainly teenagers cringe when parents correct them constantly.

"The more I tell my daughter [age twenty-seven] what she should do," Mrs. Goodtell relates, "the more she resents me and what I'm saying."

A minister of visitation asked the senior pastor to critique two sermons. So he did, taking detailed notes of two sermons on Sunday. I asked the senior pastor how he evaluated him.

"I did what he asked me. I told him what he did wrong. I had a whole list of things. I said he has got to work at his preaching—that every word is an effort, unlike myself where preaching is a joy. For me the words just flow."

Guess what the senior pastor's capability is? And guess what the minister of visitation's limability is? You're right—speaking. If you were the minister of visitation, how would you have felt in the pit of your stomach as you drove home? Most likely discouraged. Any consideration of capabilities and limabilities? None. Projection of the senior pastor's capabilities onto the minister of visitation? Correct—pure and simple, conditional supervision in action during a critique. Well-intentioned, yes, but done wrong.

I asked a field supervisor why he didn't evaluate his people periodically, like every three months or so. Giving me one of those "You must be crazy" looks, he said, "Dick, the trouble with evaluation is that too many negatives come through."

The one that takes the cake is what an administrator said to me in private, as if he had unlocked the secret of evaluation. "If Harold [their custodian] empties my wastebasket two or three times a day," he said, "rather than once, I'm sure we're not giving him enough work to do."

I have taken a special interest in Harold. His church is immaculate, and I tell him that every chance I get. "Harold, how do you see your role here?" I asked. With that pleased look he said, "I take special pains to keep our offices clean. I know they have a lot of visitors. I even make a special effort to empty the wastebaskets more than once if I hear a visitor will be around."

You may be snickering under your breath, but I hope you're getting the message. This administrator wouldn't think to "bend down," sit on a stool in front of a pail of dirty water and get to know Harold. *Talk* about serving is cheap; doing it is costly to pride and ego. And to think Jesus washed his disciples' feet. Ability hierarchies? We've got 'em!

These examples appall me. It is obvious that evaluation is slipshod and negative. It is often associated with what people are not doing. Such thinking must be turned around because evaluation such as that discourages people.

PUTTING REALITY INTO EVALUATION

Evaluation is part of positive supervision when its aim is to build up people, rather than tear down, and when the people being evaluated are an integral part of the evaluation process.

Evaluation is light years away from being precise, measurable, and clear cut. Businesses and success oriented organizations pride themselves on goals and standards being, for example, measurable, attainable, and motivational. Positive influencers seek to influence each other as equals and the extent to which we

individually influence another person or group is *impossible*—
yes, *impossible* to determine.

For example, if someone is teaching a Sunday school class,
how did the students' parents, or the last four sermons, or
their last committee meeting, or their boss at work, or the
conversation in the car on the way to church affect what
happened on Sunday? In other words, one tells his spouse a
subjective approximation when asked, "How did your class go
today?" There are many outside factors over which you have
no control.

For another example, think of all the outside influencers on
a teenager. Parents, brothers, sisters, relatives, peers at school,
peers who work with him at the pizza shop, the church, the
pastor, teachers, youth group leaders, neighborhood people all
influence. As a parent trying to be an enabling coach with
teenagers, I feel almost helpless. A fifty-two-year-old father says,
"I think being a parent is 80 percent personal example." At
least 80 percent, I would add.

Two people recently asked me, "How do you view your role
as the spiritual leader of your home?"

For twenty years, I have never consciously considered myself
the spiritual leader. Now that I've been asked that question, I
don't know how to answer. Who the leader is doesn't seem to
be the right question. Better questions are: "Am I walking with
Jesus?" or "Am I contributing to a positive climate? Is
encouragement and affirmation the main topic, rather than
correction of each other? Am I striving to be God's person in
my home? Do I view my wife and children as coequals, rather
than erect some business organization chart and have
over-under relationships?"

I also added, "How do you measure the influence of each
person's prayers in each other's life?" I'm not striving to be a
spiritual leader where family members look *up* to me, but
instead to see others as people with feelings and minds who look
to me and I look to them. Spouses, offspring, and committee
members ought to be asking the same questions.

In chapter one we said that serving influencers hardly know
they are influencing. If God's love is alive and active in one's life,
then to focus just on output and results is a sham. Why? God's
love in a person's life is impossible to measure precisely. Our aim
should be to help each other experience more of his love. Then

his evergrowing love in us produces an outflow. "For though we have never yet seen God, when we love each other God lives in us and his love within us grows ever stronger" (1 John 4:12, TLB). "For the Scriptures declare that rivers of living water shall flow from the inmost being of anyone who believes in me. (He was speaking of the Holy Spirit . . .)" (John 7:38, 39, TLB).

His love in me and the outflow of his love from me (mixed with my often selfish tendencies) depend on me, not some precise or all-inclusive definition of spiritual leadership. That is why sermons are difficult to evaluate, or a teacher's response to a spouse's question on the way home from church is tough to answer.

Evaluation begins with me—spouse, committee member, pastor, administrator, student, son, or daughter. There are questions that need to be asked:

1. Are hearts in a receivable condition? To be able to accept his
love, my heart must be soft and fertile, not hard and rocky.
"So get rid of every filthy habit and all wicked conduct. Submit to
God and accept the word that he plants in your hearts, which is
able to save you" (James 1:21, TEV). "Other people are like the
seeds sown among the thorn bushes. These are the ones who
hear the message, but the worries about this life, the love for
riches, and all other kinds of desires crowd in and choke the
message, and they don't bear fruit. But other people are like
seeds sown in good soil. They hear the message, accept it, and
bear fruit: some thirty, some sixty, and some one hundred" (Mark
4:18-20, TEV).

It is God's will that hearts be in a receivable condition to bear
fruit that varies in output—some thirty, some sixty, and some
one hundred. And what a tragedy when enabling coaches spread
the seed and see success and this world's standards choke out
his Spirit's tugging and prompting in someone's heart. It is a
tragedy when people say yes on Sunday and by Tuesday
afternoon have forgotten—choked by life-styles and time
commitments.

Positive influencers and positive supervisors should not be
discouraged by a lack of visible results. Desired results may
occur immediately or several years later. Recall in chapter 1, the
comment of one of my Sunday school high schoolers several
years later: "Now I know what Mr. Hagstrom was talking about.
It's beginning to make sense."

All that positive supervisors can do is ensure that they
themselves have receptive hearts. At least 80 percent of
leadership is personal example and the fostering of a positive
climate. "It's taken eleven years to change people's attitudes,"
a pastor said. "What I've really been doing is creating a positive
climate. I'm just beginning to see growth in individual lives."

Leadership that evaluates by first asking, "How many are
following?" or "How many came out last night?" is miles off
base. People may be following a cause or person rather than
Jesus.

Faith labored three years with a group of high schoolers with
absolutely no results. One night, totally unplanned, thirty-five
high schoolers committed their lives to Jesus.

"The subject that night had nothing to do with what

happened," she said. "I was talking, and halfway through I noticed tears in one guy's eyes. It brought tears to my eyes. Shortly afterwards, I stopped and simply asked the group, 'Would anyone like to say anything?' One after the other confessions of sin were made." Faith says, "I cannot explain what caused all this." Neither can I, and I'm glad I don't have to. But I have an inkling Faith's heart was in a receivable condition. She noticed tears in one person's eyes and in that instant caught the wind of the Holy Spirit. How do we evaluate that? We don't. We just experience it with grateful hearts. We just keep ourselves ready to receive instances of this in another's life without jealousy. "Love . . . is not jealous" (1 Cor. 13:4, TEV). Those who love encourage and build up one another rather than allow jealousy to affect their evaluation.

2. Is God really part of decision-making? If so, how do we separate what God does from what a person does, to fairly evaluate a person or situation? With a great deal of difficulty!

I functioned as an enabling coach with a friend I'll call Eric. And did I learn!

Eric dreaded going to work in the morning. Bickering in his family was commonplace. "Do something," his wife kept saying.

"But what?" Eric snapped back. "We have Cliff and Dawn in college. Where's the money going to come from?" (Typical household remark!)

We pinpointed Eric's capabilities and limabilities—a big mismatch. Values were then clarified. His wife couldn't stand their present location. Not a very ego-building situation for a Harvard graduate and company president.

Eric decided to look for another job. He told his corporate boss nine months in advance of his intended resignation. He planned a job search very carefully. Prayer teams were set up and kept informed along the way. Resumés were sent out, and friends in a position to help spot opportunities were contacted.

Nothing happened. Nothing. Many resumés were sent out, but not one got a nibble. All the while, his high blood pressure gradually returned to normal, and I think my blood pressure jumped up daily!

It went down to the wire. Two weeks before Eric's leaving his company, a business acquaintance who knew nothing about Eric's situation happened to telephone. He asked Eric if he would consider going to work for his company. It turned out to be a positive capabilities and values matchup.

A business acquaintance "happened" to call? Never. God engineered the whole thing. I tried to evaluate what happened and this is the big thing I learned. "Plan carefully what you do, and whatever you do will turn out right" (Prov. 4:26, TEV). Turn out right—most likely not the way it was planned, but as God wants things to happen. I can't prove this, but since Eric prayed, planned, and followed up thoroughly, it turned out right.

I'm stumped trying to evaluate Eric's situation. Perhaps since Eric did his part, God was able to put it all together. Without God, evaluation would be easy. With God in the picture, the evaluation gets harder to analyze, and that is how it should be. It is God's will for us to do our part and depend on him. He says he will lead us as long as we don't try to get ahead of him.

I also learned I had to give God more room in my own planning as well as when helping other people. It is tough for me to keep my hands off and to let God take over. I tend to reach for the captain's wheel and steer people to my destination for them rather than God's.

3. Are prayer requests genuine? Rob is fifty-eight. For the first time in his life, a business decision stumped him. "Do you have anyone praying for you?" I asked.

"Two or three," was his quick reply. "Have you admitted to yourself and God your need for help—God's help?" I asked. "Will you ask five people to pray for you?"

His wife jumped in defending him saying, "But Rob is reserved. He keeps most things to himself."

Then I shared how five ladies pray each week for me and how it was hard at first for me to admit to people I didn't have the answers. Down deep I wanted to do it myself. To actually reach out, to God and others, was a major breakthrough in my life. Today, when my wife asks, "What do you want us to pray about this week?" it is much easier. I didn't say easy! Those five people are silent, quiet influencers. Someone said, "I think God will have a special place in heaven for people like that."

It is considered the Christian thing to say, "Will you pray for me?" But do we mean it? To sweep out reserve and independence is the last thing to do so God can make things "turn out right." There are many people like Rob, whose conceit, pride, decision-making skills, and education make asking for prayer superficial rather than genuine.

Problem solvers encourage genuine prayer requests. Positive supervisors care more about helping people than figuring out what technique worked and what didn't work. Until the walls of self crack and tumble down, little progress is made anyway.

4. Do you have confidence in your decisions? People who preface every other sentence with "the Lord did this" or "the Lord just spoke to me about that" drive me up the wall. Everything is so rosy, almost as if they had put their brain in neutral and mouth in high gear. They seem to toss evaluation and thinking out the window. Confidence shows. It reeks with shallowness.

Let me make a confession: I'm uncertain about almost every decision I make. People often have doubts soon after making important decisions. "I'm having second thoughts," Clayton said. We all should, and this *is* God's will. Why? He wants us to depend on him *every day,* not just at decision time.

The decision to set up our own business involved prayer and judgment at every step. A hundred lights didn't go on and say, "Now, Dick, do it." People, situation, and circumstances came together and with uncertainty we made a decision.

Right now I'm redesigning a brochure (designing is a limability for me, too!). To me, it is a major decision. But it is never clear-cut. Some days I want to scrap the project. But I continue processing it toward completion until something clicks.

"But this happened so that we should rely, not on ourselves, but only on God, who raises the dead" (2 Corinthians 1:9, TEV). If we made decisions with confidence, we would soon leave God out, relying more on so-called sophisticated decision-making techniques. All our uncertainty should mean we are depending more on God.

Every goal should be set with the right kind of uncertainty. Every evaluation is made with uncertainty. Every planning process with uncertainty. We are to exercise faith at every step of the way, not just at the time we committed our lives to Jesus.

As I weigh decisions back and forth, God often speaks through people with whom I really have little in common, or who are the most unlikely source of information. Eric's business acquaintance is an example of this.

In my uncertainty, I was weighing whether or not to hire someone, realizing my personal style category is One. A person approached me to do some things that matched up with his capabilities. The five ladies and I prayed. It was one of those decisions I couldn't get out of my mind.

One Friday afternoon my wife said, "Let's have so-and-so over tonight." My sheer brilliance would have clearly predicted she is not the person I would have said has the mind to solve my weighty problem. How often I so naturally erect abilities hierarchies!

Out of the blue our friend said, "Dick, I never hear much about what you do. How come?"

I blurted out some generalities, then slipped in, "Right now, I'm trying to decide whether or not to hire someone."

She replied, "If you ask me, you sound like the Lone Ranger type."

Wham-o! Instantly I said to myself, "That's it. I will not hire that person." Her remark made me aware of how I and the person under consideration would work together. God often uses people I least expect—my ability hierarchy smashed to the ground again. My capacity to hear God from other people depends on my heart receptivity, allowing God to function outside of my plan, and within reason, my uncertainty.

Snap decision makers scare me. Decisions need to be soaked in his Word, meshed with his Spirit in prayer. Decision makers must be alert to hear him give his answer—from any source.

The person himself affects evaluation more than anything else. Positive supervisors recognize this and look at what a person does and tries to be in terms of their green, yellow, and red areas, rather than just the goals themselves.

Results of a deacon's visit are hard to measure. Literally hundreds of people affect decisions to go to church on Sunday even after a deacon's visit. But deacons, and all of us, can evaluate *do* goals and *be* goals. We can ask, "Did I visit (do) one family (goal) this month?" Evaluation can also include: "Did I pray first? Was I prepared? Did I follow up? What was my attitude when visiting?" Results of the visit may never be known.

If we consider the *be* part related to motives for doing things, only the person himself, before God, can evaluate that. It is a matter of attitude. "You may think everything you do is right, but the Lord judges your motives" (Proverbs 16:2, TEV). Only we know if we are serving out of love or not.

We don't *see* faith and dependence on God. We don't *see* results very much. All we can get a handle on is *doing* and *being*. And faith that is alive is active—doing, being, and meeting people's needs. Our spiritual fitness is the main influence on results, which are hard to see and measure. As we begin with evaluation that centers on individuals, we also may have been asked, or ourselves have asked of others, "How do you think I'm doing?"

HOW AM I DOING?

If you think I have skirted the evaluation issue, you are right! We pull away the curtains and with uncertainty dive into evaluation. Consultants I have supervised did a job that is hard to accurately evaluate, but I looked forward to evaluation time. I love evaluating other people who are my regular companions. These have been, and still are, sacred times when I learn from real life people.

There are some evaluation tips that might be helpful in answering that question. To blurt out a response to "How am I doing, boss?" without thinking first could be disastrous.

EVALUATION TIPS

1. People dislike being evaluated (judged), says Swiss psychologist Paul Tournier. Evaluation is associated with negativism and with being corrected. Carole, in chapter 1, said, "When he corrects and criticizes me, it's like pounding me further into the ground." Twenty-seven-year-old daughters often resent their mothers' advice. Kids whose parents focus on correcting them soon lose their sense of belonging. Their sense of worth drops. They sag inside and want to leave—run away. It is amazing how much some people love correcting others!

A college professor said, "Our president just met with the board of trustees. They told him four things he is doing wrong. He has been looking pretty down." I predicted to my wife that he would resign within two months. He did.

"I guess people are a lot better at wanting evaluation than taking it," the college professor said later. He is right.

When someone says, "All he does is correct me," he needs to be taken seriously. Correctors are negative supervisors. "Dear brothers, don't be too eager to tell others their faults, for we all make many mistakes" (James 3:1, TLB). Someone filled with eagerness to correct others needs tempering—maybe even a muzzle! We should try to be less eager to point out faults when we are, for example, asked to give our opinion.

I'm often asked to evaluate training programs, usually contained in a bright red binder. "So what do you think, Dick?" I'm asked as I flip the pages. I must be careful. Most likely I'm being asked to affirm and give my approval rather than my opinion. To be really honest would be tactless and irresponsible. If I turn up two or three negatives (not difficult to do when something is in writing), the bottom drops out of our relationships. He is soon defending *his* training program. It can deteriorate quickly into an argument. After he has poured his soul into a training program, I had better point out mainly good things.

On the other side, when we ask for an opinion, we should make sure that is what we want and not be defensive when the evaluation is negative.

On the other hand, people want to be evaluated. "I wish someone would tell me if I'm doing my job or not," a deaconess says.

Putting together the idea that people don't want to be evaluated and corrected, yet want to know how well they are doing, says to me: yes, evaluate me, but be a positive supervisor whose main aim is to build up, not tear down.

Let's admit it. Most of us dislike being corrected and told we are wrong. We may not show it or say it in public, but inside it hurts. A heavy knot develops in the pit of the stomach. As one supervisor said when he asked for his staff to evaluate him, "I feel as if I've been attacked." Phyllis said, "Intellectually I say, 'yes,

"Dear brothers, don't be too eager to tell others their faults, for we all make many mistakes" (James 3:1, TLB).

I want to be corrected.' Emotionally I say, 'no, I can't handle it.' " Our approach to evaluation must be done carefully and with little direct negative criticism.

2. *Be timing conscious.* In other words, if we have to correct someone, we should ask ourselves, "Should I say it now?" or "Should I say it here?" The Bible is clear that one-on-one approaches are preferred before taking someone with you or bringing it before the church. Positive supervisors will go a long way toward solving people problems by keeping this in mind, especially in our homes when company arrives and kids start behaving like kids.

Here are some questions we might consider when deciding whether to correct people at the time, to wait, or to let it go.

   a. What effect will what I say have on our relationship?
     Does the person need to hear this now?
     Does the person want to hear this?

   b. Am I simply trying to get something off my chest?
     Linus says to Lucy, "You never stop criticizing, do you? I should think you'd get tired of criticizing me." Lucy replies, "Actually, I do. But if I stop, I tighten up."

     Positive supervisors make sacrifices, such as the sacrifice of asking and listening before telling and correcting. Conditional supervisors display their correctives not only for the ones corrected but for everyone else. Positive supervisors are quiet. They do things without fanfare. They squelch their natural tendency to correct someone in a committee meeting or unnecessarily at the dinner table.

   c. Where is the person in his walk with Jesus? Certain Bible verses have buttoned my lip on many occasions. "If you correct a conceited man, you will only be insulted. If you reprimand an evil man, you will only get hurt. Never correct a conceited man; he will hate you for it. But if you correct a wise man, he will respect you" (Prov. 9:7-8, TEV). This doesn't mean we go around with a thermometer, taking people's conceit index, but that our correcting of someone includes considering where they are in their walk with Jesus.

3. Words have an effect. "Kind words bring life, but cruel words crush your spirit" (Prov. 15:4, TEV). Words like, "That's the dumbest thing I've every heard" or "Don't be so dumb" sting. They crush spirits, tear down relationships, and build walls of tension and ill-feeling. Nobody likes being thought of as dumb or incompetent. Negative supervisors use cruel words that stick a long, long time.

   Robert decided against going into the pastoral ministry one week before graduating from seminary. "So you've decided to sell shoes rather than sell Jesus," one of his peers said snidely.

   Robert told me this eighteen years after it happened. Then he also told me about the trauma of his teenage years and having to decide which parent to live with as they were divorcing. He told me how much it hurt being told he was less than a committed Christian for selling shoes. Ill-timed comments hurt people. Our advice is often unneeded, so it goes unheeded.

Evaluation includes correction, but correction is 2 percent or less of evaluation. You can see why responding to "How am I doing?" with a barrage of corrections and things they did wrong ends in disaster. People don't want to be corrected. If they are conceited (and who isn't—just a little?) we end up embarrassed too.

Research shows that if someone being reviewed is told more than one thing he or she did wrong it causes a serious negative reaction. The person is unable to handle it. In other words, unloading on someone and telling him or her one thing after another—like a repeater shotgun—is wrong, wrong, wrong! A person can handle only *one* corrective at a time. And so often, some of us can't handle one, particularly from our own family members!

Most people approach evaluation either saving up a bunch of wrongs, then dumping them all at once, or they say, "As long as we're talking about this, let me tell you two or three more things you did wrong." Bang. Shut the windows—the neighbors might hear. Or the supervisor rises to shut the office door.

Negative supervision may even be seen as "being done for their good," or "He had it coming." The way negative and conditional supervisors jump on people, particularly in a home, is shocking. It is often done better at the office.

A pastor supervising positively said, "I had a list of five or six things that our custodian needed to improve on. I took one. We talked about it, I thanked him, and I encouraged him in one area. As soon as I saw the change, I wrote him a note telling him I noticed it and said thanks again."

"It was tempting to toss in two or three more," the pastor admitted, "but I stuck to my guns—one, just one. I'm sure two or three more would have overwhelmed him."

In summary, evaluation begins with our heart's condition. How others cultivate (influence) affects growth and whether sickly stalks turn barren and fruitless or whether healthy stalks yield thirty, sixty, or one hundred.

Evaluation must also focus primarily on *doing* and *being*—not results. If results are in our hands, we are supervising negatively or conditionally. Positive supervisors assume primarily *do* and *be* responsibilities and God, *the* gardener, makes it happen, somehow.

"Only servants, through whom you came to believe as the Lord has assigned to each his task. I planted the seed, Apollos watered it, but God made it grow" (1 Corinthians 3:5, 6, NIV). We must be sensitive, caring, and grown-up evaluators.

TEN
TAKING THE NEGATIVE OUT OF EVALUATION—DOING IT

Evaluation is 98 percent positive. Notice how positive supervisors do it:

FOLLOW-UP REVIEWS

Jesus remembered to follow up after giving an assignment. "The apostles returned and met with Jesus, and told him all they had done and taught" (Mark 6:30, TEV). We might call this occasion and the one mentioned in Luke 10:17-20 follow-up reviews. The purpose was to evaluate progress to date. Parents ask hard-working snow shovelers or lawn mowers, "How is it going?" and bring them a glass of water. Committee chairmen ask, "How is it going?" soon after the assignment.

Follow-up encourages. People innately want to tell someone how it is going or show them a good job. Kids, adults, young and old people—we're all alike in this regard.

How did Jesus do his follow-up review? Apparently he asked questions and they told him what they did. *Did* does not necessarily mean results, although that must have happened too.

FOLLOW-UP REVIEW QUESTIONS

1. What is going well?
2. What is not going well? or What needs improving?

3. What are the opportunities:
   a. Not doing enough of?
   b. Not doing at all, but should?
   c. Something tried before, perhaps briefly, then stopped?
   d. New ideas?
4. What you are finding:
   a. Most difficult?
   b. Least difficult?
   c. Most enjoyable?
   d. Least enjoyable?
5. Do you feel you are developing (growing, improving)?
6. Do you feel you are contributing to this (program, etc.)?
7. Are there some things you have thought about doing, and if given the opportunity, might like to try?
   a. What would this accomplish?
   b. What problems do you anticipate, if you were to do this?
8. Have you looked at objectives, goals, and priorities, from the standpoint of other staff, their effect on other people, their quality, etc.?
9. How can I (or others) help you?

FIGURE 10.1

In Figure 10.1 are some questions positive supervisors can consider using for a follow-up review (F.U.R.). Ask appropriate questions as each primary responsibility is discussed, varied, of course, to fit the situation at hand. You'll think of other questions too.

To illustrate a F.U.R., let us return to Sandra (chapter 9) and her department heads. They already listed reasons for individualized planning and evaluation. At a meeting of both teachers and department heads, they listed on a flip-chart what teachers should consider *doing* as they carry out their responsibilities. Here is what they wrote:

Prepare during the week; be prepared on Sunday; be at least fifteen minutes early on Sunday morning.

Teach; know lesson aim and purpose and how it can be applied to today's problems.

Visit pupils in their home.

Visit parents of younger age pupils.

Prepare outside activities with class.

Pray daily for each pupil.
Attend teachers' meetings.
Share ideas to improve Sunday school.
Cooperate with department heads.
Build a positive relationship with each pupil.
As needed, meet one-on-one with pupils to encourage and
problem-solve.

This list overwhelmed everyone. "Too much to do," said
Glenn. All agreed. They decided two things. First, each one
would review the list and then, with their department head,
decide one-on-one what they could and could not do. Second, as
a Sunday school team, they all should make visitation a
primary responsibility. Some objected, saying, "I dislike visiting
people." On the spot they came up with a list of alternatives to
individual visitation: team visit with another teacher; team visit
with department head; invite pupil to their home; invite class to
their home; meet at church before or after something; encourage
parents to visit with teacher; telephone occasionally, write a
personal note occasionally.

Sandra emphasized that no one should feel forced to visit or
guilty if he said he would and then, for whatever reasons,
couldn't. As Glenn left the meeting he said to Charlene, "I'm
excited. Now I know what's expected of me. And you know what,
I'm going to start doing this with my staff at work." Harry
added, "I'm going to do this at the office."

Next, Sandra met with her six department heads, two of
them individually, and then the others, two at a time.
"One-on-one is better," she said afterwards, "but schedule
conflicts necessitated meeting two at a time. It was interesting to
note that all of them wanted to get their plans and goals in
writing. We all admitted that we didn't really know our capabilities
and limabilities but as visitation is this year's group goal,
pinpointing capabilities and limabilities would be next year's
group goal. A team spirit is beginning to form."

Each department head met with his teachers. For example,
Jackie is the junior department head. She and Frances, a
teacher, met to make plans for the year.

After reviewing what Frances could be doing from the list
put together at the teacher's meeting, Frances felt her six primary

responsibilities should be lesson preparation, teaching, visitation, daily prayer for each pupil, building a positive relationship with each pupil, and attending each teachers' meeting. Together they set plans and goals for the year.

Her preparation goal, for example is to spend a minimum of three hours weekly. She is to know the lesson aim by Tuesday night and not substitute lesson preparation for personal devotions. Two months later they had their first follow-up review. Listen as an enabling coach helps Frances review and evaluate her progress to date in lesson preparation.

Jackie: "Let's look first at preparation. What's going well?"

Frances: "I guess a lot depends on what week you ask me. You know, Jennifer was home from school all last week with a fever and cold, so last week nothing much went well. But for the most part, I'd say I know my lesson aim by Tuesday night, and the very latest by Wednesday night. You know, most of the time at least."

Jackie: "That's really a big accomplishment. How do you do that?"

Frances: "I first read my lesson while having lunch on Monday. This gets me thinking and my wheels turning. That's about it, I guess."

Jackie: "I admire your discipline. (pause) Anything else going well in your preparation?"

Frances: "Yeah. I'm having a stronger personal devotional life now than ever before; so I'm not substituting my preparation for personal devotions."

At this point, Jackie listened several minutes as Frances told about her growing walk with Jesus. Frances admitted, "You're the only one I've ever told this to." Jackie learned a lot from Frances too.

Jackie: "What's not going as well as you'd like?"

Frances: "I must admit, I'm still not doing three quality hours of preparation. Some weeks I am, but for the most part it's closer to two hours. I want to do better. It frustrates me too."

Jackie: "How can I help you?"

Taking the negative out of evaluation by doing it

Frances: "I really don't know—just keep on me. Remind me once in a while. I feel so much better on Sunday when I've put in three hours. I just need to be more disciplined. That's it, I need to be more disciplined."

Jackie: "How can you do that?"

Frances: "The main thing is watch TV less. You know what, I'm just not going to watch TV two nights—Monday and Friday nights. And would you pray for me about this, that I'll follow through on this commitment?"

Jackie: "Yes, I'll be glad to."

During the year, Jackie used other questions from Figure 10.1. Jackie said, "My favorite question was 'Do you feel you're growing and developing?' That brought out so much—and I

learned a lot. The hardest part was keeping quiet and not
interrupting. I found out people do want to talk things out."

Bill Shackelford, head of the adult department, added, "Two of
my teachers set 10 percent growth goals. One made them, the
other didn't. Both felt growth goals were secondary. More
importantly, they felt encouraged and affirmed that someone
cared about them personally and what they were doing. Making
goals doesn't represent success nor does not making them
represent failure."

Style starts at the top. Sandra is a positive supervisor, functioning
like the rudder of a ship, giving direction. She does her helping
and developing people without fanfare. The fact that Sandra
is a homemaker without a college degree and two of her
department heads have advanced degrees makes no difference.
God's love in Sandra produces spontaneity and people are
influenced positively by the climate and atmosphere Sandra is
creating.

Sandra says, in a relaxed way, "Our aim is building people.
Planning helps, but we try not to get locked into them. Plans fit
into what people need and want."

Notice the positive things supervisors do to make evaluation an
affirming growth experience:

Decide primary responsibilities as a group and individually.
   Schedule follow-up reviews to evaluate progress.
   Concentrate on a few people.
   Foster a genuine positive climate.
   *Consider end results and goals, but primarily focus planning
and evaluation on what people do and are being to achieve
results and goals.*

Results cannot be measured because no person can say,
"This is why this happened." A person's heart-receptivity cannot
be measured, just as the effect of prayer cannot be measured.
"We" efforts are experienced—not measured or analyzed. Who
did what doesn't matter. What does matter is that each is doing
his or her part to glorify God—serving unconditionally.

Evaluators measure unconditionally when it starts with people, going clockwise around the Fulfillment Cycle.

Goals developed by supervisees with positive supervisors have built-in correctives. That is, the person himself knows if he has done right or wrong. Children who see a lot of Jesus in their parents don't need a lot of correcting.

In *Workmen of God* (Fort Washington, PA: Christian Literature Crusade 1965), Oswald Chambers writes: "Jesus had never said a word about his [Zacchaeus'] evil doings. What awakened him? What suddenly made him know where he was? The presence of Jesus."

Chambers adds: "If . . . the Spirit of God is getting his way with you, other people will get to know where they are wrong, and until they learn the reason they will say you are criticizing them; but you . . . never criticized them. What has happened? . . . the Holy Spirit's presence through you has brought the atmosphere that Jesus Christ's presence always brought (like with Zacchaeus), and has thawed the ice around their minds and their consciences and they are beginning to be convicted."

The other side is allowing God's Spirit to move at his will in another's life. The Holy Spirit teaches (John 14:26; John 16:12-14; Nehemiah 9:20). "As long as his Spirit remains in you, you do not need anyone to teach you" (1 John 2:27, TEV). This verse doesn't say that instruction and teaching are unnecessary. It is saying to me: Step aside, let the Divine Teacher be primary, not me.

ON-THE-SPOT REVIEWS

There is another kind of follow-up review besides those designed to evaluate progress in planning, such as Jackie did with Francis. It is on-the-spot review. Its purpose is to give immediate positive or negative feedback. Hopefully, positive feedback is encouraging and affirming; negative feedback helps someone stop doing something (such as lateness, interrupting people, and rudeness).

In the absence of positive supervision, on-the-spot reviews often ring shallow and hollow because the supervisor is usually looking for a positive response. It is a good way to keep people at arm's length. It goes something like this:

Supervisor: How did it go this morning? Great, I hope.
Supervisee: Yeah, I guess.
Supervisor: We're so pleased you are teaching. Keep up the great
work. Call me if you need anything.

Supervisors doing this don't need to concentrate. They can hit
twenty people in two minutes, usually at the worst time to the
supervisees such as when they are getting in a car, talking
one-on-one with someone, or being pulled at the skirt or
trousers by their little daughter. Even in the absence of positive
supervision, it can be improved some. For instance:

Supervisor: How do you feel it went this morning?
Supervisee: Fair.
Supervisor: Fair? What do you mean?
Supervisee: Maybe poor is a better word. I'm mad at myself. I
yelled at Craig when he was fooling around. I
vowed I wouldn't do it again but I did today.
Supervisor: What was Craig doing?
Supervisee: Pinching Paul and a few others. I yelled right out.
On top of everything we were late getting to
Sunday school today. I was tense about that.
Supervisor: I want you to know we appreciate you and what
you're doing. You're one of the faithful and loyal
around here. And believe me, you're not the first
one to get angry at Craig-type kids. I have, and
others have. Is there anything I could do to help you?
Supervisee: I really need prayer—about my attitude and my
anger. I'm stumped about how to handle Craig.
And last week I found out another person at work
is being promoted over me. That really hurt.
Supervisor: Could I telephone you Tuesday night around eight
so we can talk more?
Supervisee: Sure.
Supervisor: In the meantime, let's both begin praying about
things you've said.

This supervisor's heart was receptive. He was prepared to
catch the wind of the Spirit of God. One person was his agenda.
The supervisee needed to talk to someone. Positive stroking in

terms of "great job" would not have helped. Inside, she knew things weren't going well. And when a positive influencer asks questions, he had better mean what he says and be prepared to follow-up—like pray and telephone at eight Tuesday night as he promised. Positive influencers care about the whole person—his job, family, problems—not just whether the class grows by 25 percent.

Positive influencers first accept the person and what he is saying. This doesn't imply approval or disapproval of what he is doing. By listening, a positive influencer is communicating a silent, strong message: I care about you, a message that is significantly affirming and strengthening to the person talking. A positive supervisor doesn't have to correct Craig's teacher. She already knows what went wrong.

In *Servant Leadership* (New York: Paulist Press, 1977, p. 17) Robert Greenleaf said that a leader who serves must first listen. He wrote: "I have seen enough remarkable transformations in people who have been trained to listen to have some confidence in this approach. It is because true listening builds strength in other people." Any wonder people appreciate being listened to? It builds us up.

"Do not use harmful words, but only helpful words, the kind that build up and provide what is needed, so that what you say will do good to those who hear you" (Eph. 4:29, TEV).

To ask, "How did it go today?" to a teenager returning from school and then immediately say, "You shouldn't say that" is to use harmful words. "Great job" approaches are harmful. The only way to find out what is needed (Ephesians 4:29) is to ask good questions and then accept and listen. Then decide, ". . . so that what you say will do good to those who hear you." Our first tendency is to interrupt, evaluate, and correct in one fell swoop. Such hit-and-run approaches cause people problems.

Here are a few other tips—some of which have already been touched on—which apply to follow-up reviews in many situations:

1. *Be specific.* The tendency is to generalize about good things and become picky-picky about negatives. Be specific when telling someone about good things they are doing also. Cite a specific example of it.

2. Pick your location. Don't automatically blare out compliments in front of everyone. It is embarrassing to a lot of people. A one-on-one "thank you" is powerful. Never try correcting someone in public if at all possible. Jesus got alone with his Twelve. He picked his location to evaluate and clarify their understanding.

3. If comments are negative, be sensitive, yet direct. Be sure to listen to their side first. And never give negative feedback if you have not previously shown you cared—such as a parent doing things with a child, or supervisors planning and doing follow-up reviews with their regular companions. This in itself cuts out 90 percent of the need for negative feedback. As we've already said, they themselves usually know already that they aren't meeting the standards. For example, Frances knew her preparation wasn't adequate—just two hours weekly. She didn't have to be told. Remember the saying: constructive interest precedes constructive criticism.

And please—no gimmicks. An approach often recommended, which I feel is gimmicky, is what I call the sandwich approach. It's used by conditional supervisors relying on positive-motivational techniques. Here's how it works:

First tell them something positive, then slip in the negative, then end up with another positive. Again, save your breath. The only thing heard is the negative. People begin expecting sandwich approaches. It is a standard business practice.

Kathy was hired as a secretary to a positive supervisor. Right off the bat, she was doing well. Barry soon started pointing out specific things she was doing well. Immediately she would respond with a questioning, drawn out "yes-s-s-s?" After the positive, she was conditioned to hearing the negative next. She admitted, "That's what my previous boss did."

So if you do have to correct someone, tell them what you're doing at the outset. Be direct, yet sensitive.

FIELD REVIEWS

Field reviews happen when a supervisor, usually someone with a lot more experience, is watching and observing the supervisee. The wheels of analysis and evaluation really turn. The number of

Follow-up encourages.

things the supervisee is doing wrong would burn up a computer.

For example, listen to a father tell his son what is wrong as son swings a baseball bat, or, a mother tell her daughter how to improve her sewing or baking. Listen to a sales manager critique a salesperson. Listen to our senior pastor unload on the minister of visitation: "I did what he asked me. I told him what he did wrong." One weakness at a time? He had fourteen correctives. Timing? Impact of words? Where is he in his walk with Jesus? Not even considered. And when someone says, "Let me tell you how *I* do it," and they insist that is the standard, I shudder.

No two people do something alike. An experienced person's

standard is far too high for someone inexperienced. Such high standards discourage people. When I hear of veterans going out, demonstrating, giving someone a model, "Ugh!" I say to myself. I hope the model tells the observer about the experience factor. If not, the observer is likely to become very discouraged.

It is important to demonstrate, but one must be realistic in evaluating the other person. When the supervisor's standard is so high, the number of things the other person is doing wrong compounds. Expect people with three months' experience to perform like a three-monther, not a ten-year veteran.

Notice how the review questions (Fig. 10.1) work in actual field conditions, where the supervisor's role is to evaluate, observe, and help out.

Imagine, first of all, a parent observing his sixteen-year-old son or daughter drive on the highway the first time. Remember what your parents did when they corrected you and got you flustered? Push the clock ahead. What did you do when you observed your sixteen-year-old? I see—you slammed your foot on the floorboard, as if it were the brake. Think how much better your son or daughter would have done if you had said you were not going to say anything and simply enjoy the ride. Then afterwards, you and the new driver would talk about it. And remember, when the "boss" is around or along, it never goes the way it should!

For example, when our son got his driver's permit, we took a drive. Mentally I noted and evaluated. A couple of times I broke the observe rule—I complimented him a couple times.

As we rolled into the garage and I stopped praying (and sweating—my glasses steamed up too!) I said, "Doug, what do you believe you did well?"

Immediately he said, "I think I shifted well. And I paused in neutral. I think I slowed down at the corners OK and I stayed within the speed limit."

Then I added, "Doug, I agree. I think you did very, very well. You also stalled the car only once. That's unusual." Then I told him how I yanked and stalled our old DeSoto my first time out. You see, this approach enables a positive supervisor to affirm things the supervisee overlooks. "What needs improvement?" I asked next.

"I need to do a better job at shifting, to get up more speed when shifting from second to third."

As we shut the garage door, I told him how pleased I was. Before I knew it, he was off telling his friends about it.

So when someone asks, "Tell me, how am I doing?" consider first saying, "I will be glad to in a moment but first, tell me, what do you think you did well?" This turns evaluation from a negative, correct-only experience into a positive experience.

There are times when a "direct hit" is necessary. As a parent, I've had to scold. As a supervisor, I've had to really unload on people when I felt they weren't doing their part. I told them—conversationally. I planned out what I was going to say. They listened. But a lot of positive supervision took place before that. And I didn't enjoy it at all. Positive supervision makes that kind of criticism a rare occurrence.

"The Lord's servant must not quarrel. He must be kind toward all, a good and patient teacher, who is gentle as he corrects his opponents" (2 Timothy 2:24, 25, TEV). Gentleness and firmness can be compatible.

HOW DOES THE TRAFFIC LIGHT CONCEPT FIT IN?

Karl is the assistant pastor. One of his capabilities is fixing and repairing engines. His pastor said, "Why is he always under our Sunday school buses? He should be out calling on people." The pastor had no idea fixing and repairing was one of his capabilities. Through various means he tried getting Karl to stop working on the buses.

This capability was viewed as a serious weakness by the pastor and church board. Karl was being constantly criticized. He left dejected. No one was willing to consider his capabilities in the evaluation process. He became another unnecessary minister drop-out. He had many other useful capabilities if the church board could have unglued themselves from their airtight job description that had smothered Karl. That is negative and conditional supervision in action.

Rich Easterland's pastoral relations committee as they evaluated his year said: "We need practical sermons and we aren't getting them. He and his wife also spend too much time away from here, putting on her plays and children's programs. Seems as if Rich is always writing something for that."

Rich's capabilities included the teaching of principles and concepts—creative writing. A yellow limability was noting. Not a very good match-up for his job—maybe 20/20/60. Capabilities, limabilities, and Rich's fulfillment were never considered in his evaluation. People even came to his office trying to correct him. They called it helping!

I don't know how much churches pinpoint capabilities and limabilities during the calling/candidating process. But my feelings are that there is not enough. I know Rich's church didn't.

"We know our pastor's capabilities and limabilities," said one church moderator. "and what a big difference this makes. We're trying to prevent people making him be jack-of-all-trades and all things to all people.

"For example, we know one of his limabilities is delegation. His personal style category is one. Another limability is administration. Another is contacting people and organizing things. This isn't a negative—just something we accept and work with him on. He has capabilities we need. His attitude is excellent."

Positive supervisors work together as a team, building each other up.

Evaluation, especially year-end or salary reviews, should take the person's strengths and limitations into account. Remember, a person will tend to do capabilities well, and limabilities not so well. To expect a person to do everything well is an impossible task for anybody. Think about the 40/20/40 concept. There is no perfect job. But to expect a person to do limabilities-using things well is to supervise conditionally with an impossible-to-reach standard.

Positive supervisors and supervisees consider capabilities and limabilities at evaluation time. (See Figure 10.2, which is an extension of the match-up checklist of Figure 6.2). The supervisee and supervisor do the rating separately. Then together they discuss the supervisee's performance. Then evaluation can be loads of fun if positive supervision is taking place. I don't know how I would evaluate someone without one-on-one planning and follow-up reviews—poorly and with a lot of guesswork, perhaps.

EVALUATION

The following instructions explain how to use the system shown in Figure 10.2.

Aim:
1. To evaluate and rate supervisees, using a common system. As in school grades, excellent is 90 to 100; good is 80-89; fair is 70 to 79, etc.
2. To take into account a person's capabilities and limabilities.

Definitions:
1. Primary responsibilities. Main responsibilities that lead to achieving aims, purposes, and goals. (Note there are six on Figure 10.2).
2. Special projects or assignments. These include both unanticipated and "someone has to do it" responsibilities that come up during evaluation period.
3. Personal growth and development. Training and development to improve attitude and competency.
4. Attitude. Willingness, cooperativeness, helpfulness.
5. Rating. Responsibilities 1 and 2 have a 1.5 factor beside the rating column. Usually there are two responsibilities of top priority in terms of time and importance, so these are weighted by the factor of 1.5. Notice there are only nine items, and a perfect rating would add up to 100 percent. Therefore, you will be giving the first two items 1.5 times as much weight as the others which will give a total of 100 points or 100 percent for the total. If the 1.5 factor is not appropriate, you may discard it, but you will have to use another method to make a perfect score of all items to total 100 percent.

Traffic Light Concept for Rating Match-up

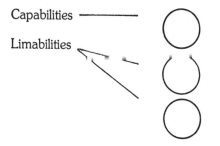

Capabilities ————

Limabilities

Green: 7 to 10 match-up
(tends to do fairly well).
Yellow: 4 to 6 match-up
(tends to do fairly well
in small amounts).
Red: 0 to 3 match-up
(tends not to do well;
takes much longer to
do it).

6. Match-up. Do not confuse match-up with rating. Match-up has to do with capabilities and limabilities. If match-up is 0 to 3 (red), the person is using a limability so has less possibility of doing something well and results usually reflect that. So if a person has tried, done his best with a positive attitude, this person should be rated higher than if his match-up was 4 to 6 (yellow) or 7 to 10 (green).

7. Overall rating. Total the scores in the rating column. For example, if the third item under the six primary responsibilities column was something you wanted to give a grade of 85 percent, you would move the decimal point over one place and record a grade of 8.5 in the rating column. A total of all these scores will give the overall rating score.

During (or before) the Evaluation: Evaluator should pinpoint capabilities (if not already done). Decide goals and plans for the six primary responsibilities and for responsibilities 8 and 9. Goals and plans for responsibility 7 may have to be set during the evaluation period itself. Figure 10.3 is an example of how the evaluation sheet might look for B. J. Supervisor.

Remember, if the match-up is poor but someone has tried and so made a best effort, it deserves a high rating. Most likely the results are less than if this were a person's capabilities. In other words, we don't want to penalize someone using his limabilities. So lowering our standard makes evaluation realistic (unconditional love in action). For example, when the church moderator said administration was one of the pastor's

EVALUATION

Name:

Capabilities:

Six Primary Responsibilities	Match-up?*	Rating**

Six Primary
Responsibilities   Match-up?*   Rating**

1. _____ |——————+——————| 1.5 ___
                      0   5   10
2. _____ |——————+——————| 1.5 ___
3. _____ |——————+——————| ___
4. _____ |——————+——————| ___
5. _____ |——————+——————| ___
6. _____ |——————+——————| ___

   Overall, the matchup is: |——————+——————|

7. _____   ___
   (Special Projects/Assignments)
8. _____   ___
   (Personal Growth/Development)
9. _____   ___
   (Attitude)
                        Overall rating: ___

                                              **Rating

*To what extent do re-   Excellent   90—100
sponsibilities match up   Good   80— 89
with capabilities? Check   Fair   70— 79
appropriate rating from 0   Below average 60— 69
to 10.

FIGURE 10.2

EVALUATION/EXAMPLE

Name: *B. J. Supervisor*

Capabilities:

Analyze.
Prepare; plan.
Catalyze; question.
Speak; teach; train.
Problem-solve.

Personal style category is (70%) one; also some (30%) category two (A yellow).
Personal style role is developer and problem solver.
Classification: People (40%) & Data (60%)

Six Primary
Responsibilities   Match-up?*   Rating**

1. *Supervise 6 consultants*   0   ✓5   10 $1.5 \times 9.5 = 14.3$
2. *Train 1st year consultants*   ✓ $1.5 \times 8.8 = 13.2$
3. *Consult with 12 companies* ✓   8.0
4. *Direct 4 schools*   ✓   9.5
5. *"Special" consulting*   ✓   9.0
6. *Write 6 articles*   ✓   7.0

   Overall, the matchup is: ✓

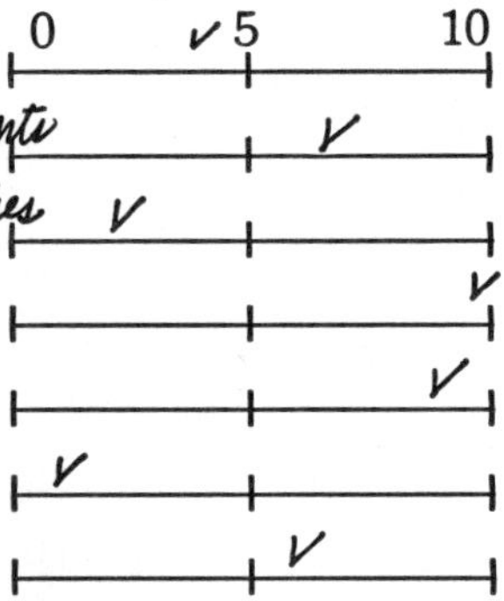

7. *Task group; write editorial*   7.5
   (Special Projects/Assignments)
8. *Self-development program with AL.*   9.5
   (Personal Growth/Development)
9. *attitude*   8.8
   (Attitude)
                                    Overall rating: 86.8

                                                        **Rating
*To what extent do re-   Excellent   90—100
sponsibilities match up   Good   80— 89
with capabilities? Check   Fair   70— 79
appropriate rating from 0   Below average   60— 69
to 10.

Copyright © 1980 Hagstrom Consulting, Inc.

FIGURE 10.3

EVALUATION

Name: *Joan Carpenter*

Capabilities:

Plan projects.
Organize committees and assign responsibilities; oversee.
Take interest in and build relationships

Excite; inspire.
Personal style category is mainly two;
Personal style role is sparkplug/organizer.
Classification is people and projects.

Six Primary Responsibilities	Match-up?*	Rating**
1. Plan and coordinate weekend programs.	0 ——— 5 ——— ✓ 10	$1.5 \times 8.6 = 12.9$
2. Teach Wednesday night Bible study.	✓ ———————	$1.5 \times 9.4 = 14.1$
3. Organize two major weekend retreats.	————————✓	9.5
4. Observe high school programs.	—————✓—	8.0
5. Promote youth programs; motivate youth to invite others.	—————✓—	8.4
6. Counsel with youth.	✓————————	8.8
Overall, the matchup is:	—————✓—	
7. Write monthly newsletter		9.0
8. _____ (Special Projects/Assignments)		8.5
9. _____ (Personal Growth/Development)		8.6
(Attitude)	Overall rating:	87.8

		**Rating
*To what extent do responsibilities match up with capabilities? Check appropriate rating from 0 to 10.	Excellent	90—100
	Good	80— 89
	Fair	70— 79
	Below average	60— 69

FIGURE 10.4

limabilities, he would lower his expectations of the pastor's work in this area. The pastor would too.

Notice how Joan Carpenter (chapter 6) rated herself after one year at her church (See Fig. 10.4). One of her changed responsibilities was No, 7, writing the church monthly newsletter.

The pastor also rated Joan. His rating was four points higher, which brings up an interesting rule of thumb. Good performers tend to underrate themselves; poor performers tend to overrate themselves.

The primary responsibilities are set between supervisor and supervisee at the beginning of the year. Expectations are therefore known and up-front. If responsibilities change, the basis of evaluation changes too.

When I was supervising consultants they would come into my office asking for an evaluation. It was fun. They would do it, then I would do it, and then we would sit down and compare ratings. The resulting discussion turned out to be more important than the rating itself.

Homemakers, husbands, students, deacons, teachers— anyone can use this evaluation. Unlike many business evaluation forms, which are usually several pages long, this is simple and straightforward. It is tailored to one person's responsibilities in terms of our original evaluation premise, which is what a person is *doing* and *being* to reach previously set goals.

"Our board is divided," a layman said. "We're trying to decide whether or not to give pastor a raise." There was no consensus of primary responsibilities, no knowledge of the pastor's capabilities and limabilities. They sat around arguing. No standards, no benchmarks, nothing—a negative experience for everyone.

Since a person has more limabilities than capabilities, people have many, many opportunities to correct one another if limabilities aren't known and considered in an evaluation. Any wonder so much correction is going on? Any wonder evaluation is viewed negatively by so many?

So I expect my wife not to sew as well as someone else. I expect myself to be mostly thumbs around an engine. People have more things they don't do well than they do well. That is just the way life is.

"Too high" standards discourage inexperienced people.

Positive supervision, receptive hearts, good questions, thinking before talking, and the traffic light concept take the negativism out of evaluation. Many seemingly big people-problems melt right before our eyes. As the saying goes, "No one ever went wrong expecting people to act like people."

I've poured my heart into these four chapters on supervision and evaluation. To write about positive supervision and evaluation is easy. To do it is another matter. Often I think I am violating concepts I've talked about. I almost think in the process, I've gotten windy—talked too much. Perhaps the readers who are praying over these things should squeeze over a little bit and let me kneel with them—I'm guilty too. I talk too much and correct too much.

Positive supervision affects positively a person's sense of worth and fulfillment—negative supervision has the opposite effect. Evaluation that is mainly negative with "stop-doing-that" approaches tears down people and, above all else, their walk with Jesus. Sometimes supervisors need to put their foot down—but not first. We need to build up one another—not push them into the ground with the wrong kind of criticism.

ELEVEN
POSITIVE RELATIONSHIPS ARE GENUINE

Their request was urgent. Seeing four full-time church staff sitting rigidly in huge stuffed chairs with their eyes fastened on me suggested something was wrong. Any wonder Fred asked, "Can you come this week?"

When I questioned them, each replied directly to me. The other three hardly expressed approval or disapproval—neither an affirming or disapproving nod. I felt the tension. They told me the problems:

"People's needs aren't being met. There is too much in-fighting between people. Our church is loaded with cliques."

"They're apathetic. No one will take on leadership roles."

"Not much happening spiritually with adults."

"Too many committee meetings. Not much is really accomplished at them."

"It's like pulling teeth to get people out for extra meetings, such as evangelistic meetings or a missionary emphasis weekend. It's push, push, push, all the time."

Two comments from the newest and least experienced person put things in perspective for me.

"I really believe they don't trust our leadership."

"People are asking about us as a church staff as to who is really in charge."

I said, "Take a piece of paper and rank the relationships that exist among you four—relationships in terms of respect, trust, and credibility. Rank the relationships from 1-poor, 5-average, to

10-excellent. Write a number between one and ten.''

The results: 2, 2, 5, and 5.5 (pastor's). No wonder church people don't trust leadership. Climate starts at the top and flows out (not down) directly and quickly, sending invisible negative or positive messages to people with either hard hearts or receptive hearts. Hard hearts love negative messages; receptive hearts are saddened by them.

No positive supervision was happening. The four staff members did not know each other's green, yellow, and red areas. In terms of our illustration of the tripod (Leg one: matching capabilities with responsibilities; Leg two: positive, caring supervision; and Leg three: positive relationships) there was no tripod at all!

Later I talked with the staff of a Christian organization. ''Without his leadership,'' Sharon laments, ''we would not have grown so fast. But then the money crunch hit and now we don't trust him anymore. He exaggerates so much and stretches the truth. He tells people (potential contributors) just so much and glosses over important facts—such as how the money is really going to be used. Our staff can hardly cope. It doesn't phase him a bit. He's lost all credibility with the staff.''

Cathleen said this about her supervisor: ''None of us trusts her anymore. She listens for a while but she always has some hidden agenda—something up her sleeve that she hasn't told us. So it always comes out the way she wants. Now we're suspicious.''

Carl is a home building contractor. ''I want no written contracts with anyone,'' he says. ''If I don't trust them and they me, it won't work.'' Carl has more business than he can do. Word has spread that Carl does what he says he will do.

''I just gave Mr. Dunn a large bill,'' Carl said. ''I had every expense itemized. Mr. Dunn said, 'Don't give me those itemized papers, just the total bill. I don't have to worry about you. I trust you.' ''

When relationships are negative, people nitpick at each other, or practice staying away. Evaluation goes haywire. People say (to themselves, of course), ''Someone like that couldn't have a good idea—and when he shoots off an idea, I'm ready to shoot it down with both barrels.''

When relationships are positive, people tend to overlook

Positive relationships are genuine. A balance of respect, trust, and credibility.

another's faults quicker, trust more (like Mr. Dunn with Carl, the building contractor), and be more relaxed and sincere when with them.

In a church, committee, family, or one-on-one sitting, relationships show, one way or the other. Our actions and words reveal how we really feel about someone. We cannot cover up forever.

WHAT IS A RELATIONSHIP?

A relationship isn't described easily but its presence or absence is highly noticeable. It doesn't take long to feel tension between four staff people or a married couple ignoring each other while sitting together. People in a home where relationships are positive experience warmth and genuineness. Objects are in second place, guests and family members in first place, food is a means, and people the end.

"I really don't know how to define a positive relationship," a pastor said. "Right now I'm too busy experiencing it."

Though a relationship isn't easily described, it is an emotional *connection,* enabling mutual affirmation and the building up of each other. Positive emotions and actions (being and doing) connect people. Negative emotions and actions (being and doing) disconnect. Positive relationships blossom when fertilized by respect, trust, and credibility.

RESPECT AND TRUST

Respect means to show regard and consideration for another. Trust means to rely on or have confidence in someone. When God's love trickles into someone's heart and flows outward, it enables him to trust people right at the start. Track records are tossed aside.

For example, people should not have to earn one another's trust. That is conditional loving. Instead, one initiates the trust action by being trusting—risking, going out on the limb for another.

Love hears inexperienced people. Love trusts the uneducated. Respect and trust are active. Not to respect and trust disconnects, causing negative relationships to get mired down in the muck of suspicion and hidden agendas. Questions prevail, and action is minimal.

Love that is always calculating discourages people. It disconnects. Relationships suffer. People problems result.

In the comic strip, Tiger says, "That's pretty sneaky," as he sees his opponent Puddinhead beating him playing cards.

"What's pretty sneaky?" Puddinhead yells.

Tiger yells back, "You haven't cheated once all this afternoon." Suspicion arouses suspicion.

A committee of eight was deciding the agenda for a larger meeting of eighty-five people. Just before the eight adjourned, Ralph remarked, "Let's remember, we need to be watching for their hidden agendas. You know, each person there will have something up his sleeve ready to push and promote."

Upset, Ron said, "That's trust? We need to go in there accepting them as needy people. Trust begins with us. Yes, there is risk, and we may look bad. But I'm not going in there trying to outmaneuver them. I'm going to listen and believe."

To believe people first is to demonstrate trust and respect. It may be very risky and become a source of embarrassment. While Jesus wants us to be secure in him, he also wants us to move away to where we're exposed and it is treacherous.

"Love one another warmly as Christian brothers, and be eager to show respect for one another" (Romans 12:10, TEV). "It [love] always protects, always trusts, always hopes, always perseveres" (1 Corinthians 13:7, NIV).

Respect and trust, balanced by wisdom and discernment, choose to step out rather than step back and be suspicious. "Love knows no limit to its endurance, no end to its trust" (1 Corinthians 13:7, Phil.). With God's help, we can trust a lot more than we first thought possible.

When a new consultant recruit was hired, the first day I told him I was going to trust him, that we would not play hidden agenda games or politics. "I'm taking you at your word," I said, "and you'll have every opportunity to get me out on a limb and then break it off."

To my knowledge, that trust was never violated. Mishandled, yes, because we're human. Mutual development thrives when people trust each other.

The same thing is true with my secretary. We have no secrets. This person is to be trusted with confidences and confidential information. To withhold disconnects. It communicates, "I don't trust you."

Even when they were young, I tried telling our children as much as possible; and just about everything in their teen years. I respect them and trust them. I must initiate being respecting and trusting.

I respect my printer. I don't haggle over prices. He's believable, even though he sometimes misses deadlines. The same is true with the person from whom I buy office equipment and supplies. I respect and trust him. He quotes a price and that is it. I don't shop around for the best deal. In my opinion, the best deals are people whom I can trust. It begins with me.

CREDIBILITY

Credible people are believable. They inspire confidence. Their motives and word meanings don't have to be questioned. Credible people mean what they say and say what they mean. Sandwich approaches and "tell them just enough to make them feel part of the team" techniques are replaced by unconditional approaches. Rapport occurs as an unexplainable chemistry fills the relationship. An already positive climate becomes even more positive. People don't have to lace every other sentence with "Why?" Trust builds respect which builds credibility.

What else builds credibility? One thing is follow-up, and that is why I like doing it so much. It is something that can be done. There is a saying: "Surprise people—do what you say you're going to do." If you can't do something, go to the person and tell him. But never let it hang.

I was swamped with work. I saw I was going to miss promised deadlines. I let those involved know it. Letting them know actually strengthened my relationship with them. "It's nice to know other people are human too," one said.

Over the years I have developed a genuine relationship with six people. When facing a decision, I go to them for counsel and advice. If I ask them to review something, it is done within ten days. These six are respected, trusted, credible people. By following up, they have become credible in my eyes.

After doing something, I ask, "How can I follow up?" I try to do a little more than someone expects. I plan and schedule follow-up time. When making out my weekly priorities, I ask, "With whom should I follow up this week?"

Positive supervisors follow up after delegating something. Committee chairmen follow up between meetings. Committee members choose to follow up. Positive, genuine relationships happen quietly. It happens when people assume responsibility for people—it begins with me. "You will earn the trust and respect of others if you work for good" (Proverbs 14:22, TEV). Working for good includes follow-up.

Florence says this about a chairman: "He really takes hold. He does what he says, and more—and without a lot of fanfare." I know of nothing that establishes credibility faster than following up. Don't assume; instead, follow up.

Follow-up is one of my limabilities. I've really got to work at completing it. For the more administrative types, it is more apt to be a capability—the traffic light signals green—so it comes more naturally. In my estimation, follow-up is a limability for 90 percent of us. Whether a green or red, let us do it rather than sit around wishing we had. Uncompleted tasks and unfulfilled promises kill relationships. Those who don't follow through start avoiding or staying away from people to whom promises were made.

GENUINE RELATIONSHIPS REDUCE FRICTION

Respect, trust, and credibility are needed for a genuine relationship. Genuine relationships are the oil that lubricates working parts—you and me. It reduces friction.

Realistically, relationships have their ups and downs. Where there are people, there will be friction. People rubbing shoulders often rub each other the wrong way. Realistically, relationships are positive and negative, up and down, high and low. Relationships change because people change. Relationships are fragile and imperfect because people are imperfect.

In *No Little People* (Downers Grove, IL: Inter-Varsity, 1974), Francis Schaeffer says, "If we demand, in any of our relationships, either perfection or nothing, we will get nothing."

A corporate executive said, "In twenty-five years of marriage, my wife and I have never had an argument." Three of the group jumped all over him for saying that. A tensionless relationship is a lie; it is phony. People living and functioning together disagree. Arguments and disagreements are neither good nor bad unless they continue unsettled.

When respect, trust, and credibility are present, patching up differences is a normal happening. Husbands who yell at wives because traffic lights turn red on the way home sour supper table conversation, but they soon patch up their differences. Wives popping off at husbands who talk too much at business meetings cause brush fires, but love soon stamps out the flame before it turns into a forest fire.

In any situation—spouse to spouse, parent to child, child to parent, president to vice presidents—if we remove respect, trust, and credibility, people will soon begin to look elsewhere (including the opposite sex) to find people who do trust, respect, and believe them. A vice president says, "I've been reduced to a functionary by my boss." His boss seldom keeps his word. The vice president is now considering two other job opportunities.

Genuine relationships soothe. Hearts abiding in Christ are sensitive. To expect ups and downs is realistic. Differences and disagreements are not disasters. They are the tough grounds that test us. The overall trend in relationships should be positive and upward. (See Figure 11.1.) Love is a choice that includes the fostering of genuine relationships. Like many other things, it is no task for the fainthearted or off and on Christians.

As there are three kinds of supervision, there are three kinds of relationships: positive—genuine; conditional—superficial; and negative—hatred, animosity.

Conditional relationships are marked by arm's-length approaches. Married couples who stick it out for the sake of the children have homes lacking warmth and caring.

Marriages sticking together for organization or political reasons are sticky and cold. Supervisors who rationalize: "I had better keep the relationship positive with my supervisees," are building conditional relationships. Deciding to tolerate someone until he leaves is superficial. The connectors are weak. Conversation is guarded. Little genuine mutual affirmation and building take place.

When I told someone I planned to have my office in our home, he said, "The place for the husband is outside the home. It will create too much tension in your marriage."

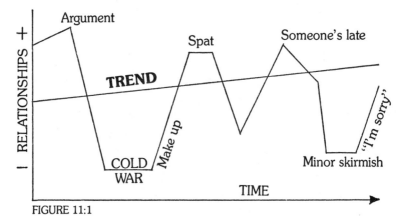

FIGURE 11:1

Just the opposite has happened. Sure, we have our differences, but I feel our marriage has been strengthened. In retrospect, our relationship would have been conditional or even negative if we couldn't do this. There is no specific place a spouse should be when relationships are genuine.

Negative relationships don't need description or amplification. When the oil of genuine relationships stops lubricating, people's effectiveness grinds to a halt. Relationships become negative. People, like gears, freeze. Action is perfunctory, mechanical, and conditional. As we are inclined to attach good evaluations about someone when relationships are positive, so people are inclined to attach bad evaluations to people when relationships are negative. For example, if the pastor visited you during the week, you are more apt to say "OK" when his next Sunday's sermon is ten minutes too long. Or, if you and the chairman spent one-on-one time recently, you are more apt to put up with a poor committee meeting he chaired. Genuine relationships allow people to make mistakes and continue to build up one another. Negative relationships pick other people apart and tear down.

One major contributor to negative relationships is our desire to control others, and one major contributor to positive relationships is caring for others.

CONTROLLING BREAKS DOWN AND DISCONNECTS

Someone has said:

To dwell above with saints we love,
That will be grace and glory.
But to live below, with saints we know,
Now that's another story.

"That's another story" is often letting our tongue say things we later regret, irritants such as loud radios, slamming of doors, or hurt egos which push people to spout off. We become conditional supervisors at the drop of a hat, we jump in feet first, rather than head first, suffering from hoof-in-mouth disease. So often it is not what is said but how it is said. Our attitude shows through loud and clear. Raised voices and negative, non-loving emotions are the little things that break up relationships. While visiting another city, I heard a parent say, "Why does that dumb kid (eighteen years old) leave his motorcycle in the driveway all the time?"

Other typical disconnecting remarks include:

"Can't you just be a little more careful with those new records?"

"When will you ever learn to put the towel back right?"

"I'd tell you, but you never listen!"

"Isn't supper ready yet?"

"Go to the store now and get milk."

"I hate my job," a tired husband relates. "I hate it, I hate it. I just can't wait for weekends."

"Oh, don't feel that way" his wife blurts out. "You know you shouldn't. You need to change your attitude. It's bad. You're the problem." Shut the windows again!

Our tongue influences others. People innately want to control others. Relationships crack and crumble under the impact of controlling people—in the driveway, home, church, playground, and office.

"In eight or ten years, I'd like to teach at a college in a rural setting," Bradley said to his company's president.

"That's the dumbest thing I've ever heard," the president replied. "In my opinion, someone with your brains and talent ought to. . . ." He suggested more lucrative opportunities.

Like a flash, Bradley was in my office and unloaded. He felt cut off at the pass by someone with good intentions trying to control and be boss over him.

In *No Little People,* Francis Schaeffer concludes, "People in the world naturally want to boss others . . . a person does not automatically abandon this mentality when he becomes a Christian. In every one of us there remains a seed of wanting to be boss, of wanting to be in control. . . ."

I, Dick Hagstrom, want to set the record straight here and now: I don't have a control problem. I simply want things done my way! Period.

"It is better to be patient than powerful. It is better to win control over yourself than over whole cities" (Proverbs 16:32, TEV). I call this tongue control. And isn't it interesting that the last fruit of the Spirit is self-control (Galatians 5:23).

FOCUS ON ME, NOT THEM

Here our "quick to change and help others" mentality gets in the way. It sounds selfish and unchristian, focusing on me. But if we first try controlling others, relationships break down. So instead we must turn to ourselves. The key principle is to focus on controlling our reaction, rather than other people.

In *The Art of Understanding Yourself* (Grand Rapids: Zondervan 1968), Cecil Osborne writes, ". . . you are not responsible for what people do to you. You are responsible only for the way you *react* to them." My reaction? Me?

In *The Calvary Road* (Ft. Washington, PA: Christian Literature Crusade 1964), Roy Hession observes, "Perhaps someone annoyed me, and I was irritated. God wants me to see that it was not the thing that the person did that matters, but my reaction to it." My reaction? Me?

Out of one side of our mouths we ask supervisees (offspring and associates), to grow up and stand on their own two feet. They do and then out of the other side of our mouth we say, "Sit down and be quiet." When we can't control others, we react—blurt out something that we later regret.

What makes us do that? Often, it is negative emotions. The splinter or log in my eye is my jealousy, resentment, hostility that ignites and flames up. So I judge and blame others unfairly. Negative emotions coupled with controlling tendencies muck up relationships.

My first responsibility then, is to get hold of myself and come under Jesus' control. I must abide during the day and whisper prayers for help and thanks to God, as I reach for the telephone, or when deciding to write a letter. I must be people-responsible. I must control me. To love others I must love God with a receptive heart. The independent "I can do it, it won't happen without me" attitude kills relationships.

HOW TO STOP CONTROLLING OTHERS

This next principle sounds backwards and it is, according to negative and conditional supervisors standards. The success mentality says, control others and you will influence more, using goals, authority, power-bases, and fabricated enthusiasm. Positive supervisors reject this. Their approach is entirely different on this point. They say, "Only by controlling ourselves are we able to influence," so they influence quietly and without fanfare. The radical principle of positive supervisors is: *control self: influence more.* Said another way; *control others; influence less.* (See Figure 11:2.) It is the opposite principle from negative and conditional supervisors, who feel that by controlling others they will influence more.

Positive supervisors believe in people. They know that other people, like themselves, prefer making their own choices, rather than having decisions made for them by others.

"When Howard (her husband) tries to force me to do something, I do just the opposite," Edna says, an example of someone who wants to make her own choices.

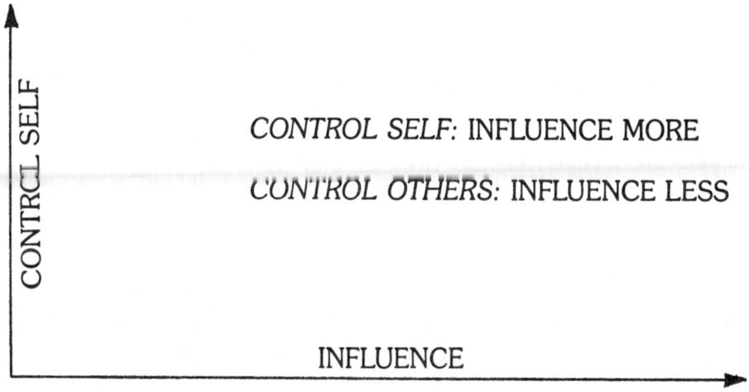

CONTROL SELF: INFLUENCE MORE

CONTROL OTHERS: INFLUENCE LESS

(Vertical axis label: CONTROL SELF)

INFLUENCE

FIGURE 11.2

For years Ann tried getting her husband to stop smoking, all to no avail. During a bout with the flu, he didn't smoke. Then on his own he decided to stop. "I just had to keep quiet and get off his case," Ann says. "I realized my barbs wouldn't help. But inside I wanted so much to get the credit." Ann controlled her reaction. Her appropriate response was silence and encouragement here and there.

In our house, I prefer keeping windows closed. You guessed it, my wife prefers the opposite. The more I push for closed windows, the more she seems to want them open. When I try "controlling her" I influence less.

When I try controlling her less by practicing tongue-control—controlling me rather than her—she is more apt to keep the windows closed or open part way. Also, she will ask occasionally, "Should I open or close the windows?" And you know what? I'll often say, "Open them."

There is within each of us a desire to not want to be pushed but instead to be free to choose. When I think before talking, my wife and I talk conversationally and then decide. When I react, rather than be quiet (mind my own business!) or ask questions, I start an argument.

Psychologists agree that we choose our reaction. I choose how I react. I cannot control other people's reactions or behaviors. Sounds selfish, doesn't it?

If I feel pushed to go to a meeting, I tend to react. When other people control their reactions and I'm free to choose, I am more apt to want to go to the meeting and with the right attitude.

We bought a heater for our home that we later found out is illegal to use in our state. I telephoned the salesperson, who had treated us fairly at the time of the sale.

"I'm not unhappy with you," I said. "It works fine and we don't want to give it up. By the way, would you buy it back? I don't expect you to reimburse us fully and if you couldn't do this, this is not the first $250 I've spent unwisely."

"No problem," he said, "I'll refund the full $250. I don't want any dissatisfied customers." We still have the heater, hoping it will soon be legalized in our state.

Garrett owns a VW repair shop. When I take our VW in for repairs, I see Garrett, a person, rather than Garrett, a mechanic. When he fixes something, and it is still malfunctioning, I choose my reaction. I can get mad at Garrett and start demanding better work. If I did, I'd be controlling him, and so influencing less. My role? Care about Garrett, the person. As an enabling coach, I can help Garrett by not pushing for a perfect job every time.

For one thing, I don't blame Garrett when something is still wrong. Rather than say, "You didn't fix it right," I'll say, "The engine is still sputtering. I know it isn't your fault. When can I bring it in?"

I also don't complain about his high prices or missed deadlines. I respect him. In my view, his is a tough business. I trust him. He's credible. I am too, as I do what he asks me to do. For example, if he wants the car there at 10:30, it is there at 10:30.

And it only takes a few moments to ask, "How are you?" And then listen.

It's almost embarrassing going there now. He drops everything and says, "What can I do for you?" Once I felt he undercharged me and I told him that. He wouldn't take any more money, either.

What takes the cake is the time I called about something and he asked, "When do you need the car?"

I said, "No hurry."

His reply was, "In that case, I'll do it right away." And he did.

In all walks of life, people are starving for genuine relationships. They're craving enabling coaches—who influence others positively by controlling their own reactions rather than others. People want to choose. Let us give them enough breathing room to do that.

CONTROLLING IS DIFFICULT

Don't underestimate the difficulty of controlling your response. Ever try going twenty-four hours without interrupting someone? Or see if you see yourself in these next situations:

Dr. Myway is the church moderator. He and his wife Marg share this job. He said, "Over the past four months, Marg and I felt strongly about two key church decisions. Twice we got voted down. And was that difficult!"

"Not insisting on our way has been a big point of learning," Marg says. "To say 'I'm sensitive to others' opinions, feelings, and attitudes' is one thing. To do it is quite another."

Don, a high school junior, dropped his report card on the kitchen table and went on to his bedroom, shutting the door.

His parents saw the results: D in English, and F in math. The immediate controlling reaction of a conditional supervisor is: "He needs to study more" or "He fools around too much" or "Let's take away his privileges—the car, for example."

His father wanted to "take action immediately" and "straighten out this dumb kid."

His mother prayed. "I'm sure Don already feels guilty," she said. "We don't have to tell him that. Let's do nothing that will jeopardize our relationship. He is a good kid. And besides, are grades really that important?"

"Of course they are" he boomed. "He'll never get into college."

Later that evening, Don's father regained his composure and perspective. "Don, I want you to know we love you and care about you," he said, "regardless of your grades. I failed a course in college. It hurts but there's more to life than grades. How can Mom and I help you?" Notice he didn't ask, "How can we get you to raise those lousy marks?"

No solutions or conditional rules were imposed. No hurting, impacting words knifed through an already guilty conscience. Instead, parents functioned as enabling coaches in a positive climate, seeing their son as a regular companion. The relationship oozes with respect, trust, and credibility.

Don's father adds, "We have few rules in our home. For example, we've asked our teenagers to be home by 10:30. If they can't, they are to let us know. You know what? Since we don't make a big deal of 10:30, they're usually home much earlier." The less we control others, the more we influence!.

"One night Don really blew it," Dad goes on, "Without telling us, he got home at 12:30 A.M. My wife and I were basket cases. The next morning I told Don that he was grounded for the next two weekends. He expected it. If I hadn't, it would have been irresponsible on my part."

People problems are solvable, but remember, style starts with parents and their influence flows outward positively or negatively.

Pauline's husband has a standing feud with his boss. "He has a good job," she says, "but this poor relationship colors everything." Pauline and two friends prayed for one year.

Then, on his own, her husband decided to talk to his boss and for once tried carrying on a conversation without blowing up. Nine months before, Pauline suggested he do this, but that suggestion sparked a long argument. At the time her husband and boss were talking, Pauline and her two friends were praying.

"Today is the first time I had a decent chat with my boss," her husband said. "The hardest thing for me to do," Pauline confessed, "was not to say, 'I told you so' or 'You should have done this six months ago.' Silently I said, 'Thank you, Lord' as he told me." Controlling self is difficult.

Roger didn't want to go to their youth group's retreat. On his return, his father asks, "How did you like it?"

"I loved it and I can't wait for next year," Roger says excitedly.

"Here you didn't want to go," his father says. "I told you you would like it."

All of a sudden, father is center-stage, grabbing the credit. Who cares about whose idea it was or who told who what? Besides, many people influence—not just parents. People seem to love jamming words at people.

How much better if he had said, "Tell me about it" rather than to take credit. "Let us have real warm affection for one another as between brothers, and a willingness to let the other man have the credit" (Romans 12:10, Phil.).

Lloyd consulted Fred about buying a Brand X car. "I wouldn't buy it," Fred advised, "I've heard of people at work having lots of problems with them."

Since the price was right and he needed a car, Lloyd bought Brand X. It turned out a lemon, as Fred had predicted.

When Lloyd meets Fred, what is the natural thing to say? That's right, "I told you so." That makes Lloyd feel like a dummy. "I told you so" remarks are designed to humiliate others and make the speaker look good and smarter than the other person. Controlling that natural tendency is difficult, particularly for those who love to spew out their expertise on anyone at any time! "A fool does not care whether he understands a thing or not; all he wants to do is show how smart he is" (Proverbs 18:2, TEV).

"I told you so" remarks break down relationships. Positive supervisors strive to build up people rather than to show others how smart they are. Tongue-control is self-control.

A woman expressed her concern about her role as minister's wife and mother: "Ben isn't having daily devotions. Before we were married, we would even pray together."

"With all the pressures on Ben," she lamented, "I don't feel I can talk to him about this."

"There's one thing you can do," I replied, "Pray that Ben will want to pray, to find the time."

Then I projected ahead. "If after praying Ben comes to you and says, 'You know what, I've started having personal devotions again, and what a difference it's making,' what will you tend to say at this point?" I asked.

" 'Ben, I've been praying for you' " she replied quickly. " 'I'm glad you're doing it.' " I suggested this response gives credit to her. All of a sudden it is her idea. What precipitated his positive action on personal devotions is unimportant. What is important is that Ben is doing it.

We discussed a better response. "Ben, how did you decide on doing this?" or "Is there any way I can help you?" She replied, "Being a quiet positive influencer is different, isn't it?"

Shelby is a positive supervisor who plans and does follow-up reviews one-on-one with each of the seven people reporting to him. "In my day-to-day contact with my seven," Shelby says, "I sow seed thoughts here, drop an idea there—then sometime later, they'll come into my office saying, 'I just had an idea about so and so.'

"Most likely, their ideas sprang up because I gave them the initial idea. It would be easy for me to steal the show. I must continually close my mouth and remind myself that supervision is developing people, rather than crediting my idea-account." Most likely Shelby talks only to his wife about these things. Shelby's appropriate response is one that facilitates their idea, rather than bringing it all back to him for credit.

Shelby is experiencing genuine relationships. He would like telling his seven staff people that he precipitated the idea. He cannot, since he recognizes this would be his own conceit reaching out to be patted and stroked. He knows too he is maybe only one of fifty other people influencing one person.

HOW TO BE MORE SELF-CONTROLLED

Controlling *me,* rather than them, is one way of maintaining respect, trust, and credibility. Below are three suggestions that may help us to be more self-controlled.

1. Trust God first. Lorna's marriage crumbled. She and her husband are together again, although in Lorna's words, "It's still pretty rocky." I asked her what she is learning through this.

"I wasn't aware how much I depended on my husband, Dennis. When I saw him fail, I almost went under. I am learning the hard way it's all Jesus, and it's a matter of choosing, as an act of my will, to depend on Jesus. It all starts with me. Today trusting God is not a second thought."

2. Recognize your green (traffic light) tendencies. The inner pull to do what we do well, in almost any situation, may see us controlling others. Unrecognized and unbridled, it causes problems.

Gifford's green (capabilities) areas include initiating and speaking. The committee leader was not leading, so the meeting floundered. Gifford stepped in and took over. "Since he wasn't running the meeting," Gifford said, "I filled the vacuum." The meeting objectives were missed badly. Committee members got discouraged. Without realizing it, Gifford was controlling others rather than himself.

Another example is Wesley, whose green areas include resolving conflict. He enjoys crisis problem-solving. So when there was no conflict in his organization, he would wander around looking for conflict. When he caught a whiff, he would automatically move in to create a stir.

"I hardly knew I was doing it," Wesley said. "Since I don't get enough crisis problem-solving on this job, I've had to do this outside my job. It's really true," he added. "We often sin at our point of strength."

Unbridled, in any situation, people will try doing the thing they do well—teachers teach, counselors counsel, sales people sell, and promoters promote. Go to a board meeting when a promoter is promoting if you want to see such a person dominate and control.

As I already mentioned, how often I've unknowingly and unthinkingly raised questions, stirred up people in situations where I should have shut up. Knowing and recognizing our green areas helps us control ourselves. It also helps if we ask ourselves:

What is my role here?

What is my natural tendency? What should I avoid saying or doing?

How can I contribute to our purpose rather than try to appear as the star of the show?"

What can *I* do to follow up what is happening here?

3. Avoid letting negative emotions take over. Negative emotions coupled with controlling tendencies break up relationships.

Jealousy is cancerous. Win or lose standards set up barriers. Competition makes controllers of people—only a few win or come out on top. Jealousy sets in. The losers are told, "Do better next year." Such guilt-creating statements tear up genuine relationships. Field people, for example, try proving head office people wrong. Pastors try making their church successful, to qualify for teaching at seminary or pastoring a larger church.

"Was I shocked when I got on campus," Dr. Surprise relates. "The competition among professors for students was fierce."

"At our convention," a pastor confides, "I really can't tell others how I'm feeling. You see, our denomination has established goals and the pressure and competition among pastors to meet them is intense. It's creating rivalries and factions."

"Anger is cruel and destructive, but it is nothing compared to jealousy" (Proverbs 27:4, TEV). "A wise man controls his temper. He knows that anger causes mistakes" (Proverbs 14:29, TLB). Reactions sparked by jealousy break up relationships.

Parents may resent their own children when friends' and neighbors' children grab the limelight. A father may resent his son's being a substitute rather than a starter. A spouse may become resentful when someone else gets the promotion.

"Love . . . is not jealous . . ." (1 Corinthians 13:4, TEV). Anything that creates competition, rivalries, and jealousy is wrong. Bitterness is also deadly. An eight-year veteran said, "I've come to the conclusion that I've been too critical and negative. I must stop being so bitter. Worst of all, it has affected my spiritual life. Will you pray for me?"

"Guard against turning back from the grace of God. Let no one become like a bitter plant that grows up and causes many troubles with its poison" (Hebrews 12:15, TEV).

It is not wrong to ventilate feelings and blow off steam occasionally. We all have days we get up on the wrong side of the bed. Negative emotions come and go. But by putting God first, we don't allow negative emotions to control us.

Trying to control others breaks down and disconnects. Our approach so far has been mainly what not to do, such as don't control, don't act impulsively, and don't overreact. Consider now a more positive approach. Notice how encouragement builds up people and fosters positive relationships.

CARING BUILDS UP AND CONNECTS

God's word is our primary encouragement (Romans 15:4). And people who care also encourage. People who don't care discourage. Encouragers build genuine relationships, something which happens over a period of time. The motto of an encourager is: "Love is caring about another person as though it were happening to me." Loving encouragers concentrate on one or two people, busily doing little things that build up people. Encouragers raise people's sights, helping them shake loose from everyday tasks, or help someone get above their problems, bringing hope to the discouraged. The effects of encouragement are impossible to evaluate; its powerful positive influence goes beyond even our imagination.

A pastor became increasingly concerned about congregational rumblings that were caused by some emotionally disabled people coming to his church. The deacons and pastor couldn't explain why they were coming or what to do about the problem.

"I committed myself to pray each morning for twenty minutes," the pastor says, "to literally talk to God and to listen. One day, on my knees in my office, came the solution to the problem: 'Stop loving them.' I wept. I was ashamed. These people were not problems. We were living the Lord's teaching about loving and caring. They were there to be loved—if we stopped loving them they would go away, but that wasn't a solution that we could accept."

Lynn is fifty-seven. Her mother, who is eighty-one, still has her own apartment and Lynn does her shopping. Lynn says: "Every time I go to see my mother she corrects me. My husband thinks she's a pain in the neck. I hated seeing her. But then I realized she is my mother and I have a responsibility to take care of her. Taking a good hard look at myself was the hardest thing I ever did. I thought I could be Christian without God's help. How stupid of me to think that. Today, I pray daily for Mother. My reaction was terrible, but with God's help that is changing. Rather than looking at her as a critical person, I need to be Christlike with her. My reaction should be one of love and compassion."

Encouragers try overlooking other people's shortcomings.
Despite knowing many of his disciples' weaknesses, Jesus
picked out three good things about his disciples as he prayed for
them: (1) they *obeyed* your word, (2) they *received* it (the
message from God), and (3) they *believed* that you sent me
(John 17:6-8, TEV).

Encouragers can pick out at least one good thing about anyone.
Encouragers don't dwell on a person's shortcomings. We hope
others don't dwell on ours either.

"I really don't like Ted," Mary confesses. "He rubs me the wrong
way. But you know what? We have a positive relationship." I
asked how that could be. "When he asks me, 'How are you?' he
means it," she answered.

James works with underprivileged teenagers. "People always
ask me about the work and how it's going," he confides to his
Sunday school teacher. "You're the only one who asks, 'How are
you?' It's encouraging to me to know you care."

Encouragers concentrate on one person. I guess they would
make lousy politicians! After church, I like talking to one
person, rather than shaking hands with fifteen people. Ten
minutes with one person encourages me.

Coffee is served between Sunday morning church services.
Charlie has been responsible for the coffee and rolls for years.
His pastor takes him aside and asks: "Do you see what's
happening out there?" pointing to the people talking and
fellowshiping. "You're the one responsible for that fellowship
and people getting acquainted. You are making a key
contribution each Sunday."

"I've never looked at it that way," Charlie says. "I saw my job as
buying rolls and making coffee."

Encouragement builds up relationships and people. Now a
Sunday sees Pastor and Charlie exchanging knowing glances.
Charlie has new spark; and the coffee new perk.

Bill owns a business. He has been chairman of the trustees two
years. He noticed how clean Carl the custodian keeps the
carpets. He realized he never expressed his appreciation to Carl.

The next day, Bill wrote Carl a note. "Now Carl can't do enough for us," Bill relates. "He asks, 'Is everything OK? Are there some things I should be doing differently?'

"Our church shines more than ever," Bill says. "Carl is part of the team and now even more cooperative than ever."

My wife Marion received this encouraging note: "Your visit last night, Marion, delighted me. It was nice to talk, but the high point of the evening was the prayer time. I am so glad you suggested it. You do talk to God in such a beautiful way.

"You did give me an idea, although I do not want to impose on your time. Sometime if we could arrange a convenient time, would you pray with our little group? I told the other two women about you."

Peggy struck up a relationship with Jill. Then Jill moved to another city and lost contact with her for several months. In the mail came this note from Jill to Peggy: "I just wanted to get off a tiny little note to you, in case you'd ever wonder what became of me. You were so faithful and such a caring Christian sister to me. I just felt the need to let you know that all is well."

Encouragers follow up, doing little things that go unnoticed in today's busy world. I try writing notes to two people each day. To receive a note, or to hear a positive word from someone pushes personal worth up a couple notches. Encouragement is part of positive supervision. People encouraged feel they belong on the team. Positive supervisors give positive feedback and point out specific things people do that are appreciated.

God tests us mainly through people. Did you ever notice how God puts people into our path we immediately dislike? Then we try hiding behind excuses such as, "We have no common bond" or "Our personalities clash" or "There isn't a chemistry between us." We try sticking to "our kind," or "our types."

Our excuses hold no water. A beautiful sixty-one-year-old black lady said to me, "I don't know why so many white people avoid me. I've never hurt anyone." We embraced.

Encouragement connects. Building positive, genuine

relationship means respecting, trusting, and being credible. God sees people, not color, titles, or position. We hurt the people we avoid. God is calling us to put aside excuses and reach out to people, to go the second mile and more. If more of us would do our part and do little things for each other the friction between people would be reduced. Opportunity is mainly the person next to you now.

TWELVE
WHAT TO DO ABOUT CONFLICTS

There's a saying: "Watch a married couple approaching. The one four steps in front is the one who is angry."

Millie and Wendell have been married twenty-one years. Each dumped a load of hate and hostility in separate two-hour sessions at my office. Each blamed the other. Wendell wanted to move to another city. Millie did not want to move . . . she loves her job and where she's living. Both admit drinking too much.

"I thrive on being alone," Millie said. "He loves being with people."

"It's difficult for us to talk now," Wendell lamented. "We end up arguing. She'll say, 'I'm sorry' and that opens the floodgates and I lash back. We have no communication."

I went with Millie to the car. I got up courage to ask, "Why did you come here tonight?"

She paused. "I don't know." To myself I said, "Oh, oh. Dumb question!" But then I added, "For you to do this was very mature. I admire you."

Another pause. "Maybe there is hope," Millie said with a slight sparkle in her eye.

Unknown to either of them, two separate groups were praying, started by a caring pastor and loving neighbor. Millie and Wendell stopped getting outside help. Divorce proceedings were dropped. They are now living together, in that city to which

Millie did not want to move. The ice in their relationship is thawing slowly. Can I explain all this? No, but I think it started with one word: hope.

"You can't go up front with the other kids," Mrs. Harper said. "You missed both practices. You know the ground rules, Danny. Sorry." That Sunday morning Danny walked, with his head down, out to the family car in the parking lot. He thought of his grandparents who had just bought his first suit, who would soon be bobbing their heads around whispering, "Where's Danny?" As the next week wore on, Danny's grandmother's patience stretched thinner and thinner. She couldn't hold it any longer, so she telephoned Mrs. Harper, Danny's teacher.

"You drove Danny away. You should have . . ." comments burst from her pent-up emotions. She also called the Sunday school superintendent and the pastor to "gun down" Mrs. Harper.

Now five months later, Grandma is saying, "My relationship with Danny's teacher isn't the same. It's like a tear in a shirt. I don't think it will ever be the same. Now I'm wondering what the confrontation really accomplished. What it really did was fracture a good relationship. I hate going the other way when I see her now."

"If I said the sky was blue," a runaway teenager relates, "Dad would disagree. If he said a book had a red cover, I'd say it wasn't. I really think he hates me, or I'm some intrusion in his life. He's never hugged me. He's never said, 'I'm sorry.' He's always telling me what to do. He treats me like a four-year-old. I hate home."

Four steps between people separate. Without hope, people become stubborn and faceless. Uncontrolled tongue lashings boomerang. Well-intentioned rationalizations backfire. For example, people say, "I'm speaking the truth in love," meaning "They're wrong and I'm right."

Conflict hurts people. Volcanic eruptions between people spew their deadly ash of bitterness, hate, and jealousy even onto innocent bystanders, particularly children or new people in a situation.

What to do about conflicts

I've had serious conflicts. I find confrontation seldom works; in fact, it usually makes matters worse. I hate conflict. I hate confronting people. I come away wishing I had never said what I did.

I have been confused about how to handle conflict. Down deep, I think some writers on conflict have never been directly involved in one. Their approaches seem aimed at getting the other person to cough up a confession, or to totally unload one's feeling on someone. One did that on me and I remember feeling like I had been run over by a steamroller.

To blame conflict on sin or the devil or selfishness is both easy and unworkable. When in a conflict, I have difficulty sorting out whether it is sin, the devil, or the selfish me.

I still have many unanswered questions about conflict. But out of this stew pot of confusion and indecision have boiled up two conclusions: (1) I should confront myself before them. (2) I should care enough to keep my mouth shut. Confrontation ought to be a last resort, rather than a first resort.

Those of us with strong tendencies to control and tell others what to do and those who are practicing conditional supervision may find the following six guides for preventing and resolving conflict hard to swallow. But we should examine them anyway. You may even want to call it "advice." Remember the saying: The desire to give advice is insatiable, but the ability to ignore it is universal.

SIX GUIDELINES FOR PREVENTING AND RESOLVING CONFLICT

1. Am I doing my part? That question jarred me after reading "Do everything possible on your part to live in peace with everybody" (Romans 12:18, TEV). That verse scored a direct hit on my heart. It is up to me to do my part. My strategies and checklists designed to resolve conflict were going down the tubes like Drain-O is supposed to do. Only this time, my cluttered mind-pipes were being cleaned.

Now back to my part. "When you please the Lord, you can make your enemies into friends" (Proverbs 16:7, TEV). That is one verse I hadn't underlined. At first I rationalized, saying that only supersaints would accept that one. But when in the middle of a conflict, we will consider anything. So I did. And the final answer was that my part is to please God.

My memory brought back an experience of ten years ago. After many years of so-called Christian living, my wife and I decided to take Jesus and Christianity seriously. Then that inevitable question hit, "What is God's will? How do I find out what he wants?"

That answer came from *Man to Man* (Grand Rapids: Zondervan) by Richard Halverson. He said that the key verse is Genesis 24:27: "I being in the way the Lord led me" (KJV). He said, "Knowing God's will is not complicated. Man's side is to be 'in the way.' God's side is 'to lead.' " That realization lifted a

"The start of an argument is like the first break in a dam; stop it before it goes any further" (Proverbs 17:14, TEV).

twenty-ton burden. In other words, when I do my part, God does his. Since then, doing my part means daily Bible reading and prayer.

I've also concluded that solving people problems, particularly conflicts, is an intensely spiritual process. It is God's love and spirit within people that repairs relationships. I can't explain exactly how that happens. It takes two people to break relations and it takes two to restore them. So, not all attempts at peacemaking end up positive.

Chuck didn't click well with Howard, the committee person. "When I spoke up," Chuck said, "he ignored what I said. The meetings became perfunctory. I decided to try spotting things Howard did well." Chuck adds, "Three or four times I complimented him. All I got was a blank stare. No response—not even a thank you. I guess we never achieve perfection in relationships, do we?"

I agreed. But first and foremost, it is our responsibility to initiate peacemaking and relationship building. As I can't control others (chapter 11), so I also can't control a relationship.

Quarrels erupt into explosions. People abiding in Christ try resolving things at the disagreement stage. "The start of an argument is like the first break in a dam; stop it before it goes any further" (Proverbs 17:14, TEV).

2. Am I willing to change? We resist and avoid this question. Our human nature resists rationalizing: "They are wrong; I am right." We also resist by getting used to thinking that helping other people change for the better is a noble ambition—and it is.

For example, one thrust of Christianity is to win others to Christ. This means someone else changing. Parents want their children to change and learn. Learning is a change in behavior (attitude too). We want them—child, parent, organization—to change for the better. It is often the right thing to want.

But conflict situations have a different starting point—me. Ouch! That hurts as feet hurt when pinched by new shoes. Pinched human nature and pride strike back, urging me to avoid asking: "Am I willing to change?" But we must, even though ego and pride get bruised and pinched. Conflict is never solved by expecting others to change first.

"I'm in favor of progress but it's all this change I'm against," said the gray-haired college professor. We are often naturally against change when it hits us personally, but we can accept it with God's help (Ephesians 3:20), even in conflict.

"Should the new church wing be on the east side or west side?" Pastor Argender asked. "That was the bone of contention between Paul, the building committee chairman, and me. Heated discussions turned into a serious rift.

"I agonized between meetings," Pastor added, "and I soon found myself dreading them. So often, my wife's question proved pivotal: 'What's really causing this conflict? What is God teaching you?' I felt pinned down. It forced me to ask, 'Is the issue really east side or west side?'

"I concluded that the problem is relational. We don't know each other. We've spent no one-on-one time together. It's got to start with me.

"Asking him to have lunch was the hardest thing I've ever done," Pastor sighed, "but soon we were relating and even exchanging prayer needs.

"Oh, yes, about the east side or west side problem. Funny thing—he soon shifted to my views and I to his. After we started seeing each other as people, rather than opponents, the decision came easy." A conflict resolved itself quietly and privately. And all the while Mrs. Argender and three prayer partners were praying.

Winnie is a loyal churchgoer. Her husband Dean goes at Easter and Christmas. Over the years, Winnie has been urging Dean to be more serious about God. "My words are like water off a duck's back," she says. Their arguments and heated debates brought on long cold wars.

"I'm finally realizing I must change completely before expecting Dean to change," Winnie says. "The other night I wrote a long critical note and left it on the kitchen table for him to read when he got home."

"I went to bed," added Winnie, "and soon fell asleep. Suddenly I woke up, got up and tore up my critical note. I really believe the Holy Spirit woke me up, not only to stop sleeping but also to get me to quit trying to change Dean."

All discussion of separation has stopped. Dean still doesn't go to church very often. 'I've got peace now," Winnie says. Her spirit is humble and gentle, replacing pride and harshness.

Bette is twenty-two and still lives with her parents. The conflict between her mother and her deepened. But that is changing.

"Things are better now," Bette says. "I had to realize she has feelings and ups and downs—good days and bad days. I now expect less of Mom. Somehow, I felt she was superhuman. And she isn't."

Matt's parents were unhappy. In their opinion, their seventeen-year-old son Matt was completely dominated by his girl friend. Matt often worked out schemes to be with her. When his parents heard of it, cold conversation around the supper table made hot soup taste lukewarm.

I decided to do nothing for a while," his mother said. "All our attempts to restrict him failed."

At the suggestion of a close friend, she and her husband tried being nicer to Matt's girl friend. They asked two others to be praying. The negative home climate turned positive.

Five months later, Matt suddenly dropped his girl friend. "She's telling me what to do all the time," he said. "I've had it with her." I can't explain this either, except that his parents were willing to change.

It's not who is right or wrong, but what is right. It is right for me to change before expecting others to change.

—The more I try changing others, the less I influence.

—The more I try changing me, the more I influence.

A pastor put it succinctly: "I can't relate to him yet. But I've done a complete turn in my attitude. I'm here to minister to him and his needs. I'm optimistic that we'll get along better in the future."

3. Am I forgiving enough? "Honey, about that argument we had. I want to apologize," Dagwood says kissing Blondie good night. "And remember this, it takes a big man to apologize when he knows he's right."

Saying, "Yes, I'll forgive you" or "I'm wrong, I confess" is often done flippantly. Like Dagwood, we don't mean it. It is being a conditional supervisor.

Jesus tells us to forgive "seventy times seven," not once or twice. He tells a parable about a servant whose master punished him for an unforgiving spirit. Then came the clincher: "That is how my Father in heaven will treat you if you do not forgive your brother, every one of you, from your heart" (Matthew 18:35, TEV).

To say, "I'm sorry" or "Yes, I'll forgive you" is the *toughest* thing a Christian does. It is not automatic; it is an act of will. Someone has said, "We're never closer to Christ than when we

forgive someone." I say that forgiveness epitomizes
Christlikeness.

"Forgive from the heart? How?" some may be asking.

In my view, it is summed up in 1 Peter 4:8. "Above
everything, love one another earnestly, because love covers over
many sins" (TEV) (See also Proverbs 10.12.) Most Bible
commentaries say the essence of this verse is forgiveness. "If you
want people to like you, forgive them when they wrong you.
Remembering wrongs can break up a friendship" (Prov. 17:9,
TEV). Have you ever consciously tried letting Jesus' love put a
lid on someone's wrongdoing?

Being forgiving to an outsider is easy. "For two days I've
been trying to figure you out," said Bert, a participant in a
seminar. "I've been angry at you and now at myself. Will you
forgive me?" Forgiving an outsider like Bert from the heart is easy.

But to forgive insiders, people we rub shoulders with all the
time, is tough. The longer married people are married, or
committee person works with committee person, we see more
and more of their faults. Reality strikes after the honeymoon,
whether it is husband-wife, pastor-church, or supervisee-
supervisor. Even two-year-olds irk more than seven-month-
old babies!

I once read, "On their honeymoon, the groom took his bride by
the hand and said, 'Now that we're married, dear, I hope you
won't mind if I mention a few little defects that I've noticed about
you.' 'Not at all,' the bride replied with a deceptive sweetness.
'It was those little defects that kept me from getting a better
husband.' "

Unlike this couple, God's love in a person enables
unconditional loving, overlooking, tolerating, and covering up
another's defects and faults. God's love quietly plunges in and
heals leaks in the dike, and stops finger-pointing and direct
confrontation.

At our daughter Kristen's sixteenth birthday party I flared
up. Relatives and friends were just going to sit down for "cake and
coffee" at 4:30 when Kristen said, "Isn't someone taking me to
church for my five o'clock meeting?"

"You're going to church now?" I said with disappointment
and frustration showing with every word. A verbal battle broke
out, and my wife stepped in and said that I would take her to
church at 5:45. So we ate.

Ate? Yes, but mostly thought and prayed, "Lord, teach me what the love that covers a multitude of sins means. I'm helpless. I blew it an hour ago; I need you." I anticipated a conversation-less ride to church.

How wrong I was. In a mysterious, beautiful way, God's love filled our car and us. We had a great conversation on the way to church. We didn't bring up our argument—it seemed to pass and evaporate into thin air.

"Thank you, thank you, Lord," I prayed on the way home. It was a great experience for me, being warmly and snugly enveloped by God's love. A new day dawned in my walk with Jesus.

The Ripley family had a sharp, heated argument the evening before leaving for a family vacation together. The four-hour trip to their destination warmed up a bit at the three-hour point.

Two days later, Mrs. Ripley said, "You know what? God's love moved in and healed. The Sunday night fight wasn't brought up again. We had the best vacation ever.

"It took me two days to realize God's healing power was doing it," Mrs. Ripley said. "Looking back, it was a beautiful experience." All the while back home, Grandpa and Grandma Ripley were praying.

Jesus died to forgive us. It was costly. To let love cover is costly and sacrificial. For example, we will no longer keep scores that add up to another's failures, since ". . . love does not keep a record of wrongs" (1 Corinthians 13:5, TEV). Also, we will tolerate their behavior more. "Be tolerant with one another and forgive one another" (Colossians 3:13, TEV). And more important, we will forgive and trust, forgive and trust—seventy times seven.

Love covers a multitude of sins, not all sins. Some sins must be uncovered and exposed. But if we were all being more forgiving, perhaps the need to uncover and expose them would lessen.

We should not press someone to forgive us, for that would be trying to control the person. We should say, "I'm sorry" and let it go at that. We should never say, "Will you forgive me?" Let them make their own decision because they will anyway.

When is the last time you said to an insider, "I'm wrong" or "I'm sorry" and meant it? When is the last time you said, "Yes, I

forgive you" and meant it—from the heart? Love covers.
Heated arguments shut out God's healing. As Mrs. Ripley said,
"The bottom line is me." I caused the dispute between Kristen
and me. Who is right or wrong does not matter. All I know is my
part was to cover and love. Kristen did her part, too.

4. Is confession to God required? Perry and Dexter serve on a
church committee. Perry grew up in the suburbs and has a
management job. Dexter's background is farming. Unlike
Perry, he never went to college. Over the years, Dexter has done
well in real estate. His worth is now estimated at $1.5 million.

A serious rift broke out between Perry and Dexter. "We'd listen
to the two of them first," said Charlotte, "before voicing our
opinions. Then we would take sides. It's really pretty silly, but it's
happening."

Perry searched his heart. "Why is this happening?" he asked
himself. "We aren't competing or jockeying for position. He
hasn't hurt me nor I him. And I said to God I can't simply chalk it
up to a personality clash. While we have never gotten along
that well, somehow the issue is not personality differences." Perry
alternated thinking and praying.

It happened in his office. "I had this big report due," Perry
relates, "but this conflict held me in bondage. It was draining
me. The rift, rather than the report, grabbed my attention."

Lightning struck. "I'm jealous," he said out loud. "Jealous
because Dexter is a millionaire, which I think is all dumb luck."

In his office, Perry confessed to God his jealousy of Dexter.
Some relief. He finished his report.

"OK, God, now what?" he prayed two days later. No answer.
"God, I'm still immobilized by this rift. I don't know what to do.
OK, God, I'm simply going to trust you. I want your peace
again in my heart," Perry pleaded.

God's silence lasted nine months. After a committee
meeting, Dexter asked Perry for a ride home. "Have you got a
minute?" Dexter asked. Perry turned off the car ignition.
Dexter unloaded a heavy personal burden he had been carrying
around for four years. "For some reason, I didn't feel I could
talk to Pastor about this, and you know how much I love and
respect him. I felt you were the only person I could tell."

A relationship healed over and a prayer partnership formed. "It all started on my knees in my office," Perry says. "I was frozen stiff in my tracks then."

Perhaps we would confront less and do our part more if we first asked these questions:

Have I really cared for them and encouraged them (a parent, relative, supervisor, offspring)?

Have I considered that they may be facing a problem they can't share, even with me? A problem in their job, personal health, marriage, or peer relationships?

Have I ever tried doing some little thing for them— compliment them, give them a ride, or volunteer to do something for them?

And to what extent am I loving unconditionally? Are their minor irritations really that important? Am I ballooning things way out of proportion?

In *Run Today's Race* (Ft. Washington, PA: Christian Literature Crusade, 1968), Oswald Chambers writes, "Whenever you come in contact with the great destructive sins in other lives, be reverent with what you don't understand. There are facts in each life you know nothing about and God says: 'Leave him to me.' "

No one tried to settle the Perry and Dexter rift. Perhaps unconsciously, people who knew about it left it to God. No one gets the glory, no one can say "I did it."

"You will never succeed in life if you try to hide your sins. Confess them and give them up; then God will show mercy to you" (Proverbs 28:13, TEV). Perry's confession got the ball rolling.

"For me, becoming a Christian was a complete turnaround" Franklin said. "I had an overwhelming sense of cleansing, a lifting of a burden, and a feeling of wholeness."

Christians get dirtied up fast in today's world. Tempers flare, conflict happens. Perhaps more of us should clean up our own act more often, rather than rush out to restore and change other people.

5. Have I consistently prayed for them, with the right motives?
Don prayed diligently about a break between himself and the owner of a competitive firm. No answer came from God, and counsel from other trusted friends left him confused.

Balancing faith with reason, we take one wobbly step at a time.

Then the thought came to him. "Down deep, I really wanted his firm to fail," Don said. "I was hoping they would bite the dust and go into bankruptcy. I alone would rise the victor. I even found myself hoping his beautiful car would be sideswiped by an old pickup truck. Any wonder my prayers didn't go beyond the ceiling? My motives were bad. In fact, I wanted God's worst, rather than best for him. I read Philippians chapter 2 and felt ashamed. I had selfish ambitions. I had no constructive interest in him. My attitude was unchristian." Three years later, the relationship mended when both happened to meet at an airport coffee shop.

"I was so bitter and negative," Don recalls, "I constantly had to ask myself, 'What did God put in him that was good?' "

Motives impact the effects of prayer. "And when you ask, you do not receive it, because your motives are bad" (James 4:3, TEV).

Positive supervisors want to help others rather than fight to win. A helping, caring attitude scrubs clean impure, unhealthy motives that sneak into our prayers.

James tells how we should pray for wisdom. "But if any of you lacks wisdom, he should pray to God, who will give it to him; because God gives generously and graciously to all" (James 1:5, TEV). Asking God's wisdom in an age of information explosion sounds ridiculous to those who never look to God. Wisdom is the most underused weapon in our fight to solve people problems.

Dean manages a store where Beverly is a salesperson. Beverly is excellent doing inventory, stocking, and straightening out merchandise. But Dean began hearing customers complain. "She's so abrupt," they said. "She doesn't seem to care. What got into her today?" Two other staff members dropped "not so subtle hints" about Beverly's sour attitude. Conflict was escalating fast, between Dean and Beverly, Beverly and customers, and Beverly with other staff. These tiffs would soon be tremors; the first break in the dam was happening.

"What are we going to do?" Dean pleaded. "This store is going to erupt any minute."

I pulled out a list of possible causes. (See Figure 12.1.) I looked them over. But what worked in the past didn't seem right here. All options were explored, including letting Beverly go, to Dean having a frank, heart-to-heart talk and laying things on the line. That didn't seem right either.

"We need wisdom. Have we prayed for it?" Dean asked. We both had not, so we agreed to pray for wisdom thirty days.

"Guess what?" Dean reported two weeks later. "Beverly came to me today and opened up the whole problem. What a relief that she brought it up. She admitted having a sour attitude that needed correcting."

We both said we would continue praying for wisdom. About three weeks later came a frenzied telephone call. "Beverly's daughter tried to take her life last night. Although critical, she is expected to live." Dean's voice trembled.

CAUSES OF PEOPLE PROBLEMS

A. Supervision

One-with-one planning and follow-up reviews? Person centered? Appreciation expressed?

B. Personal strengths

Screened (selected) for responsibilities? Know capabilities? Capabilities and interests match responsibilities?

C. Poor relationships

Does not trust, respect others? Have trust, respect of others? Negative opinion of others?

D. Personal priorities and values

Reasonably clarified? To what extent being realized?

E. Expectations

To what extent has what was expected to happen actually happened?

F. Poor sense of worth

Feels incompetent? Lacks confidence? Lacks sense of acceptance by others? Feels like "doesn't belong"? Feels inferior? Compares self with others? Indecisive? Lost sense of purpose?

G. Negative attitude

Critical? Jealous? Resentful? "Pulling down" people's attitudes?

H. Interferences

Noise? People? Interruptions? Enough time? Spread "thin"—too many responsibilities? Poor equipment?

I. Time management

Plan adequately? Set weekly and daily priorities? Late starting preparation? Procrastinates? Follows up poorly?

J. Lacks motivation

Lost respect for organization and/or leadership? Job no longer challenge? Feels future opportunities limited? Lacks career direction?

K. Training

Too much? Too little? Responsibilities related? Focus on developing capabilities and strengths? Help overcome weaknesses?

L. Spiritual

Quiet time? Pray enough? Read and study Bible enough? Unclear about "What is God's will?" for their life?

FIGURE 12.1

Together we wondered what would have happened if Dean had confronted Beverly earlier and botched things up and then this had happened to her daughter. What if the decision had been to fire her? Neither one of us could take the credit. "Isn't it nice to know God is still on the throne?" Dean said reverently and thankfully.

This situation taught me more about solving people problems than any other. I felt helpless when Dean asked, "What are we going to do?" But God only helps helpless people who pray believing. "But when you pray, you must believe and not doubt at all" (James 1:6, TEV). To believe and pray for wisdom doesn't mean unscrewing our brain or ignoring facts. It does mean putting God first when solving people problems. Solving conflicts is an intensely spiritual process.

Beverly was also loaded with guilt. She teaches family counseling part-time at a local college yet almost lost her own daughter.

Guilty, insecure people need special handling. While they need advice, direct confrontation or "hit and run" approaches don't help anything.

Solving people problems means "walking by faith, not by sight" (2 Corinthians 5:7). Solving conflict and people problems is like walking a tight rope—balancing faith with reason. We take one wobbly step at a time. God uses us and others to be healing agents and peacemakers. God will frustrate methods and deadlines to solve conflict.

This illustrates why avoidance and direct confrontation seldom work. Between these two approaches are ways to solve people problems that recognize that our approach must be thought through carefully. We are dealing with people, not pawns on a chessboard.

6. Is this relationship my "thorn"? Garrett has had an ongoing conflict with Frank for two years. Garrett decided to go to Frank and clearly, gently, and conversationally tell him why he felt he was wrong. Garrett felt Frank talked too much, was jealous and conceited, and never followed up. "Lot of wind and talk," Garrett concluded about Frank.

Garrett's former pastor dropped in to see him. Pastor Stopper, his spiritual father, serves a small, rural church. "Not very good in the pulpit, but does he love Jesus," is Garrett's glowing evaluation of him.

Garrett soon was unloading his problem about Frank. Then Pastor Stopper asked his first penetrating question: "Is this relationship your thorn in the flesh?" Together they read 2 Corinthians 12:7-10, "There was given me a thorn in the flesh, a messenger of Satan to buffet me—to keep me from exalting myself" (v. 7). "Exalting myself? Do I do that?" Garrett thought.

Pastor's second question was, "Will your actions to confront Frank directly—clearly, gently, and conversationally—glorify you or glorify God?" Pastor Stopper told Garrett about two relationships that he views as thorns. "They are to humble me and keep me on my knees before God," Pastor says. The silence between them lasted two minutes.

Garrett and Pastor Stopper couldn't think of one way Garrett's decision to talk it out with Frank would glorify God. It would only "glorify" Garrett.

Shortly afterwards, Garrett got a nasty, condemning letter from Frank that he felt was a cheap, low blow.

"King Hezekiah took the letter from the messengers and read it. Then he went to the temple, placed the letter there in the presence of the Lord, and prayed" (Isaiah 37:14, TEV). Immediately after reading this, Garrett took Frank's letter, placed it on his office chair, got on his knees, and prayed. "It's all yours God. I'm open to do what you want."

Never before had Garrett submitted like this before God. The truth of "when I am weak, then I am strong" (2 Corinthians 12:10, NASB), didn't become evident for another eleven months. Frank suggested that a third party be brought in as mediator. "That was a second major point of submission," Garrett says, "doing something Frank suggested. But I had to trust, God and Frank."

It took another eighteen months to resolve this conflict. "The power of Christ's love just flooded the mediator, Frank, and me. It was the high point of my walk with Jesus. God controls, if we'll let him."

We have all experienced times we've exalted ourselves, and put down others because the internal conflict within each one of us rages on. "For the sinful nature desires what is contrary to the Spirit, and the Spirit what is contrary to the sinful nature.

They are in conflict with each other, so that you do not do what you want" (Galatians 5:17, NIV). We want resolution, but our way!

Our sinful nature wants nothing to do with submission, to God or others. On the other hand, God wants us to submit, to him and to others. This conflict within us and the other person is real. Not only is the visible conflict external but there is a bigger internal battle conflict between our wanting it our way or God's way. The big question is: Are we trying to control the other person? If so, we are starting at the wrong end. Instead, we should be asking, Are we submitting? Are we doing our part? All cooperative efforts start with us. Garrett submitted. Pastor Stopper cared enough to stop by and see one person. Stopping to see Garrett was done on impulse. God's Word gave specific direction (2 Timothy 3:16, 17) to two needy people.

There are many conflict-situations for which I don't have answers and which I've never faced. For example, conflicts caused by a spouse who drinks heavily, or travels too much, or has been unfaithful. How quiet, positive influencers remain faithful and loyal to Jesus in terribly difficult conflict situations is beyond me. "May God's love bless and keep you," is all I can say.

I hope you do not see these six guides as advice to ignore; instead I hope they are guides to encourage you to help others to deal realistically with your situation. These guides are not models on which to depend, because we must depend on God first.

THREE COMMON MISTAKES

People often make three mistakes when resolving conflicts.

1. *Everything will be forgotten.* "We're friends again," Marie says, "but there is always that area (conflict) we avoid in our conversation." Earlier in this chapter, Danny's grandmother said, "It's like a tear in a shirt."

We don't forget, but neither should we dwell on past records of wrongs. "I've quit holding it (grudge) against him," Jane said. "I'm trying to wipe the slate clean, but I still remember. I truly feel I've forgiven him."

Past sins and conflict should instruct us. When someone
says, "Forget it," if you can, fine. If you can't, admit it. Jesus'
love enables us to forgive and cover. Forgiveness is the real
issue, not forgetting.

2. *Trying for resolution too soon.* "After our terrible argument,"
Doris said, "I went right back to her house the next day and
tried to apologize. What a mistake that was. Another fight broke
out."

Cool off, let emotions simmer down so minds can regain
control over emotions. Days? Weeks? I don't know—whatever
it takes. Remember there are two sides to most conflicts—theirs
and yours. And the conceit factor—yours and theirs—often
raises its ugly head.

"People who do not get along with others are interested
only in themselves; they will disagree with what everyone else
knows is right" (Proverbs 18:1, TEV).

Fred got blamed by his associates for their company's financial
deficit. Rob in particular expressed anger and hostility. "If I'm
going to do what research says," Fred says, "I should go into
Rob's office first thing this morning and try settling our
differences."

"Have you prayed for wisdom?" I asked, referring to James
1:5. "And have you asked that love cover it?" referring to
1 Peter 4:8.

"Then I guess I'll do nothing," Fred replied.

The relationship between Fred and Rob is better than ever
now. "I can't explain it," Fred says. To myself, I said, "It's God's
grace."

So we should cool off before we start out to prove ourselves
right and others wrong. We should put the brakes on our
enthusiasm to get it over with. Patience is still a virtue and a fruit of
the Spirit—love, joy, peace, *patience.* . . .

3. *Not admitting being a "misfit."* Dan's capabilities include
promoting a program and selling products. His red-limabilities
include supervision and administration. Rather than being
40/20/40, he's 5/20/75. He's a misfit.

Listen to his staff's comments: "He's never in the office; he's
always late and unprepared; he blows up at staff meetings; he

criticizes us in public; we aren't involved in decisions—he announces them."

Dan's side sounded like this: "They're all negative thinkers; they're talking behind my back; they argue with me all the time—no cooperation and team spirit; I never received training like they're getting so what's their gripe; they only look at my faults."

This situation oozes with conflict. "Everything went wrong when I found out my capabilities," Dan says. "I can rise to the challenge. There's nothing I've tried in life where I haven't succeeded. I know God will help me." Dan feels he can do anything, with God's help. It sounds Christian, but it is questionable when functioning mainly in red areas for long periods of time.

As a supervisor, Dan is unfulfilled, insecure, and indecisive. His "I can do everything" mentality is creating conflict. Unfulfilled people cause horrendous conflicts because they take it out on others. Dan is using his staff as a whipping boy. Family, a neighbor, or a committee, may become a whipping boy to unfulfilled people. So far I've failed with Dan. So has his supervisor. Eight of his nine staff members quit.

I raise this question about misfits because one reason for today's high divorce rates may be caused by an unfulfilled spouse or both spouses unfulfilled. Role models emerge out of capabilities and strengths. Once more: we must fit the job to the person, not the person to the job.

QUICK TIPS ABOUT CONFRONTING SOMEONE

Direct confrontation to resolve conflicts should be a last resort. There are always exceptions, but self-confrontation usually works best. However, if your decision is to confront someone to resolve a conflict, here are a few quick tips, some of them mentioned before:

Do it privately and without fanfare.

List the other person's good points.

Talk over with a trusted friend what you are considering.

Watch your language. Never say, "You always . . ." or "You never . . ." to them.

Reverse the roles. Ask yourself, "How would I react hearing

what I feel I should say if I were in their shoes? What attitude would I appreciate?"

Ask yourself, "Am I willing to listen to their advice? Am I willing to learn from them? If not, is it because I feel superior to them?"

Don't try to resolve it all at once or at one sitting. A championship fight is fifteen rounds, not one!

Follow up. Encourage each other to do something specific such as pray about one thing for each other.

Listen at least 50 percent of the time.

Get five people praying for you.

Spend thirty minutes daily in Scripture. Ask God to lead you when deciding what to read. If in doubt, reread your favorite verses.

Expect not to enjoy it (welcome to the group!).

People often go counter-clockwise around the Fulfillment Cycle, supervising negative and conditionally. People also tend to use counter-productive approaches to resolving conflict by confronting others before confronting themselves.

Jesus confronted first on occasions. He got angry; you and I do. But confrontation and anger are the exceptions rather than the rule.

Conflicts and struggles between people are turning points. They bring us nearer to Jesus or push us further away. We choose our reaction to conflicts. Methods in themselves are not the answer.

Jesus said, "Father, forgive them for they know not what they do." Later Peter, who many agree talked the most, wrote this about Jesus' reaction, ". . . for Christ himself suffered for you and left you an example, so that you would follow in his steps. . . . When he was insulted, he did not answer back with an insult; when he suffered, he did not threaten, but placed his hopes in God, the righteous Judge" (1 Peter 2:21, 23, TEV).

Criticism gets under our skin. When Jesus hurt and suffered, he gave us an example to follow by forgiving. Rather than lash out verbally, he chose to love those who mistreated him. He didn't answer back. People must have thought he was crazy, but Jesus knew verbal eruptions hurt people.

We may rationalize, "They have it coming to them." Jesus too could have said the same thing. Their verbal barbs must have hurt more than the sting of the actual thorns around his head.

Our role is not to "straighten them out" but to be like Jesus, unconditional supervisors and lovers in any situation, practicing tongue-control. If conflicts turn us to Jesus, they are positive turning points

Smede in *Love with Limits* (Grand Rapids: Eerdmans, 1978), wrote:

The power of agape love drives us to a new beginning. Love lets the past die. It moves people to a new beginning without settling the past. Love does not have to clear up all misunderstandings. In its power, the details of the past become irrelevant; only its new beginning matters. Accounts may go unsettled; differences remain unresolved; ledgers stay unbalanced. Conflicts between people's memories of how things happened are not cleared up; the past stays muddled. Only the future matters. Love's power does not make fussy historians. Love prefers to tuck all the loose ends of past rights and wrongs in the bosom of forgiveness—and pushes us into a new start.

CONCLUSION
BROKEN PEOPLE
INFLUENCE POSITIVELY

Several years ago, I thought I had the world by the tail. After I returned from an overseas speaking engagement, Scott, our son, asked me, "Dad, what is management?"

That question stumped me. How do you communicate that to a seven-year-old? I asked myself. "Scott, management is helping people," I replied. He then darted off to play.

The next day, Scott died instantly in an automobile accident. For the first time in my life I felt completely helpless. I had absolutely no control. My dreams for success and my views of success began changing. My success world was shattered and breaking down. The main thing I learned was about brokenness.

Up to that point, I never knew what it meant to be broken. I had read a book by Watchman Nee, *Release of the Spirit* (Sure Foundation Publ.) but after this experience, it meant something. Watchman Nee wrote, "The Lord Jesus tells us in John 12, 'Except the grain of wheat falling into the ground die, it abides alone; but if it dies, it bears much fruit.' Life is in the grain of wheat, but there is a shell, a very hard shell on the outside. As long as that shell is not split open, the wheat cannot grow." Mr. Nee made the point that the greatest hindrance to serving God is "not others but himself. . . . the cross must destroy all that belongs to our outward man—our opinions, our ways, our cleverness, our self-love, our all."

Then he adds this about one who is broken. "You are not only able to give help, but in giving you also are helped. You are asked a question, and in answering it you are helped. . .   this ability to receive help—allowing another's spirit to touch our spirit—is proof that one is broken."

I had to admit that I thought I was a good supervisor, but supervision as helping people? Never. Scott's question triggered a new world for me. Helping people, expecting nothing in return, being helped while helping someone—this was new territory for me. I had to reevaluate some sacred conditional definitions. Now I laugh at speeches I had written—they zoomed counter-clockwise around the Fulfillment Cycle mentioned earlier. It sounded good, but it was wrong.

Another thing happened in the breaking process. Scripture came alive, such as the familiar John 14:6. "Jesus said to him, 'I am the way, the truth, and the life; no one comes to the Father, but through Me" (NASB). I had read that verse many times. Today I believe it. Jesus is central. It is God's will to believe in Jesus.

Problem solvers are broken, wobbly people. Their outer shell of self is broken. The life of Jesus springs loose from their lives—fostering an accepting, positive climate.

Broken people often have nothing to show for it. They serve, doing little things quietly. They are applying Sunday's lessons on Tuesday. "Live a quiet and peaceful life with all reverence toward God and with proper conduct (1 Timothy 2:2, TEV). Fruit on a tree grows quietly.

Before brokenness hit, I was good at upsetting people—with questions for the sake of questions, rather than being helping, caring, and sensitive. I remember a committee chairperson saying to me, "Dick, the night before a church deacons' meeting, I don't sleep a wink." I didn't hear that, didn't even bat an eyelash. The traffic light concept hadn't dawned. To myself I said, "Anyone can lead a committee meeting. I can, why can't they?" My heart was hard.

My success-mentality said, "If people try hard enough, work hard, and are committed, goals will be reached." But I failed to ask where people fit in.

You and I wobble as branches attached to the Vine. But the "accept me, accept you" mentality makes us listen more to God and others, rather than first giving advice. Now when I look at people, I try seeing a person, rather than a manager, caretaker,

". . . live a quiet and peaceful life with all reverence toward God and with proper conduct" (1 Timothy 2:2, TEV).

carpenter or cook; a human being rather than a spouse, teenager, president, or treasurer. People are people.

This is a dumb question but it makes a point: What is the highest compliment one person can pay another? I think it would be that when you are with them you feel you are at Jesus' feet. You know they know Jesus.

For example, when I'm with Karen, she'll say, "I was just reading in Ezekiel, or in Micah, and it really spoke to me. . . ." When I'm with Karen, they are sacred moments. People like Karen say to me that they love Jesus. He is first in their lives.

Phil received this note from Jay: "I think you know how

much I enjoy you. I see a lot of Jesus in you and it is really fun experiencing that."

Do people see Jesus in you? Often enough? "Have a reputation for being reasonable, and never forget the nearness of your Lord" (Philippians 4:5, Phil).

"When they saw the courage of Peter and John and realized that they were unschooled, ordinary men, they were astonished and they took *note* that these men had been with Jesus" (Acts 4:13, NIV).

People note when you have been with Jesus, in his Word and in prayer. Problem solvers are continuously being broken of self-will and pride. They admit failure, yet like Peter and John they are courageous. They step out and help people—at times walking where angels fear to tread. They are active.

Karen, a member of my Sunday school class, said: "Heat, unlike cold, is a separate entity. Cold exists because heat is absent. In the same way, good is a separate entity and evil exists when good is absent."

Problem solvers are active. They are doing good, going the second and third mile, and recognizing traffic signals getting there. In God's sight they stand tall and broken. In man's sight, they go unnoticed, trafficking among needy people, giving and expecting nothing in return.

"If anyone has material possessions and sees his brother in need but has no pity on him, how can the love of God be in him? Dear children, let us not love with words or tongue, but with actions and in truth" (1 John 3:17, 18, NIV). Abiders accept God's resources and actively give to needy people.

People-problem solvers help other people-problem solvers do and be better. They are spiritually fit leaders who influence positively—serving, helping, and building up—in ordinary, day-to-day ways. Like Jesus, they concentrate on a few people. They see one person's need.

"For God is at work within you, helping you want to obey him, and then helping you do what he wants" (Philippians 2:13, TLB).

People with clean, broken, receivable hearts experience Jesus. Others experience Jesus too as they come in contact with such people. They don't have all the answers, but they do their part solving people problems. Broken people influence positively for God is at work within them.

APPENDIX A
DISCOVERING YOUR CAPABILITIES

Follow a three-step process:

STEP ONE: Look back.

a. On a separate sheet of paper, divide your life into four time periods. Do not try being exact with figuring your time periods.

b. List two or three positive experiences for each time period.

c. Review all your positive experiences (disregard time periods) and rank them in terms of enjoyment and fulfillment (number one: enjoyed the most; number two: enjoyed a little less; and so on). Put a number beside each positive experience. For example, if you have listed eleven positive experiences, they should be ranked number one to number eleven.

STEP TWO: Look at.

a. Look at your five top-ranked positive experiences. Do one of two things:

(1) Write eight to ten brief sentences about each one, or

(2) Tell someone you trust what you did. Let them ask you the three (next) questions.

b. In either case—writing or talking—use the three questions from chapter 4:

(1) How did you _____ ?

(2) Give an example of _____ .

(3) What was your role?

c. (Optional) You may want to write or talk about more than
five positive experiences. This will give you more information
for step three.

STEP THREE: Look into.

a. Look closely at what you listed (all your positive
experiences), wrote about or talked about (some people use
a recorder and listen back).

   (1) Note (circle or underline) your abilities. Refer to
Appendix C.

   (2) Note the Classification—people, data, or things (or
some combination of the three). To get more specific,
ask: What kind?

   (3) Note personal style; category one, two, or three (or
some combination of the three). Also note personal
style role.

   (4) Pinpoint your capabilities; look for what repeats: Write
down four or five abilities, your classification, and
personal style.

b. Helpful hints to pinpoint capabilities.

   (1) When in doubt about what to pinpoint, look more
closely at your top ranked positive experiences.

   (2) Think of examples and times you did it; this helps you
get specific.

   (3) Take enough time to do this. There are no shortcuts. It
is hard work. It should pay fulfillment dividends in
days ahead.

   (4) Once a year add one or two positive experiences
from the past year. This will affirm and encourage you
and you will see your capabilities being used over
and over.

APPENDIX B
DISCOVERING YOUR LIMABILITIES

Follow a three-step process:
STEP ONE: Look back.
- a. On a separate sheet of paper, list at least five of your negative experiences. Do not consider time periods and when they occurred.

STEP TWO: Look at.
- a. Look at your negative experiences. Do one of two things:
    - (1) Write a few sentences about each one, or
    - (2) Tell someone you trust what you did. Let them summarize your answers.
- b. In either case—writing or talking—give one example. Do not go into a lot of detail.

STEP THREE: Look into.
- a. Look closely at what you have written or talked about.
    - (1) Note (circle or underline) your red abilities (see Appendix C), your red classification—people, data, or things (or some combination of the three), and your red-personal style—one, two, or three (or some combination of the three).
    - (2) Write down some of your limabilities.
- b. Helpful hints to pinpoint limabilities.
    - (1) Locating limabilities is less precise than spotting capabilities. This will give you some handles.
    - (2) Once a year add one negative experience from the past year. It will help you accept yourself and be less guilty about not enjoying something like that.

APPENDIX C
ABILITIES

administer
advise
analyze
arrange
assemble
assist, help
befriend
bookkeeping, accounting
build
care for
clean, maintain
clerical, type
coach
compete, sports
control
convince
cook, bake
coordinate
counsel
create
design
develop
direct
draw
edit
empathize
encourage
entertain
evaluate
facilitate
follow-up
homemaking
lead discussion
listen

manage
memorize
moderate,
    preside over
operate
organize
paint
perfect
perform
physical agility
plan
plant, grow
ponder, mull over
problem solve
produce
promote
recruit, select
relationship building
repair
research
sell
serve
shape, make
sing
speak
study
supervise, oversee
systematize
teach
train
understand
visit
visualize
write

APPENDIX D
QUESTIONS FOR DISCUSSION

Look at these questions when you finish reading a chapter. They are designed to (1) be thought provoking and (2) encourage application of ideas in real-life situations.

These questions are helpful answered either individually or in discussion groups—where the discussion leader uses the questions as discussion starters. In either case, an individual, discussion leader, or discussion group may decide to concentrate on a few selected questions instead of answering all of them. Do what meets needs best.

Some questions are marked P for personal. This means a person or group may decide to skip answering that question in a group setting since it applies mainly to one person.

CHAPTER 1

1. Besides patience, what attitudes and actions must characterize someone who wants to solve people problems?
2. How realistic is it to say that everyone is a supervisor? Give reasons for your answer.
   (P) Do you consider yourself a supervisor? If yes, in what ways? If no, why?
3. Recall trying to help someone with a problem when you were on the horns of a dilemma of whether to advise or not. How did you decide? What did you do? What happened?

4. Is striving to follow the Golden Rule idealistic or practical when solving people problems? In the home? church? business? Give reasons.

   (P) Where is it most difficult for you to follow the Golden Rule? Why?

5. Think of two people who have influenced you positively. Why do they stand out?

   (P) What application is there in their example for you?

6. Compare how solving people problems in volunteer settings differs from in business settings. Be specific.

   Does this affect someone's approach to people problems? Why?

7. In your opinion, are two-hat approaches to solving people problems common or uncommon? Give examples.

8. Give two examples of people problems from the Bible (Example: 1 Samuel 18:4-16). Why do these two stand out? What can be learned from them about solving people problems?

CHAPTER 2

1. Do you feel personal fulfillment and fruitfulness (Galatians 5:22-23) go hand-in-hand? Why?

   Do you feel the opposite is true: unfulfilled people are not fruitful (Galatians 5:19-21)? Why?

2. Do you feel someone unfulfilled and dissatisfied can "pick up his cross daily" (Luke 9:23)? Why or why not?

   In general, what prevents "cross-bearing"?

3. In your view, what is personal success? Support your answer from Scripture.

4. With reasons, describe your initial reaction to the Fulfillment Cycle. Is it realistic? complex? simplistic? Why?

   How would you define "sense of worth"?

5. (P) Look at Fig. 2.2. List and rank your top five to eight values. On a scale from 0-none, 5-some, to 10-a lot, ask yourself: To what extent am I realizing that value now? Put your number rating beside each value. What are you finding out?

6. (P) How are you helping other people realize their values? Be specific.

7. In what ways should 1 John 2:15-17 affect values? Think of

one other Scripture that should affect values. Discuss how.
8. Describe Jesus' life-style. What enabled him to do that?
   (P) Describe your life-style. In what areas of your life should you stop, look, and listen?
9. (P) If you could get away for one day to evaluate and plan without interruptions, what would you do? Schedule an ideal day. What would you bring along? What prevents you from "getting away" occasionally?

CHAPTER 3

1. Describe what you mean by (1) program-centered and (2) people-centered. Is it easier to be more program-centered or people-centered? Why? What attitudes must prevail so people and program are balanced?
2. Think of two different situations when you felt (1) no one listened to you and (2) someone listened to you. How did this affect your willingness to take on responsibilities? Your follow-through?
3. (P) Look at 1 Timothy 4:8, Philippians 3:10, and any other Scripture. Write your spiritual-fitness goals. Tell a trusted friend what they mean. Get his reaction.
4. Read Matthew 25:31-46; zero in on verse 40. What is the central teaching?
   (P) Who are your "least of these"?
5. List people needs that concern you. How can you realistically set in motion plans to meet them?
   How do you help other people meet people needs that concern them? Be specific. Include family members.
6. How did Jesus form realistic expectations? For himself? For others? Why did he do that?
   How do unrealistic expectations contribute to people problems? Give examples.
7. Look at the Guilt Cycle. Tell how guilt affects attitudes and willingness and give your reasons. How widespread is the guilt problem? Why?
8. In your opinion, did Walter, minister of Christian education, make a bold decision asking Lorraine to pray rather than immediately take a position? Why?
   If not bold, how would you describe Walter's decision?

CHAPTER 4

1. What did you learn from the Phillip Mack example?
2. React to the concept of "fitting the job to the person, not the person to the job." Is it practical? Why?
   What often prevents implementation of this concept? Should it? Why?
3. Define a positive experience. How does this definition tie in with Galatians 6:4; Ecclesiastes 2:12-13; 2:24?
4. What is Romans 12:3-6a saying to you? How should these verses affect acceptance of other people? family members? committee members? Do these verses limit people? Why or why not?
5. Explain how the concept of capabilities and green traffic light signals go together.
6. When helping others discover their capabilities, why is listening and first accepting what they are saying so difficult?
7. Do you feel some people reluctant to pinpoint their capabilities? Why?
   Think of two ways their reluctance may be constructively dealt with without turning them off or making them feel guilty.
8. Think of one way the green light concept can be implemented in groups in which you function. What obstacles must be overcome for this to happen?

CHAPTER 5

1. Define a negative experience. Contrast negative and positive experiences.
2. List attitudes and behaviors characterizing someone using their limabilities. Give examples from your life.
3. In your opinion, what is the main cause of procrastination? Also list other causes.
4. How do you deal with the procrastination problem? Give examples.
5. Explain the 40/20/40 concept. Why is it important that at least 40 percent of a person's responsibilities be green, capabilities using? "I enjoy creating and writing," Peggy says, "but I hate editing." How does the 40/20/40 concept apply? How should this help Peggy?

6. (P) List your daily responsibilities. Review your positive and negative experiences and list of capabilities and limabilities. Estimate your green, yellow, and red ratio and compare to 40/20/40.
   Are you fulfilled enough? If not, what changes need to be considered?
7. Give two reasons people should not avoid responsibilities requiring them to use their limabilities.
8. Why is first accepting one's limabilities difficult for many people?
   (P) Is it difficult for you? Why?
9. What is the main thing you learned from this chapter? (P) How can you begin applying it?

CHAPTER 6

1. Do you believe only God completely understands people? Give reasons for your answer. How should this affect ways people function with one another? Give an example.
2. Look back at the three examples—George, Charlene, David—in the Educational Choices section. List two things you learned.
3. Agree or disagree with this statement and give your reasons. Roles and models emerge out of a person's capabilities and limabilities going clockwise around the Fulfillment Cycle.
4. Look back at the example of Glenn in the Changing Responsibilities and Careers section. Why was his decision tough? What special personal qualities are needed to make tough decisions like this?
   How do people benefit from making decisions knowing their green, yellow, and red?
5. Look back at the example of Myron in the Changing Responsibilities and Careers section. What impressed you about Myron's decision? What did this example teach you?
6. Why do you think people downplay their capabilities?
   (P) Have you? If yes, how did you feel about yourself? About others? What can you do to avoid doing this? Be specific.
7. List ways to encourage and affirm someone who is downplaying his capabilities.

8. Do you feel people tend to rank some capabilities more important than others? Why?
   Does this ranking contribute to people problems? Give examples.

CHAPTER 7

1. Describe whether you agree or disagree with the breakout of three supervisory practices—negative, conditional, positive. Give your reasons.
2. How does negative supervision affect people's attitudes and willingness? Give two examples from your experience.
3. In your opinion, what is the purpose of positive supervision? Back up your answer with Scripture.
4. Why is Luke 6:35 so difficult to apply with the right motives?
   (P) How does Luke 6:35 apply to you? Be specific.
5. What are reasons you feel helping others is a sacrifice?
6. Why do some people resist being supervised? How can positive supervision help overcome that resistance?
7. Give two reasons why you feel everyone needs a positive supervisor.
   (P) Do you have a positive supervisor? If not, why not?
8. React to the statement: "I have no right to hold someone else accountable unless we have a positive, genuine relationship." How does this apply in homes? churches? offices?

CHAPTER 8

1. In your opinion, what was Jesus' main goal functioning with the Twelve? How does Jesus' goal affect your supervision? at home? church? office?
2. How can positive supervisors "take charge" without coming across as dominating dictators? Give examples.
3. List ways a positive supervisor functions in the role of an enabling coach. Do you really think parents are enabling coaches? Give reasons for your answer.
   (P) Where is it most difficult for you to be an enabling coach? What can you do about it? Be specific.

4. (P) In the light of your capabilities, limabilities, and values (from chapter 2), answer the question, "Where is my heart?" Write out your answer. Pray about it. Read James 4:1-3.
5. (P) Write out your interests. Make a file to include your capabilities, limabilities, values, heart aspirations, and interests. Use it when setting goals.
6. Do you think some people try accomplishing too much? If yes, how can an enabling coach help such people?
7. How do you recruit? Why? How should you recruit? At home? church? office?

CHAPTER 9

1. Do you feel positive supervision helps in solving the follow-up problem? Why or why not?
2. Why is evaluation often a negative experience for both the supervisor and supervisee? Give an example from your experience (home, office, or church) and how you felt after being evaluated.
3. In your opinion, what is the purpose of one-on-one evaluation? Do you evaluate with that purpose in mind? Often enough?
4. Describe why evaluation is so imprecise. Give an example from your experience.
5. In your opinion, how do Proverbs 4:26; 16:1, 2, 9, and 2 Corinthians 10:5 affect evaluation? Be practical.
6. Agree or disagree that a person's spiritual fitness is the main influence on results, which are hard to see and measure. Give your reasons.
7. List the three evaluation tips. (P) Which one affects you the most? Why?
8. In what situations has correction been helpful to you? Not helpful? Be specific. Describe a situation in which you asked for correction but did not want it. What made you ask? What did you learn?
9. If you had a choice, what attitudes and qualities would you appreciate in a person from whom you wanted correction? (P) Are you that kind of person to people you correct? What needs changing or improving?

CHAPTER 10

1. Read Ecclesiastes 4:9, 10; Mark 3:14-15, 6:30; 1 Peter 5:2-3; Hebrews 13:16-17. List specific attitudes and behaviors that should characterize (1) supervisor and (2) supervisee.
2. What is the purpose of a follow-up review? Describe how you do follow up reviews with your supervisees—spouse, children, or friends. What needs improvement?
3. Do you feel positive supervision cuts out 90 percent of the need for negative feedback? Give your reasons.
4. In what ways do "experienced models" produce unrealistically high expectations in other people—an observer, for example? Give an example from your experience. How can this be avoided?
5. Do you feel gentleness and firmness compatible qualities of a positive supervisor? If yes, why? If no, why?
6. What lessons are there for you in the example of Karl, the assistant pastor, who was always repairing the Sunday school buses?
7. (P) Evaluate yourself, using Fig. 10.2, Evaluation. Use a practical time period as you look back—three months, six months, or one year. Review it with your supervisor and/or a trusted friend. Put your evaluation in your personal file.
8. Assume a person is doing something with a positive attitude. Do you think it fair or unfair to evaluate him highly when he is using his limabilities but results are not good? Give reasons for your answer.
9. React to the statement: Since a person has more limabilities than capabilities, people have many many opportunities to correct one another. What are the implications of this concept to solving people problems?

CHAPTER 11

1. Evaluation was discussed in chapters 9 and 10. List specifically how evaluation of people is affected by (1) positive relationships and (2) negative relationships.
2. Describe what you feel is a positive relationship.
3. Cite an example when you loved unconditionally in the face of risk and embarrassment. What did you learn about being unconditionally loving?

(P) How do you measure up to 1 Corinthians 13:7?

4. In your opinion, is follow-up one way of being credible? Why? What else builds credibility between people?

5. Describe what you feel is a realistic relationship. Give an example.

6. If people are starving for genuine relationships, why are there so many lonely people?

7. Describe your reaction to the way the parents of Don, the high school junior, handled the report card incident. What did you learn from this example?

8. Kimberlee is often late for meetings. She is greeted by, "Glad you could make it this afternoon" (for a 9 A.M. meeting) or "the late Kimberlee Clark." How do comments like this contribute to people problems? Read James 3:1-12. Can jest and cutting remarks be overdone? Why or why not?

9. What attitudes should characterize encouragers? Think of two people who encourage you. What do they do? How do you encourage others?

CHAPTER 12

1. Describe a serious conflict where you were directly involved. What did you do that worked? Did not work? How did you feel during the conflict? How did others feel? What did you learn about conflict?

2. Do you feel people first confront too often? Why? Give examples.

3. (P) Read Proverbs 16:7. Discuss its meaning and application in your life.
   (P) Read 1 Peter 4:8. Discuss its meaning and application in your life.

4 Why is change that starts with me doubly difficult during conflict?

5. Describe a situation you faced when it was tough saying, "I'm sorry" or "I forgive you." How did you get to the point of actually saying it and meaning it?

6. When in conflict, do you rely more on prayer and his wisdom or techniques? Give examples.

7. Why is submitting to God and others especially difficult during conflict?

8. How should Jesus' example affect our attitudes and actions during conflict? Be specific.
9. What is the main thing you learned from this chapter about handling conflict? (P) How do you intend applying it?

CONCLUSION

1. Describe a people problem (in any situation) you are facing. Look at the Fulfillment Cycle (Fig. 2.1) and consider especially the three primary causes for people problems: (1) mismatch of capabilities and responsibilities, (2) lack of positive supervision, and (3) negative relationships. Decide what is causing the problem. How can you (and others) go about solving it? Be specific. Work out a plan of action.
2. Read James 3:13-18. Discuss its application to solving people problems.
3. What do you think is the central theme/message of this book? (P) Discuss its application in your life.